A SLENDER THREAD

D I A N E   A C K E R M A N

A Slender Thread

RANDOM HOUSE   NEW YORK

Library of Congress Cataloging-in-Publication Data is available
ISBN 0-679-44877-2

Random House website address: http://www.randomhouse.com/
Printed in the United States of America on acid-free paper
9 8 7 6 5 4 3 2
First Edition

Book design by J. K. Lambert

The narrative that follows is based on my actual experiences. However, to protect the privacy of callers, I've changed their names, whereabouts, and some circumstantial details of their lives, and my colleagues on the crisis line have been kind enough to check the manuscript to ensure confidentiality. Any similarity to real individuals arises from the wealth of experiences and feelings all people share. I have not attempted to disguise people and events reported in the newspapers or other media, since these dramas are already public knowledge.

DIANE ACKERMAN
August 1, 1996

CONTENTS

A SLENDER THREAD

At the edge of the town I live in, a converted depot restaurant called The Station reminds us of days when train cars shuffled in a long conga line to Manhattan. A clock outside the restaurant froze at 6:22, when the last iron fury left town, but the trains of circumstance have never stopped running.

Towns are like railroad stations, where at any moment hundreds of lives converge—people carrying small satchels of worry or disbelief, people racing down the slippery corridors of youth, people slowly dragging the steamer trunk of a trauma, people fresh from the suburbs of hope, people troubled by timetables, people keen to arrive, people whose minds are like small place settings, people whose aging faces are sundials, people desperate and alone who board a bullet train in the vastness of nothing and race hell-bent to the extremities of nowhere. In time, everyone meets everyone, either by repute or in person. When they are at their most frightened, desperate or alone, they sometimes phone Suicide Prevention and Crisis Service.

Its phone number can be easily found in the telephone directory or on posters strategically placed around town, but its whereabouts is a closely guarded secret. It's as if the people who worked there belonged to a mystery cult. Their names may not be spoken. Their ages may not be given. Their professions may not be hinted at. Because they touch the lives of desperate people, as well as of normal people in desperate moments, the address of the building may not be revealed. Counselors enter and leave it discreetly, even furtively at times. Yet in that building the blood and guts of human life, the minor sorrows and the bright catastrophes play themselves out. It is an emotional landscape that alternately expands and shrinks; one moment it may swell to the size of a remembered battle in Zaire, and the next it may huddle in the corner of a dorm room. The faces of the callers and counselors must be masked, but I can tell you about their struggles. The same is true of the building. I am not free to describe its façade, but I can tell you about its inner life.

CHAPTER 1

Borrowed Hearts

The telephone room sits on the top floor of this rambling old house, whose wooden staircase creaks no matter where or how gently you step. The walls once were cream-colored, and the varnish on the stairs, windowsills, doors, and woodwork have aged into a deep resiny brown. There's something comforting and old-time about the creakiness, the drafty hallways, and twisting staircases. Downstairs are administrative offices and rooms where the counselors meet; upstairs, a kitchen, a bathroom with shower, the counseling room, and three more offices.

I climb the stairs one evening, shrugging the knapsack off my shoulders. The crisis lines are located in a room with two simple polished oak plank desks arranged in an L-shape. The walls are tan, mottled by hand with a feather duster dipped in green and white paint. Stare at them long enough and you will see a snowfall in a field of tall grass. A shadow might be a rabbit bolting between the dry stalks. Wilderness, not an urban room. A foldaway bed covered with a quilted green fitted cover serves as couch for day counselors and sleep spot for overnighters. I put my knapsack there and wave hello to Frieda, one of the agency's new counselors, who is talking quietly with a caller. A slender woman in her sixties, a music teacher, she wears her gray-blonde hair in a ponytail with bangs.

In many ways, it is an ordinary room. A fitted brown-and-white twill industrial carpet, whose nap has been worn smooth, has a strange stain (in the shape of a pug-nosed man looking left) near the door. In one corner sits a small green velveteen armchair. In another, a golden-yellow hassock, torn at the seams and with the stuffing hanging out. Black steel filing cabinets contain the "current monthly write-ups" (a brief report on each call), referral information, emergency telephone numbers, clippings of interest. Two phones sit in the middle of each desk. Beside them, a black goose-necked lamp offers a little extra light. Along the rear of the desks are more files and folders, a tan box of "Counselor Communications Cards" (in case staff wishes to comment on some call a counselor has received), a digital clock radio with red numbers on a field of black, bowls filled with M & M's and miniature Tootsie Rolls, a silver-and-red flashlight, a tabletop air cleaner that's never on, a copy of the *American Heritage Dictionary*—the edition with Indo-European roots at the back. A well-thumbed green logbook lies ready for the next entry—all calls are noted according to date, time, and counselor. A red spiral-bound binder, the "Emergency Resource Book," steers counselors through everything from rescue procedures to the locations of local bridges. On an open-frame steel bookcase, which might once have held power tools, back issues of the journal *Suicide and Life-Threatening Behavior* lie in stacks among various magazines and books. On the floor, a black boom box, silent, coated in a thin layer of dust, sits beside a Dustbuster. A gray school-model pencil sharpener is attached to a doorjamb. And near it, hanging on the door, is a large desk calendar on which counselors sign up for their shifts.

"Whew, that was exhausting," Frieda says, putting down the phone. She rubs her hand across her forehead and pushes her bangs straight back, pulling the skin tight. "Mary Jo is having a tough day. We talked for about an hour. I'm out cold." Putting both palms on the desktop for support, she slowly stands. "I did the write-up as we were finishing." She tucks a sheet of paper into a folder, hoists a smile onto her face, and says in a weary drawl, "Bye-eye."

"Good-bye," I respond, and sit down at the desk. The chair is still warm, and as I settle into it, it squeaks like a porpoise.

Darkness has just begun to envelop the town. Overhead, a saucer-shaped glass fixture with a pretty etched-leaf design covers two light-bulbs. The light it showers down on the room is soft and yellowy. A silver mobile hangs in one corner of the ceiling, its seventeen seagulls perfectly motionless. I blow hard at it and soon the birds begin to glide.

One tall window faces the driveway and the other, behind one of the desks, looks out onto the yard next door. Both are covered with thin tulle curtains which have grown so dingy they've lost their ability to shimmer. Cork bulletin boards on the east wall provide a guide to who is available for "Emergency After Hours"—that is, who can be reached by beeper if a consultation is needed or an emergency unfolds. On the west wall, a white poster offers a list of important places and their numbers: the Task Force for Battered Women, the emergency room at the hospital, the Poison Control Center, the Mental Health Clinic, Family and Children's Service, and so on. One of the most important filing cabinets, stationed between the two sets of phones, holds a laboriously gathered and researched library of special support groups, private organizations, and public agencies in the area. So it's possible to refer a caller to a support group for cross-dressers, or find help for a sexually abused child, or give a caller a list of places that will help him or her find a job, or a meal, or a safe house, or friends in similar circumstances. The business lines ring in the normal way, but the crisis lines ring with a sudden loud two-part jangle that's startling. It's the telephone equivalent of a fire alarm.

—

7:45 P.M. First call. A single father phones about his sixteen-year-old daughter, who has become too wild for him to manage. She stays out late, even on school nights, drinking heavily with her friends and taking drugs. Though he's tried to talk with her about her addictions, she won't listen. Last night she returned home with a black eye and refuses to say how it happened. Seeing her physically hurt is more than her father can bear. We speak for an hour or so, during which he unfolds his deep frustration and fear, then anger and guilt. When he feels calm enough to make plans, we discuss his joining a support group like Al-Anon, where he would find other people who have loved ones abusing alcohol or drugs. I cannot help his daughter, who did not call. The father is suffering; my job is to try to help *him.*

"Do you think it might give me a better relationship with my daughter?" he asks.

"I don't know," I answer. "But you would meet people in circumstances similar to yours, and they might be able to give you some ideas about what has worked for them, or not worked. At the very least, you won't be facing this problem all alone."

"What's their number?" he says, his voice strong for the first time since the conversation began. I give it to him, and then I invite him to call back if the support group doesn't work out, or if he just needs to talk. He thanks me, and we say good-bye.

Although I suggested an agency that could help him, I did little talking through the hour-long call. SP counselors are not therapists. Our job is not to search through psyches, picking problems apart and making sense of their origins and patterns. We don't engage the caller in the usual give-and-take of a conversation, or offer advice. What we do is listen. Sometimes it feels like auditory braille, and I can see the callers' faces in my mind's eye, and read their expressions. Sometimes it works like echolocation: I send out small reconnoitering sounds—a leading question, perhaps—and wait to hear in what shape and from where it echoes back. There is an art to making listening noises, which I have not yet mastered, and after a long silence, a caller may ask, "Are you still there?" "Yes," I answer, "I was just thinking about what you said."

We do not listen passively, the way one does during a lecture. We're not much distracted by personal thoughts, as one is in normal conversation—listening while thinking about what to say next, perhaps something about one's own related experiences. We listen actively, and it is physically exhausting. It feels like a contact sport.

Listening athletically, with one's whole attention, one hears the words, the sighs, the sniffling, the loud exhalations, the one-beat-longer-than-normal pause before a difficult or taboo word, the voice-falls of misgiving, the whittling of worry, the many diphthongs of grief, the heavy tongue of drunkenness, the piled ingots of guilt, the quiet screeching of self-blame, the breathlessness of fear, the restless volcano of panic, the fumings of stifled rage, the staccato spasms of frustration, the sidestepping anger of the "yes, but"-ers, the tumbling ideas of the developmentally disabled, the magic dramas of the hallucinator, the idea shards of the psychotic, the harrowed tones of the battered, the bleak deadpan of the hopeless, the pacing of the ambivalent, the entrenched gloom of depression, the distant recesses of loneliness, the anxiousness that is like a wringing of the hands.

One hears the silences and the spaces between the words, as well. They have a rhythm and shape all their own. And one hears many inanimate things, too—ice tinkling in a glass, a cigarette being smoked, the television set on in a nearby room, the traffic outside the caller's window.

Perhaps it seems a little odd to be touching other lives and analyzing their condition simply through sound. But listening in this way is what many animals do, communicating over long distances: whales, frogs, wolves, birds. Just as doctors auscultate by pressing their ear to the patient's chest, or listening down the line of a stethoscope, we press an ear to the warm receiver of the phone and listen for the heartbeat beneath the words. The words are the surface of an ocean of grief, and they may sound like a squall, a doldrum, a typhoon; we listen for hidden currents below.

8:47 P.M. A developmentally disabled woman calls; talking in a slow staccato, she is upset that some children teased her today. We talk for half an hour, and she decides it's time to go to bed.

9:22 P.M. The telephone rings, and I answer it briskly, only to find no one there. "Hang-up," I jot down in a logbook on the desk. Hang-ups are frequent—not everyone is ready to make contact, but they want to know someone is here for when they *are* ready.

In the lulls between calls, I page through a notebook of press clippings and find the obituary of a young man I'll call Allen, troubled by depression and loneliness, who called SP often over a period of three years. I touch my fingers to the printed words, which suddenly look strange as hieroglyphs, flat as a tombstone. We could not save him. Perhaps we had for some while, for those three years when we were his lifeline. It reminds me of the time I was driving home from a shift at about eight o'clock on a Sunday morning. The streets were empty, but on one, near a bridge, I saw a group of ambulances. Sure enough, somebody had jumped. And I thought: Why didn't that person call us? We were there all night! Why didn't he call? The painful truth is that people irrevocably bent on suicide tend not to call. We are there for the people who still have some precarious, tenuous connection to life left. That's what we speak to when they call. We don't tell them not to kill themselves. Suicide is certainly one option open to them—and we respect their right to choose when to live or die—but it's not the only option. Suicide is a permanent solution to a temporary problem, as we like to say. The part of them that clings to life called us, and so we explore what other options still remain.

9:15 P.M. A middle-aged woman calls. She is restless and on edge; her speech sounds a little slurred, perhaps from drinking. She has phoned often before, and I recognize her voice.

"This is Melissa...have I talked with you before?" she asks.

"Yes, Melissa. How are you feeling today?"

"Not so good."

The last time I talked with Melissa, two weeks ago, it was early morning and she was savagely depressed. I have been worried about her for quite a while because she seems terribly fragile, and I'm afraid we may lose her. In her early forties, she is intelligent and articulate. She has two young children and is in a second marriage, this time to an alcoholic husband who sometimes becomes violent. She has a poor relationship with her parents. She is going back to school to finish a college degree. She is breathtakingly sensitive, very critical of herself, pummeled by self-doubt, and often lonely. Her life is riddled with stress, and it's only when something hits unbearable proportions that she phones. After all, we are a crisis service. But "crisis" is a relative term. Everyone's emotional thermostat is set differently.

By definition, a crisis is what impedes the normal flow of someone's life, and that may be as public as a divorce, as physical as an overdose, or as subtle as a nagging worry. We think of crisis as something gone awry, as an illness of circumstance or fate. Yet, when we watch wild animals, we see lives storied with crises. For them, crisis is part of the usual fabric of their existence. It is not rare or special. Although they seek to avoid crises, many more will arrive. Crisis is normal, but painful and disruptive. In that sense, a crisis service is unnatural. As unnatural as living in a heated house in winter, and wanting to help others stay warm, too.

When people call in crisis, I want to help them regain equilibrium. There was a time when extended families played this role—kin and neighbors, peers and elders—offering solace and understanding in times of trouble. With so many generations and in-laws on hand, one could always find a confidant or an advocate. Families expected crises to emerge from time to time, because crisis is a normal part of human life and cannot be wholly erased or relieved. In evolutionary terms, it provides turning points, it allows necessary change. When we say wistfully that *we are creatures of habit,* we rarely pause to consider the biological truth of the statement. Habit is the great deadener; but habit also assures an organism that what worked before will work again. It is the best survival technique. *Eat the berries on that tree,* it argues, *they didn't poison you before.* But habit can lead to boredom and frustration, which is also adaptive. Contented creatures don't feel driven to change their lives, as they often must to survive in a changing environment. It is also adaptive to hate crisis and strive for calm, when no one is threatened and the children can safely grow. So crises may be normal, and even liberating, but they are painful and frightening, and we are compassionate creatures.

I cannot stop the crisis Melissa finds herself in when she calls. All I can offer her is a breather, a temporary safety zone in which to help explore her feelings and help review her resources and options. I can be with her in the long corridors of the night, when troubles can take on monstrous proportions. I can be with her in the morning, when she phones from a bed she is unable to climb out of, because her day is an avalanche waiting to fall. I can be with her at noon in a phone booth, just after she has been laid off from work in midwinter, with no job on the horizon and a family to help feed. I can be with her when her husband has stormed out to go drinking, and she is shaking in the aftermath of his violent rage. I can be with her when she gets an F on an exam and decides death is preferable to her disappointing future. All I can do is be with her telephonically. I listen. At times, I have urged her to call one of the agencies in town that provide support groups, legal advice, and ongoing help. On rare occasions, when I believed she was in physical danger from herself or someone else, I intervened and sent help. But my goal is not to intervene. My goal is to make intervention unnecessary because I've helped her reach a safer place—mentally or physically. My goal is for her to keep control of as much of her life as possible. I do not give advice, and sometimes I actually say that.

"I don't know what to do," Melissa sobs tonight. Her husband came home drunk and beat her in front of her small children. She is terrified to stay with him, and terrified he'll find her if she leaves. In any case, she has no money of her own, no full-time job, no way to feed the children. She is afraid he might even get custody if she runs off and isn't employed. "What should I do?" With all my heart, I want to tell her, *Leave him! Take the children and get out now! Now before he comes back home. Get out as fast as you can!* But I would not have been the first person to give her such advice.

"I can't tell you what to do," I say, "but maybe together we can figure something out. Let's explore what your options are tonight." Then we review several plans that have occurred to her, and some that occur to me. In time, still frightened but a little more focused, she decides at least to talk with someone at the Task Force for Battered Women, who have a safe house where she and her children can go while they help her put her life back together.

10:15 P.M. "Suicide Prevention and Crisis Service," I say. "Can I help you?"

"No." A male voice.

"What's on your mind this evening?"

Suddenly irate: "A bigoted society. Vicious, rotten, loveless, sucking-on-a-gun society. You're no good at all! Anyone who doesn't love me doesn't love God. Louis Armstrong said that. If I were evil, I'd understand it, but I'm not. Anyone who hates me doesn't have the love of Jesus in them. You're all bigoted!" Caller hangs up.

10:17 P.M. Same caller: "Another thing. Women are the most vicious members of society."

"You've had experiences with women who were vicious?" I ask in a level voice.

"No. Just a general observation. They don't even deserve to be called human beings."

"What do they do that's so vicious?"

Caller hangs up.

10:19 P.M. Same caller: "I've been the recipient long enough."

"The what?"

"The recipient." Long loud scream like a lightning strike.

10:22 P.M. Same caller: "You're a monster. You're all monsters! You're monsters!"

"You sound like you're in so much pain." I say.

"PAIN? PAIN? You don't give a fuck about my pain, you cock-sucking bitch. You're all monsters!" Caller hangs up.

10:25 P.M. Hang-up. Probably the same caller. He phones every now and then, insults a counselor for a shift, then doesn't call for days or weeks. Some of the counselors dread his calls and are rattled by them; some look forward to them as a challenge, one or two have even managed to engage him in conversation long enough to discover a little of his bizarre story. Apparently he is a Vietnam veteran, suffering from Agent Orange exposure, who works as a night watchman at a factory, and lives in a cabin in a small farming community. He has four children, and we're worried about all of them, but especially the two girls. He claims to have facial tattoos and a mechanical hand. We don't know his name, but one counselor labeled him "Edward Scissorhands" on a write-up and the tag stuck. "Edward" I jot down in the logbook, and on the write-up sheet I note simply: "The usual."

10:30 P.M. I hear the front door open, the stairs begin creaking. Soon a woman with short red hair appears in the doorway to start the next shift. We say hello and she goes into the kitchen to fix herself a cup of coffee. There are seventy-five counselors on active duty, and we take five-hour shifts—except for the overnight shift, which runs from 10:00 P.M. to 8:00 A.M. We have very little in common when it comes to background, education, family life, religious upbringing, personality, or income. Many of us have experienced great trauma or hardship, survived it, and want to help others. Each of us knows pain, heartache, humiliation, shock, fury, the unspeakable. Who doesn't? One might imagine that crisis-line counselors lead more stable, less troubled lives than the callers, but that isn't always true. This was a surprising and powerful discovery for me. For example, a young man in my training class told with a visible chill how he had returned from classes one day to find his roommate lying dead in a pool of blood, and a suicide note on the counter. He had loved his roommate dearly, and knew he had been depressed, but not *that* depressed. How could he have missed the danger signs, been deaf to the appeals for help? In retrospect, they seemed obvious. It took years for him to make peace with horror and guilt. A mature woman in the same training class described a lifetime of coping with an alcoholic mother who was violent, unpredictable, and needed to be mothered herself much of the time. Long after training was over, a gifted counselor confided that she has been struggling with depression for many years, takes medication for it, and usually feels strong and good-humored. Although her spirits were fine when she volunteered for SP work, by the time training classes began she had tumbled into a perilous depression, one of the worst of her life. By day, she suffered bloodcurdling lows. But she was able to shake them during the intensely dramatic hours of training. I trained in the same class with her and never detected her private suffering. None of us did. She always seemed cheerful and devout about counseling. Faced with the pain of others, she could shelve her depression, vacate her prison of worries, reach deep into a generous, nurturing part of herself, and provide help. Depression waited for her at home, but it vanished when the crisis line rang. After a couple of months, the low ran its course and the doldrums lifted. Hers was an extreme example of how much distress a person can be in and yet triumph as a counselor. But it taught me an important lesson: One does not need to be stronger, fitter, morally better, or untroubled to come to the aid of people in crisis. One has to be able to put one's own problems on hold and listen heartfully, nonjudgmentally, and focus entirely on someone else's need. In fact, there is a relief that comes from being able to get your mind off your problems as you do work that's worthwhile. Many big-hearted people are drawn to public service of a more visible sort, but SP attracts people who prefer altruistic anonymity, who don't want to be singled out. Because no one else is applauding or even eavesdropping, you become your sole judge; you must decide for yourself if you are worthy.

Most counselors volunteer simply because the work makes them feel good. What does that feeling consist of? It's slightly different for everyone, but for me it's equal measures of compassion, accomplishment, a sense of myself as a good person, and a curious sleight of mind: the chance to renovate my past by helping others change the present. When I was little, I had a chromium ball on whose equator was inscribed the Golden Rule: *Do unto others as you would have them do unto you.* As selfish as that axiom may sound, it inspires good works. Symbolically, I'll grant you. But we often attempt to revise our history in someone else's life. A counselor once told me that although she isn't a naturally compassionate person, on the phones she becomes a version of herself she can admire.

Although I've tried to be candid in this book, I've also chosen not to reveal some details of my own story, out of respect for the people in my life who would be hurt. Unlike the callers, who have the luxury of being anonymous, I do not. You see my face. Suffice it to say that I've experienced a wide range of suffering, some of which I've carried with me all my life and probably always will. Trauma early in life is written in indelible ink. Trauma later in life stays with one in powerful ways, too. My life also includes joy, love, adventure, fulfillment, and discovery. No boredom. Never a dull torment. But I've seen enough of the dark side to identify with a wide range of callers. Many of them are trapped in nightmares I have survived. Their stories, flowing along the telephone lines in this small town, have been complex and fascinating. It's unbelievable what predicaments human beings get themselves into. So I find crisis work simultaneously heart-wrenching, frightening, stressful, and deeply rewarding. None of these rewards are public, of course. Being a crisis-line counselor may be one of the most emotionally demanding things that human beings do for one another, but unlike paramedics or firemen, say, who receive public praise for their death-defying efforts, my counselor colleagues act in secret; ours is always a private drama, a vicarious relief, an inner triumph.

Suicide hasn't touched the lives of all our counselors, some of whom volunteer for other reasons, but enough have felt death's heavy hand on their shoulder to recognize the feeling. If it doesn't kill you, surviving your own death or someone else's can be a tonic, a metallic drug that makes the world shine brighter, your heart beat stronger, and the knowledge that you can face down death a formidable tool.

Frank Drake was a typical counselor. Married, the father of two, he was a professor who divided his time between teaching and research. He made jewelry, scuba dived, and had other hobbies. A tall, slender man with an easygoing manner, he was already a renowned astronomer, playing a vital role in the search for extraterrestrial intelligence. Using radio telescopes as giant ears, he explored the silent tundra of outer space for signs of life. If you sit in the domed darkness of a planetarium, listening to a lecture on the heavens, odds are the speaker will refer to the "Drake equation," which calculates the likelihood of other planets being inhabited.

From time to time he had been stationed at observatories around the world, remote spots that were perfect settings for nervous breakdowns. He had met people who were alone, away from home and family, under stress, and dealing with overwhelming questions. A few had attempted suicide, or were contemplating it. With his prematurely white hair and gentle manner, he looked like someone distressed souls could turn to, and they did. This had happened to him so often that he thought formal training might be helpful and so he joined SP. But once he started answering the crisis line, it got into his blood, and he stayed on for nine years. He preferred the overnight (never referred to as *graveyard*) shift, which stretches to 8:00 A.M, and often includes the most dangerous or depressed callers.

None of the callers ever knew his name. His neighbors and friends didn't know he was a volunteer. As all counselors must, he took an oath of confidentiality. For the hot line to work, callers have to feel safe and discreet. They want to talk to a person they will never meet. (That is one reason why I have changed the callers' names and any identifying details.) Although I had known Drake for a decade, I only learned of his night vigils after he left town and took a job at the University of California at Santa Cruz.

One August, we both happened to be aboard a ship off the coast of Baja, waiting to view a total eclipse of the sun. Lasting seven minutes, it would be the longest eclipse of the century. Drake was at the height of his career. Soon his voice would brim from loudspeakers all over the ship and guide 500 passengers through one of the great spectacles of the ages, the kind of event that had stirred civilizations and changed history. But for the moment his mind was on a different kind of gloom—the eclipsed spirits of the callers he had handled at SP— and in the failing light, he spoke about those days.

"Some of the calls were real heart-pounders," he said. "A caller would already have taken a lethal dose of pills, or be threatening to shoot a dozen people with a rifle he had brought into the phone booth with him, and I'd be thinking hard: What question can I ask, what trick can I play, to get this person to say where he *is*?"

Detective work is difficult when all one has to go on is sound, but background noises do offer telling clues. Once, dealing with a violence-bent drunk, Drake heard the downshift arpeggios of passing cars, and pieced together which intersection the man might be calling from. Sure enough, that's where the police found and disarmed him. On another occasion, a woman in the process of committing suicide called him. Although she was ambivalent enough to call, she wouldn't say where she was. There was nothing left to interest her, she had moaned after a long time. Desperate, Drake said the first thing that came into his head: "How about astronomy? Astronomy is full of interesting things." She agreed, and they talked a while about the stars and planets. When she referred in passing to the moon-shaped window across the street from her, something clicked in Drake's memory. He had driven past that window. The police arrived in time to rush her to the hospital. A month later, when she regained her equilibrium, she sent a heartfelt note to SP, thanking whoever was on duty that night for saving her life.

"What would you do after a harrowing shift?" I asked Drake. "How could you calmly go about your life?"

"You'd think that after eight or nine years you'd get so calloused, so hardened by other people's grief, that it wouldn't have any impact on you any longer. But for me it was actually the other way around. At home, trying to sleep, I found myself getting upset for those people all over again, and that wasn't good. After a night of dealing with really heavy stuff, I'd be nonfunctional the next day. So I finally burned out." He paused. "But there were these major moments in people's lives that I was sharing. I often think those were the most important hours I ever spent in my whole life."

Returning home, I couldn't shake my curiosity about an agency that, according to Drake, performed quiet acts of mercy and heroism, but also transformed the lives of volunteers. Who were these people? One fall morning I phoned SP to ask if they could use a laptop computer I didn't need. Marian van Soest, who was then director, proclaimed the call heaven-sent, since SP urgently needed another computer, and she graciously accepted mine, adding, to my astonishment, that there was one condition: I would have to agree to speak at the annual meeting. Odd way to accept a donation, I thought, but charmingly full of chutzpah, so I agreed and gave a talk on altruism to a merry gathering of SP's counselors, staff, and governing board. They had a relaxed, somewhat macabre sense of humor; they played hard, and they *felt* the world's troubles in an unusually candid way. I liked their spirit. After that, one thing led to another, until at last I found myself taking the training.

———

There are two or three training classes a year, and I trained in the winter. Tuesday and Thursday nights and Saturday mornings, for six weeks, we met in a city building down by the lake. Buses and vans were parked outside and the only lit part of the building was a conference room in which fifteen chairs were arranged in a circle. My fellow trainees included an ex-mortician, a social worker, a combat photographer from the Gulf War, a musician, a premed student, an ex-radio announcer pursuing a degree in psychology, a volunteer firefighter, a biogeneticist, a carpenter with a literature degree, an air traffic controller, and a man who had delivered three of his own children. They ran the gamut of ages and ethnic backgrounds. The oldest was fifty-eight, the youngest twenty-two. Kate, Fred (who works many overnight shifts), and a changing crew of up to four additional counselors and staff people were the trainers. At our first meeting, we did listening exercises, including one in which we formed two circles, so that half of us stood facing the other half.

"You'll have three minutes," Kate said. "The inner-circle person must talk continuously for that time about the topic I'm going to give you. The other person must only listen. Ready? Okay . . . talk about your mother."

I shake my head with a laugh, as I recall what a challenge that deceptively simple exercise was—talking for only three minutes nonstop—how my mouth had opened and I began at the beginning, where my mother was born, her circumstances, her probable emotional life, how that affected her choice of husband and how she related to her children. I remember that Fred listened intently, his face making interested, encouraging expressions. By day, he taught small children, whose astonished lives were all future; by night, he listened to the misfortunes of the world, and helped people whose lives seemed all past. When Kate called "Stop!" the inner circle stepped a pace to the left, and I had the job of listening this time to the genial stranger facing me, a conservatively dressed woman in her fifties, with a pleasant but somewhat strict face.

"Ready?" Kate had asked, stopwatch in hand. "Okay...talk about masturbation."

I remember how fast the color drained out of the woman's face, how long it seemed to take her eyebrows to relax, and yet how gamely she managed somehow to talk about masturbation for three minutes solid. My job was to make encouraging, accepting, interested, listening noises and facial expressions without showing disapproval or embarrassment. Not so easy! Some of the topics that day, as I recall, were suicide, loneliness, depression, and homosexuality. Among other goals, this exercise helped us practice the subtle art of communicating without words, conveying such things as trust and lack of judgment. Other exercises emphasized other skills, and much time was spent during the first weeks in explaining ourselves to one another, so that we were more than the name tag worn at every session, more than a set of ears or a whispering mouth. Two of the trainees started dating. One trainee (who couldn't bridle her strong opinions during calls) was asked to leave. Three others dropped out. The rest of us practiced following a six-step crisis model, which involves making contact with the caller at a feeling level (by reflecting and identifying feelings), exploring the current problem (through open-ended questions), summarizing the problem (and agreeing on a common understanding), problem-solving if possible, exploring resources (such as past coping techniques and agency referrals), and agreeing on a plan of action (or perhaps arranging a follow-up call). At every session we received a short lecture; watched two experienced counselors, sitting back to back in the middle of the room, role play calls relevant to the evening's theme; and we practiced role plays ourselves, with a counselor monitoring each twosome and giving them feedback. We learned about the different parts of a call and practiced the opening moments as well as the endings. We practiced talking with depressed callers, suicidal callers, gay callers, cross-dressing callers, addicted callers, masturbating callers, battered callers, developmentally disabled callers, violent or abusive callers, obsessive callers, and a caravan of others. We discussed our own feelings and prejudices, the need for banishing them when we're on shift, and various ways of empathizing with, empowering, and widening the world of the caller. We learned how to send rescue, and where to find referrals and resources. Stumbling and tongue-tied at first, sometimes disheartened and unsure, we discovered in time that techniques clicked into place. And yet, when training ended and we signed up for apprentice shifts, not one of us felt fully confident. How would we react when it wasn't practice, when lives were at stake? Each of us was riddled by self-doubt. Nonetheless I began counseling fifteen hours a month, and sifting deeper and deeper into the soul of the agency.

Nine thousand calls a year now flow into SP, and about a thousand of those are related to suicide. This in a town of 18,000 people, a county of roughly 95,000. The agency began in the late sixties, after a rash of student suicides. Stunned by the death of a friend who had hanged himself, a student begged Jack Lewis, a local minister, to *do something*. Lewis approached a psychologist, George Miller, and before long a small group of concerned people coalesced to establish a crisis hot line. They installed a single telephone in an upstairs bedroom at a parsonage downtown, and took turns answering it, using whatever counseling techniques they could agree on or improvise. They used to pass the hat at board meetings to collect money to pay bills, and they often counseled callers in person, even if it meant going to a motel room at 3:00 A.M. or meeting someone in the park at midnight.

"We lived on a sort of love and pale moonlight," Jack Lewis once explained to me. Now eighty, still a practicing minister, Lewis vividly remembers his early years with SP. There were no six-week training sessions, no counselor support groups (attendance is required, since burnout is always a potential problem), little financial support. "But we shared the crises of the community, it drew us together."

And it tested his courage. For example, one Sunday morning in 1971, Lewis was summoned to a terrifying scene. A man was holding a loaded gun on his family, threatening to kill them and himself and anyone else who got in the way. Lewis walked right into the man's house, sat down beside him, and said quietly: "Tell me your story." Ten hours later, the man gave him the gun. The truth buried in this drama gets to the very heart of Crisis Center work: each of us has a story, each of us has a loaded gun that we aim at ourselves. After hours, or years, of talking, the story can at last be told in its fullness, and the gun can be laid down. The story has both happy and sad chapters, and parts of it may be forgotten. Sometimes it takes an outsider to help remember or clarify it. Lose your story and you lose the pageant of your life.

Lewis also told me about a chilling incident that he had witnessed. A deaf, epileptic young man intent upon ending his life had parked his car at one end of a bridge and climbed over the railing to perch trembling on a parapet. Soon the city police arrived, and parked at the north end of the bridge; the campus police parked at the other end. Whenever someone tried to approach, the man threatened to jump. SP was called and a counselor hurried to the bridge. Jack Lewis arrived a little later. By then night had fallen, and flashlights held the young man with ropes of brilliant dust. The counselor had insinuated herself closer and closer to him. Because he was deaf, she turned a flashlight on under her chin so that he could read her lips as she talked with him. Depressed and desperate, but indecisive, he would turn to jump, feel her concern, turn away from the gorge, only to reject her words and turn back again. But in time she got through to him, and at last he began climbing up from the parapet. It was precisely at that moment— as he was throwing one leg up over the railing to safety—that he had an epileptic seizure ... and fell to his death in the gorge. The counselor screamed all her breath out and her screams echoed down the stone canyons. After heroic hours, she had saved him, and then in seconds, in a terrifying flash of complete helplessness, had lost him.

10:48 P.M. The phone rings. "Suicide Prevention and Crisis Service," I say in a welcoming voice, an achieved voice. "May I help you?" For a few seconds, only silence answers, and I glance out the window. A thick shoal of meteors is due before dawn. It will drift too close to Earth, brush violently against air particles and explode into a firestorm of shooting stars. Severe friction, that's all it takes. Unconsciously, I press my ear more tightly to the phone, as if I could lean closer to the caller. I think I can hear the choked breath of someone crying.

A distraught woman says, "My husband just..." The voice hovers, searches for bearable words, then settles on: "...hurt me."

"Your husband hurt you?" I repeat calmly. "Could you tell me about it?"

In a voice half-whisper, half-sob, she tells me—a stranger—the intimate and horrifying details of her day, how her husband came home drunk and brutal. A sarcastic remark made him erupt into a violent rage, during which he had torn off her robe and beaten her. Terrified, she ran out into the street and just kept running. She is in a phone booth, in her nightgown. It is a clear March night and there are frost warnings. She does not want an ambulance or the police. She does not want anyone to know. She feels humiliated and desperate. She refuses to say where she is. She is afraid her husband will come after her. Her voice trembles from cold, anger, and fright.

"I'm so glad you phoned," I say, trying to press my concern through my voice and down the slender thread of the phone wire. I want it to be an invisible arm wrapping around her. "You sound scared and upset."

"Scared to death," she whispers, adding under her breath, "I shouldn't have said what I did...it's my fault, I provoked him like I always do."

"No one deserves to be beaten," I say. "Look, I'm worried about you, and I'd really like to get somebody to come over and be with you."

"No, I can't face anyone...my life is such a mess," she says, crying. "I'm so confused. I don't know what to do."

"That's okay," I say. "I understand how frightened and confused you're feeling. How about if we just talk for a while. How would that be?"

Twenty minutes later, a little calmer, she agrees to let someone escort her to a safe place. When help arrives with a blanket, they find her standing nearly naked in a phone booth, shivering in the greenish light of a nearby streetlamp.

CHAPTER 2

Squirrels, and the Dark Night of the Soul

Awakening to a misty day, I fix myself a cup of Peruvian coffee that smells loamlike and bitter, and remember the noisy streets of Cuzco, where chic ladies in stiletto heels strolled beside farm laborers. Swiveling my memory, I can also picture the rain-soaked mountains and coffee plantations, then peer farther inland to the dense, teeming Amazon. Or is it the Brazilian Amazon I'm picturing? Or the Colombian? I'm sure it's not the Mata Atlantica rain forest northeast of Rio, where the last surviving golden lion tamarins scamper—which I remember in vivid detail down to the sloths and orchids. In my heart I know these regions vary the way humans do; they have essential natures in common but different cultures, different personalities, and they're endangered in uniquely different ways. Yet in my memory they've all begun to blur into one throbbingly beautiful, vine-clad rain forest, and that saddens me. Memory is such a damned good collector and organizer. How quickly the unique One becomes the indistinct Many and then the Many an emblematic and impersonal One.

Carrying my coffee into the garden room, I crank open a window, and call the squirrels as usual, warbling to them in a melodic two-note that starts high and slides lower: "SQUIR-rels, SQUIR-rels, SQUIR-rels." Then I quickly scatter a mix of peanuts, hazelnuts, Brazil nuts, and almonds in a wide arc. The nuts are unsalted and still in their shells, just as squirrels would find them in nature—that is, if they happened to live simultaneously in New York State, Georgia, and the Amazon. Scufflings begin deep in the two acres of woods as squirrels leave the warmth of their leaf nests and rush down tree trunks, leap across brush and woodpiles, and run along telephone and electric wires toward the house, using their tails to balance, tightrope-walker-style.

Knowing this unseasonal bounty will soon be devoured, I sit back and survey the dawn. There's nothing like the fecund beauty of spring in New York State. Separate raindrops lie along the twigs of a maple branch—round, brilliant globules—trembling without falling. All the light of the morning seems trapped in their small worlds. You can smell the mixing fragrances of spring, bud-luscious and full of growth. But it's a difficult time for animals. Spring means waking from the long coma of winter into a land of hardship and haste. Roused from their winter stupors, they find food scarce and little yet in bloom. Locating a mate becomes an urgent quest. Humans suffer in this season, too. At the Crisis Center, we receive more calls in spring than during any other time of year. No one is sure why. I think it may be the stark contrast between the blossoming world outside and the perceived desert of the callers' lives. Sometimes I picture their lives as complex emotional ecosystems, like rain forests, and their hurts as huge fallen brown leaves among the undergrowth. A masseur once told me, as he walked the palms of his hands up my spine vertebra by vertebra, that he visualized a healthy green force coursing through him when he worked, pictured it flowing into the body of his patient, healing and strengthening her. I wish I could do that with callers, send a green force down the line, wish I could heal by hand, the way surgeons do, reaching into the Armageddon of the body and declaring peace. How beautifully Shakespeare turned that wish into a question in *Macbeth*:

> Canst thou not minister to a mind diseased,
> Pluck from the memory a rooted sorrow,
> Raze out the written troubles of the brain,
> And with some sweet oblivious antidote
> Cleanse the stuffed bosom of that perilous stuff
> Which weighs upon the heart?

The last time I heard from my friends at Interplast—the volunteer cosmetic surgeons who operate on the faces of deformed children—they were still flying into small Peruvian towns to resculpt the lives of kids who have cleft palates, burns, or other facial disasters. This has become exceedingly dangerous, now that the Shining Path guerrillas are on the prowl for Americans. I make a mental note to call Interplast and suggest they add a social worker to their trip rosters. Fixing a deformity may improve a child's face, but there are bound to be less obvious scars. When I went with them to Honduras a few years ago, to help out with the children and to write about Interplast's mission for *The New York Times Magazine,* there was so much laughter and fun surrounding the nerve-racking work. That's true of the Crisis Center crowd, too. The counselors laugh easily and tend to be very sociable. A dozen of them have planned a trip to a nearby city next week to visit blues clubs, and another group is taking swing-dancing lessons. I've signed up for a bird-watching hike through the state forest, led by an emeritus professor who is a superb naturalist.

A drumroll across the roof grows louder and then stops. I feel something watching me, look up, and see the Pleader—a large muscular male gray squirrel—on the roof, examining me, the morning, and the sudden appearance of manna. Whiskers twitching, he leans over the edge and fixes me with shiny dark eyes.

"Breakfast?" I ask.

He coils up fast, raises and lowers his head rapidly, springs off his haunches, and leaps eight feet to a slender hickory, is down its trunk in four strides, and at the window in two more. It's not that the strewn nuts aren't appealing, it's just that the Pleader prefers walnuts, and, as he knows by now, I keep those indoors.

I hold a walnut lightly between thumb and forefinger and offer it to him, feeling the gentlest tug as he lifts it free. Twisting around fast, he takes a watchful position on a rock, turning the nut on the lathe of his teeth and paws until he finds the exact spot to drill a hole. This he does with his two chisel-shaped front teeth, then he carries the nut like a bowling ball as he runs to a large hickory and scampers up its shaggy trunk to the first branch. From that lookout post he can see a mob of squirrels arriving, grabbing nuts, squabbling over territories. He widens the hole in the walnut and attacks the meat, spitting out a plume of husks.

"What a buzz saw," I say out loud, smiling. He continues to watch me with a look of uneasy vigilance. When he finishes half of the nut, he holds the remainder like a bowl of porridge and carefully lifts out the lung-shaped meat.

I call him the Pleader because of the way he always finds me in my study or in the living room, and gives me a look insistent as a placard. When he gets my attention, he runs to the glassed-in garden room, races up to the window, and stares. He stands up on his back feet, arms held at his chest, stretching to look in, face alert and expectant. Above all, the Pleader is daring—brave enough not to flee when I open the creaky window. Brave enough to take a large walnut from my hand. Brave enough to drive off competitors from his small pile of food.

Often when I open the window he comes up and puts his head inside, watching me as I reach into a half-barrel of nuts. If I leave both the window and nut barrel open, he will climb right in, help himself, and dart outside to eat. When the window is closed, he puts his bulging eye up to it like one of the horses in Picasso's *Guernica,* and peers in.

I'm halfway through a two-year research project for *National Geographic* (which provides the nuts and a photographer), studying the secret life of gray squirrels, taking field notes, and trying my best to fathom their ways. How could they not become familiars? I haven't exactly adopted the squirrels, it's just that I worry about their well-being during the hard winters, and I've become fascinated by their relationships, instinctive behaviors, and antics, especially the Pleader's. A small irregularity on his left ear is his only marking, but I always know him by his unusual alertness, muscular shoulders, and eager, exploratory verve.

Mind you, this is nothing compared to the legendary nerve and insight of squirrels. *Daylight Robbery,* a British film about gray squirrels, reveals the high jinks of one who figured out how to break into a vending machine. The squirrel enters through the wide metal flap at the bottom, climbs up inside, and moments later returns with a Baby Ruth bar, which it calmly unwraps and eats. I've known of people setting obstacle courses for squirrels—the most ingenious one requiring them to climb up a greased pole, leap a wide chasm, tunnel inside a pipe, and, finally, fly across the yard in a red rocketship—all to get hazelnuts. It took the squirrels only two weeks to master. Myself, I put up a squirrel gymnasium, which includes a Ferris wheel of four corn-cobs, a picnic table with a chair the squirrel must sit in if it wants to eat from a corncob, a "Pandora's Box" filled with peanuts (the lid is too heavy for birds but easy for a squirrel to lift to remove nuts one at a time), a two-armed seesaw with a corncob at either end, and a trapeze with a corncob in the middle. They figured out all five within half an hour and seem to enjoy the challenge each offers. It gives me a better chance to study their stretchings, agility, and underparts.

Although when I'm in a rain forest I caress it with all my senses, and am grateful for the privilege, I also love temperate forests, scrublands, lake shores, glaciers, even city parks. One doesn't have to leave home to encounter the exotic. Our human habitat encompasses rolling velds and mown lawns, remote deserts and the greater wilderness of cities—all "natural" ecosystems. Many animals inhabit the small patch of woods out back, from deer, raccoons, skunks, wild turkeys, garter snakes, and other large fauna down to spiders, moths, and swarming insects. I spend happy hours there watching the natural world bustle about its business. The animals all seem caught up in one intriguing drama or another, especially the squirrels. Their small distresses echo the ones I see among my neighbors, their small triumphs teach me about the indomitableness of life.

In a flash, the Pleader returns for a hazelnut and scampers back up the tree, barely disturbing the large gang of assembled squirrels. Busily feeding are "Mr. Tatter Tail," a male whose tail falls in a scruffy shag; "Narrow Nose," with his plier-shaped schnoz; "Black Chin," who reminds me of a helmeted British policeman; "Red Tail," a female with a rusty stripe down her tail; "Collops," one of my favorites, the largest female, who always seems to be pregnant (hence her nickname, which means *rolls of fat*); "Snow White," who has a white scar across her nose; "Topple" who stands up too tall when he eats and usually falls over backward as a result; and twenty or so unnamed others. I admit it's anthropomorphic of me to name them when numbers would do as well. But most naturalists I know resort to names at some stage of their relationship with an animal, be it whale or chimpanzee, lion or hyena. The urge is irresistible. Lewis Thomas once wisely noted that labeling us *Homo erectus,* the creature who stands, wasn't exactly right—we are the creature who worries. We also seem to be *Homo nomenus,* the creature who names.

At the Crisis Center, for instance, we have nicknames for many of the frequent callers whose real names we don't know. Not only "Edward Scissorhands," but "Prisoner," "Endless Love," "the Fall Guy,"

"Don't Lie to Me," "Ten Years," "Garter Man," and dozens of others. We need a shorthand to be able to keep callers in mind as individuals when their names are unknown. Indeed, this is probably the way in which naming began. John the arrow maker (the ancient word was "fletcher") became John Fletcher. Agnes, who lived a short walk up a steep hill, was called Agnes Walkup. It says something about our need to organize and label. Though we live in a chaotic world and sometimes feel overwhelmed, we are tidy by design. Adam's task was to name all the creatures in the world. Sometimes the nicknames we invent for SP callers are funny or ironic, sometimes sad, sometimes factual, but they do enable us to discuss a caller's problem or history when we need to with staff or other counselors. Giving callers names also forms them into a community in our minds, it cuts through the potential blur of voices and distresses, and allows us to think of them as individuals with unique quirks, problems, fine qualities, and needs. Separate ecosystems, not a collage of rain forests.

Mr. Tatter Tail and Collops shuffle a little, putting a few more inches between them as they eat. I always scatter nuts widely so that a few grays can eat side by side without feeling boxed in. They keep their distance from one another by invisible force fields. Minimum separation seems to be three feet. At that distance, squirrels will happily munch a pile of peanuts, but face one another and keep their tails arched high overhead in a self-enlarging display. Any closer and they feel obliged to drive off the claim jumper. Heaven knows what they'd make of fashionable restaurants where the tables are so close diners rub elbows when they lift their forks. We do feel uncomfortable in such places, with not enough separation distance between us as we eat and indulge in "grooming talk," as anthropologists call our public version of gossip and intimacy.

Sometimes I think of this part of the yard as a sort of tavern for squirrels. "Grays" it might be named. But there are no tables. Squirrels prefer to carry their food up a tree to a low secure branch, arrange themselves with their tails curved in a question mark, and scout the ground below as they dine. When they eat, they hold a nut with both paws together like mittens. Squirrels have three fingers and a thumb on each hand, but they don't flex or bend them to eat. Fastidious about skins, they carefully peel grapes and apples while eating. When they chew, their mobile cheeks move a lot and their long whiskers twitch. Whiskers are sensing organs, and squirrels feel the movement of air, snow, wind, and rain as they eat, which probably adds to the pleasure. On the ground, squirrels face upwind when they eat, so that their fur will be ironed shut by the wind, not ruffled up, and they wrap their tails around them like thick fur cloaks.

Today a dozen grays are dining. Males and females look the same color and size—fourteen to seventeen ounces of fur and appetite. Happy with about two pounds of nuts a week, they also enjoy mushrooms, buds, flower shoots, berries, apples, catkins, caterpillars, and other delicacies. I've seen red squirrels lay mushrooms along a tree limb to dry them in the summer and grays in winter peel the bark from a tree to suck the sweet sap underneath. We may pretend our fare is higher brow, but *we* also relish nuts, berries, insects, and seeds. We eat lots of shrimp—an ocean insect. We love the sweet sap of maple trees. And we eat meat, too, especially if it's still a little rare, by which we mean slightly bloody, like a fresh kill. Old habits are hard to break.

Four grays, bounding in from a neighbor's yard, pause to make a sudden detour. Masters of circuitousness, sly indirection, the long way around, squirrels don't like to head straight for anything. They move by innuendo, running past and sweeping around from the side. And that's just what one husky gray is doing, running a circle around the other squirrels to sees if there's room enough to squeeze in behind. There isn't, so the only alternative is to challenge one of the others by running at it until it leaps straight up in the air, jumping right over the challenger, launched by the trampoline of its fear and aggression. For humans, taste is a social sense; not so for squirrels. "Husky" takes a position with nuts and the others soon find new places. They're a little too close together, so they all eat with their tails folded into pompadours high over their heads. The purpose, again, is to make themselves look taller, like big bad butch squirrels, and I guess it works.

Soon another intruder arrives, a medium-sized gray with a brown chin strap, and takes a spot close beside Collops. Her personal space threatened, Collops faces her foe and sits still, but rapidly twitches her cheeks and, with them, her whiskers: a visual growl. Even though her mouth is busily chewing almonds, she makes small insistent harmonicalike noises that sound like a chugging train. "Too close! Too close! Too close!" they warn. Chin Strap doesn't retreat, and Collops cheek-twitches while bending her tail right up and over her back and head into a war bonnet, growling a syncopated terror whine that sounds like a swarm of insects. Still Chin Strap won't budge, so there's nothing left but a tussle, and tussle they do—first leaping high to kick box, then shrieking while nipping at ears and flanks. The other squirrels watch and make elbow room but continue eating. In a moment it is all over—the lunging, the chasing, the scolding—and Chin Strap swiftly gives ground. Though there are no serious injuries, it seems to be a technical knockout. Collops picks up a peanut, rips the husk off, and settles down to eat, while keeping a steady eye on Chin Strap, who circles around the crowd and finds a less-than-ideal spot at the edge of the banquet.

———

While the squirrels continue feeding, I dress, pack a lunch, and head down to the Crisis Center. The minute I sit down at the desk and rest my feet on the hassock (which someone has repaired with silver duct tape), the phone rings. A man's voice greets me. It sounds like he's talking from the moon. In a sense he is. He feels alone and troubled enough to call, and thus his voice seems to come from a distant reality, but he must also feel strong enough to seek help from others. "Only connect!" E.M. Forster once wrote, reducing all of our human quests, hardships, and fears to a basic need for contact with others. And this caller? His plight could be anything: a worry about sexual orientation, a child in trouble, a bout of depression, a fight with his boss, a death in the family. My thoughts hover in midground, waiting to learn which direction they'll be taking.

"I don't know why I'm calling really . . . ," he says.

"Would you like to tell me a little of what's on your mind today?"

Slowly, he reveals that he's calling from his car, on a cellular phone. He is parked at the edge of a scenic overlook outside of town. His wife has left him and taken the two children with her; he has no idea where she's gone. Laid off four months ago, he hasn't been able to find a new job. And that's meant living on welfare, which he feels ashamed of. Because he can't make his car payments, he's going to forfeit his car, too. That was the last straw, the car repossession notice arrived yesterday. Something about losing his mobility, the iron-clad freedom a car represents, has hit him viscerally. Now he is planning to drive himself, his marriage, and his soon-to-be-repossessed car over the cliff.

"Why shouldn't I?" he asks angrily.

It is a counselor's nightmare, and I wish to God a genie would appear to guide me, someone with more years of experience, one of the trainers who lead novice counselors through an intense six-week course of psychodrama, role-playing, self-examination, and discussions. I feel I'm in the middle of a dangerous intersection, without knowing which road to take. In desperation, I pull a rabbit out of an old hat.

"Tell me your story," I say, and then wait through the longest silence I can remember. To my amazement he starts to speak, slowly, beginning with his childhood. When we get to the here and now, we discuss a couple of agencies in town who could help him temporarily, with his legal and financial problems anyway. It's not much hope to salvage from the wreckage of his life, but it's something. After a while, his voice changes from frantic to worn-out.

"How are you feeling now?" I ask.

"Exhausted."

"Maybe it's time to go home and get some sleep. Will you be all right driving home?" I picture him in a blue Chevy, driving erratically, too fast on side streets, too slow on highways.

"Yeah, I'll be okay."

"Would you like me to have someone call you tomorrow morning, just check in on you, see how you're doing, see if you need any advice with those calls?"

His voice chokes. "Yeah. That'd be good...I hate to be such a bother..."

"It's no bother. That's why we're here," I say, trying not to sound dutiful or perfunctory. I want him to stay calm, but I also want him to feel comfortable about calling. As usual, I wish I had more control over my voice, wish I could sculpt its nuances so that, regardless of the exact words I used, the tone would tell a caller like this one, *You're not alone. We're here to help you, or, if help is impossible, at least to understand.* I think it's possible to insinuate your emotions into your voice wholeheartedly like that, to speak sentences charged with pure emotion, as if they were part of an opera in which indecipherable words float on waves of heart-stirring and meaningful music. I just can't figure out how best to do it.

"If you have trouble sleeping later, don't hesitate to call us back. Someone's here all night, okay?"

"Okay."

Something reticent in his voice worries me. He probably won't call. "I'm concerned about you," I add tentatively. "How about if we make a contract that you won't do anything to hurt yourself without calling us first. Could you make me that promise?"

After a long silence, he does. It's a funny thing about promises. People tend to keep them. Even time-consuming, awkward, or dangerous promises. Even a promise they know will interfere with self-destructive plans. "Promise," from the Latin *promittere* ("to send

forth"), runs back through the ages to the needs of our earliest ancestors, hidden inside the Indo-European word *smeit-* ("to throw or
send"). It is an ancient idea, to make a promise to another person, to
oneself, or to one's god. Our species has survived partly because of
our great skill at negotiating and working together. Most of our laws
are based on contracts, the paper form of a promise. Because their
lives revolved around exchange and reciprocity, our ancestors had
many contractual obligations, and Indo-European is thick with legal
terms. There is *wadh-*, "to make a pledge," literally "to lead someone
back home," which evolved into our word *wed* (leading a new wife
back to her husband's home). There is a word that means *vow*, which
has more religious than social connotations, a word for taking an oath,
and even a specific word for compensating someone for an injury.
What do we "throw" when we make a promise? What do we "send
forth" into the world? Because a promise foretells how one will act, it
allows us the relief of knowing a small shred of the future, of relax-
ing some of our anxieties. Without promises we would constantly be
in a fret. They allow us to solve some of the future in the present,
thereby controlling it, and making it seem less arbitrary, mysterious,
beyond our grasp. A promise signals trust: We entrust the promiser
with some measure of our anticipated happiness or well-being.
Therefore a broken promise warrants punishment or shame. Children
are taught how to promise. I think promising goes back to the un-
stated contract between a mother and child. It's no use her telling a
child, "You must not go near the edge of the cliff, or touch fire, or
wander off," unless the child agrees that it won't. If the child doesn't
agree, then the mother must be more vigilant than is practical. What
the child promises is to try to stay alive. What the mother promises, in
return, is to love the child and try to keep it alive. That is the earliest
contract humans make, or have ever made. So when we ask a caller to
promise, we are touching an ancient nerve. The equation written in
our cells, in our bones, is that keeping yourself safe will lead to love:
It is the oldest and simplest promise.

Many people in our callers' lives have betrayed them in one way or another, the system has let them down, and life itself has broken its unspoken word. Their future no longer holds any hope. Yet callers trapped in that nightmare usually act honorably with us. If they make a contract not to kill themselves without calling first, they keep it. Sometimes a caller, bent on suicide, will say "I promised to call first, and, out of respect I'm calling, but I'm heading for the bridge now." That leaves just the narrowest chance for a counselor. A lifeline only a few minutes wide. Sometimes it's enough, sometimes not.

———

At last I have a breather. Wandering into the kitchen, I microwave a frozen bagel and pour myself a cup of tea. When the phone rings, I hurry back into the counselor room, sit down, glance at the clock, jot the time down on a piece of paper, collect myself, lift up the receiver.

"Suicide Prevention and Crisis Service. May I help you?"

No one speaks.

"This must be difficult for you," I say at last, "take your time."

My heart starts to pound when I hear, almost outside the range of hearing, a tearful voice whisper, "I can't go on any more." A small sob fills the blackness. "I've tried so hard," she says in a strained voice, a girlish voice that fragments into a whimper. "I've been holding on for so long. But nobody would want me to live in this pain, this pain that never goes away. Anyone who loved me would want me to die and not suffer this way."

I recognize the voice as belonging to Louise, a fragile woman who has been calling the agency for a few years. Sometimes Louise introduces herself when she calls. Tonight she is beyond names. She is a part-time baker who sings in an a cappella group, volunteers as a stage-hand during the local theater's summer season, and sits on several boards serving the homeless, flood victims, handicapped children. Although she lives close to the poverty line, she somehow manages to raise a difficult teenage daughter on her own. She occasionally writes insightful and spirited letters to the editor of the newspaper about important local issues. Going about her public life, she appears confident, talented, attractive, smart, apparently on an even keel.

That seems incomprehensible. We hear from her only when she's in the quicksand of her depression, when she has laid pills out on the counter and is a hairbreadth away from taking them. In most of the write-ups after Louise's calls, the counselors predict that she won't be alive by morning. Although she calls every few weeks in a desperately suicidal state, it is not an act. We all agree: she is holding on by her fingernails. She has no money, no steady job, no boyfriend, a prickly relationship with one of her daughters, a long parade of antidepressants that haven't worked, and something organic—a depression hard as mineral that can appear suddenly in the vein of her day and stop her life cold. From time to time she has checked into psychiatric wards, but they never really help much, just sedate her for a while. She fears that the stigma of her being "a mental patient" is keeping employers from hiring her, and she may be right.

Louise is special. Some of the callers are quirky, many of them are suffering with great dignity, and I tend to like them for one reason or another. Louise is caring, funny, sensible about most things, big-hearted and decent with people. She's smart and sensitive, a real peach. How can I be uninvolved when she phones? Even in the densest thicket of her depression, her brave wonderful self shines through. I long to go knock on her door when she's feeling sad and drag her out shopping or biking or to a show. I long to insert myself into her life and heal her. But that is taboo, of course. All I can do is hope to be on shift when she calls. It would kill me to lose her.

"I'm so sorry you're suffering," I say. "What's made it tough today?"

"Everything, everything," she says. "My life is in ruins. I'm at work. In a phone booth. I keep going through the motions, but inside I'm dying. It's time to make the inside and outside match."

I sigh audibly, an exhalation of sorrow. "It must be horrible to feel so much pain that you want to die to make it stop."

"It is. It's so horrible." She sobs. "I picture myself at the bottom of the gorge, picture myself hitting the rocks, and I don't feel any pain, I just feel grateful that it's finally over."

Without meaning to, I also picture her lying broken on the rocks. I hate it when callers describe a horrible fantasy or event in their lives, because then it takes shape in my imagination, I witness it with them, and sometimes it haunts me for quite a while. I always picture the callers in my mind's eye. The lines and rhythms of their voices paint living portraits of them and I see them clearly, as if in a movie, see the emotion on their faces, how they're holding the telephone, when they look out a window, smoke a cigarette, glance at their watches, fight to keep their eyes from tearing up. I know what every caller looks like—not accurately of course, but in an emotional geography or landscape. To me, Louise is an attractive woman of medium height with curly, shoulder-length brown hair she has parted on the left side, and a delicate complexion that blushes easily. She's about thirty-five years old, needs glasses to read, and likes to wear skirts and sweaters. She prefers earth-toned makeup and colors her lips with a brownish-red pencil that she covers with a tinted gloss. She has long slender arms and a graceful gait when she walks. None of this may be true. It's fascinating how the sound of a voice obsessively expresses itself in vivid images. We are so visual a species.

Even though I don't know what the callers look like, they are not disembodied voices or crises. I only administer to one facet of a caller on one day, but I see him or her whole in my mind, and in my understanding I try to see each of them as more than their pain, more than this narrow self their depression has flattened them to. Often I recognize the voices; some of the callers are familiar and each new call adds another chapter to a long narrative of struggle, survival, obsession, anxiety, and grief. I may feel comfortable asking Louise, "Has your daughter been much help with this?" even when she hasn't mentioned her daughter. The caller knows my voice too, and replies with the ease of a confidante. We are intimate strangers.

Louise mentioned a bridge near where she works, and I think I know the one she means. Shouldn't I send the police? But if I do, will she lose her job, a job she desperately needs? If I don't, will she lose her life?

"Have you pictured loved ones finding you?" I ask gently.

"My daughter, I've thought about what it would do to her, and some days that's the only thing that's stood between me and the rocks."

"She needs her mother."

"It doesn't seem like that right now. We're always fighting."

"How old is she?"

"Fourteen."

The age of my goddaughter. Instantly I see her perfect peaches-and-cream complexion, her lovely blonde hair, which she endlessly tends and frets over. "That can be a tough age for girls. What was she like as a child?"

"Oh, she was a wonderful little girl, so huggy. We were really close there for a while. We went everywhere together." Her voice brightens a little.

"Do you think it's possible this might be a stage she's going through, that it will pass?"

"It's possible."

"How do you think she would feel if you killed yourself?" I know this is the cheapest of cheap shots.

Louise does, too, and her voice breaks into a soft whine as she says, "It would be really hard on her, but I think she would understand. 'Love is a religion with a fallible god' someone once said. She wouldn't want me to go on living in so much pain."

My cheeks fill with air and I glance out the window as I slowly exhale. The sky couldn't be bluer and an intricate thatch of clouds hovers over the lake.

"Are you standing outside?" I ask.

"Yes," she says.

"Look up."

A moment later she laughs a little, distracted from herself. My heart drinks in her weak laughter.

"That's amazing," she says. "It looks like someone has been writing up there, using clouds as ink. That's really neat."

All over town the trees are surging with buds, some of them folded into mysterious and beautiful shapes. She responded to the clouds; maybe she would respond to the trees. "You said there was a tree nearby. What kind is it?" I ask.

"It's a ginkgo. It has fan-shaped leaves."

For a few minutes we talk about how ancient the ginkgo is, how its leaves are brewed into a tea and drunk three times a day as a brain tonic beneficial for circulation and short-term memory. I didn't realize Louise was so knowledgeable about homeopathy, but apparently it's one of her hobbies. *Marry the moment,* I think, *it's your only hope.* She gradually calms down a little and we take some deep breaths together. Depression works like a lens, narrowing one's focus to a grim, painful obsession. It's as if the senses become blocked, and stop feeding in information from the outside world. All the irrelevant perceptions and idle thoughts that normally bustle through one's life seem to disappear. Reattaching a few can sometimes ease the sadness for a short while, or suddenly shake the logjam free. Today that works for Louise, who, feeling a little better, decides to hang up and return to her work. But how about next time? For the rest of my shift I keep worrying when she will call again. Not this afternoon anyway, thanks to the clouds, the ginkgo tree.

———

We think of salvation as a large heroic drama. But in depression one clings to life by such humble knots. Sometimes retying one of them will be enough. I remember a day five winters ago when depression had been working on me all week, slamming doors inside me, closing off my future, magnifying the simplest slight into a rosary of woe, making me feel rejected and alone. It began as a sort of loose sadness, then by week's end I woke up crying and couldn't stop. All day I sank lower and lower. Despite that, in an effort to hold on, I kept my appointments, I told almost no one. But the next day the depression was so bad that I could barely move. My mind had begun mulling over grim ironies. As I knew from years before, when my dear friend Martin had died in a plane crash—despite his dentist appointment, his dinner plans with me, and all the ropes and anchors we use to bind ourselves to life—death doesn't require you to keep a day free. People die even if they have appointments, even if they have newborns, or unfinished business, even if it's the worst possible time for everyone they leave behind. "Stopping by Woods on a Snowy Evening" is a beautiful poem, but having promises to keep won't save you.

I looked out on a smattering of snow. *Light,* I thought, *drink the light.* Tossing my cross-country skis into the car, I drove to the golf course and set out on the thin, wet clumpy snow. It stuck to my skis so that I couldn't glide, but I could snowshoe and shuffle. For half an hour I stomped toward the woods. It was then that I heard a sound that can only be described as honking. Geese honking. Nothing else sounds like it, not a bike horn nor a city of penguins. I closed my eyes. For a long moment I listened to the sound, as a smile of wonder crept up my face. The honking grew louder and I opened my eyes to see a large wedge of Canada geese low overhead, flapping, skiing through the air, and honking like mad. I said the word out loud: "*hon-king, hon-king,*" as they passed, savored the sound, nestled it in my memory. It was a wonderful crazy combination of trombone and kazoo.

Sometimes the smallest thing can be enough to glue you back to life. On that day, a dark, wispy storm cloud began to clutch low in the sky, and I started for home, trying to retrace my steps. I had thought the way back would be easier, since I could use the same path I'd blazed out, only with less effort, without needing to devise a route. But to my dismay I discovered that this wasn't possible. My skis cut a new set of parallel lines, slipped and spread the outbound tracks. I could not glide or skate; with so little snow base all I could do was shuffle. The going back was just as hard as the setting out. But in time it brought me to the same place, the horseshoe drive, and overhead the geese kept honking. It can be enough, one small lifebelt: a salvation of geese, the snow polished by daylight, a signature of clouds above a budding gingko tree. But one doesn't know where or which or when or if.

CHAPTER 3

All the Bright Catastrophes

"Honey, I'm home!" a basso voice calls from downstairs, as Bob arrives to take the evening shift. Then two sets of doors rattle closed, and soon afterward size thirteen feet start climbing the creaking stairs. I know it's Bob from the schedule posted in the counselor room, but he doesn't know who is on afternoon shift, and I'm tempted to yell down something clever. After all, he is a sculptor who works exclusively with cement—someone who likes to watch things harden in his hands—and the temptation to tease him about it is strong. But before my brain can sharpen itself, he appears, a tall, thin man in his forties, with shoulder-length brown hair and the largest hands I've ever seen on a man, wearing jeans and a red-and-white T-shirt that shows a drawing of a snarling schnauzer, under which are the words BAD DOG-GIE, NO BONE.

"Hi, how's it goin'?" he says.

"Busy day." I turn the logbook so that he can read the seven new entries. "Louise called. I don't think she'll phone back tonight, but I'm not sure. And there's a teenage girl named Jesse who may call. Her classmate phoned, worried because Jesse has been cutting herself." Both of us winced at the word "teenage." We know the number of teen suicides has skyrocketed, know it only too intimately, since there were four suicides in one local high school last year. After each tragedy, SP sent in their postvention team to talk with the shell-shocked classmates, the grieving families and friends, the mystified school officials, the worried teachers and guidance counselors. Since then, more teenagers have phoned us for help, but the suicide rate continues to be alarmingly high. For every 660 depressed teens, one commits suicide. Researchers have found that over half of all teens think about killing themselves. Indeed, suicide is the third cause of teen death in the US. Only accident and homicide claim more lives. Depression plagues both village and city teens, and the very young have become especially vulnerable. Gang members, interviewed after a brutal killing, often explain their actions by pointing out that they don't expect to be alive past their teens. With such a death of hope, it's not surprising how many inner-city kids speak in a disconnected present tense—"we be going"—since they have no usable past or recognizable future.

Our local teens also find the world a frightening place. What with raging hormones, school pressures, family problems, world events, and such normal identity issues as who they are and what they should do with their lives, it's a miserably confusing and stressful time of life. Mind you, depression isn't the only risk factor for teens. Withdrawn, lonely perfectionists sometimes kill themselves out of shame or guilt. Anorexia, bulimia, and self-mutilation are reaching epidemic propor-

tions, and that's ironic, since these are often the afflictions of the edu-
cated, accomplished, "good" families, in which parents relentlessly
demand excellence from themselves and their children. However,
since body piercing has become fashionable among teens in the US,
some forms of self-mutilation aren't worrisome. After all, people all
over the world have been stretching, piercing, or carving their body
parts into unusual shapes and emblazoning them with fashionable
emblems throughout the ages. It's when the person loses control and
pain becomes its own end, a habitual lure, that we worry.

"Cutters are tough," Bob says. "Had one the other day. Lordy, that's
a tough call." I like the way Bob mixes "lordy," "land's sake," and "holy
smokes," with hip nineties talk. I doubt callers have any idea of his
age, he slides so smoothly into their lingo. "He was this upright dude,
a banker, who would sneak out to the bathroom at work to burn himself with his cigarette. Called here instead."

"At least he phoned first. That's a good step." I tell him about the
woman caller I spoke with recently who had burned herself minutes
before the call. She had a history of cutting, but had only recently
started burning herself, and she was afraid her problem was escalat-
ing, that she was crossing a new and dangerous threshold, afraid of
what she had become and of what her two young children would
think. In a weak voice almost too quiet to hear, she explained how
emotionally exhausted she felt, how upset and frightened. We talked
about what she felt when she burned herself, how overpowering a
compulsion it was, what might have precipitated it, if anything helps
when she senses the urge coming on. Sometimes she would spend
days thinking about hurting herself, brood on it for hours, and go
through curious rituals of preparation—stroking the area of the arm
she meant to cut or burn, arranging the knives or razor blades or cig-
arettes in a tidy way. She was seeing a therapist, but progress was slow.
Self-mutilation is a stubborn addiction. It has something in common
with eating disorders: people who suffer from one frequently suffer
from the other. My caller confided that she was sexually abused as a

child, and I responded with how heavy a burden that must be to live with, but I didn't pursue motives or history. Cutters tend to be women who were sexually abused as children, tend to be people who can't complain about the torment in their family, can't fight back at their abuser. One theory about cutters holds that, as children, they received nurturing only after they were badly injured, and thus as adults they injure themselves because subconsciously they associate harm with kindness, protection, love.

Or this strange affliction may be due to a physiological glitch. Cutters almost always report that they feel relief afterward, possibly because endorphins flow in response to the pain. They say that it makes them feel alive, in touch with reality, and that they otherwise feel dead inside and disconnected from life. Is there something off-balance in their chemistry? Thrill seekers have been found to have unusually low levels of serotonin and other neurotransmitters—to feel "normal" such people apparently risk danger just to wake up their system to a state we would regard as ordinary. I became especially aware of this years ago, when I was learning to fly and was hanging out at airports and visiting air shows. When they aren't flying, even the most daring pilots tend to be surprisingly calm and quiet people—golf is their favorite pastime; they probably fly planes to boost their low metabolism. So could it be that cutters don't have enough neurological feedback to have a physical sense of themselves in the world? Or is it, after all, a psychological problem? Cutters seem more driven to hurt themselves as a response to rejection, anger, and helplessness, which to some analysts suggests that they may be consumed by an emotion like rage or resentment, and are enacting the desire to symbolically punish their abuser by punishing themselves. Whatever their motives, their actions are horrifying and leave me and other counselors feeling both helpless and sad. We know they rarely commit suicide, though sometimes they're so disgusted by their addiction, which seems unstoppable, that they do end their lives to end their misery. Ironically, when that happens, they choose an overdose or some other swift method unrelated to their condition.

My cutter had caught me off guard and I didn't know how to help her, except to persuade her to flush her matches down the toilet, which she did while I waited. The next immediate problem was what to do to keep her hands busy. Remembering advice my mother once gave me—"There's no problem that can't be lightened by doing two sets of windows and two sets of floors"—I gently asked the caller how she would feel about accomplishing something around the house. She said she'd put off cleaning her bathroom and her kitchen was a mess, and yes, she might feel better about herself if she mopped and scrubbed them. After that she might take her sleeping three-year-old daughter out for a walk. By then it would be time to pick up her son from school and make dinner for the family. That was her plan of action when we hung up. I had asked her, begged her really, to call us *before* she hurt herself next time, but she confessed with remarkable candor that she couldn't, that at such times she entered a remote place mentally, far from help or self-control. That's probably why she responded so well to taking control of her life, if only for an afternoon, in even such small ways. It's possible she may need us again tonight, but it's more likely that the young cutter, Jesse, will call, which is what I tell Bob.

Alerting the next counselor to people who might call back makes it possible to prepare a little, perhaps devise a strategy for dealing with them. Sometimes it feels as if we are all part of a slow-motion relay race, and the baton we pass to the next person is made not of matter but of energy. I envy those who can take off concern's thick lenses and leave the callers behind when they go home. Some days I can, with a heartlessness that surprises me; today, I feel as if I'm carrying ingots on my shoulders.

On my first shift three years ago, when I heard the crisis line ring for real I reached out a finger ET-style to the phone, and my hand trembled so much I was afraid I'd hit the wrong button. Suddenly, it was not a role play. A live, hurting, unpredictable human—who didn't know the crisis model—blurted out her suffering, offering it up for my understanding and acceptance. Breathlessly, she bemoaned her predicament, and seemed to be sliding into a well of despair. Frantically, I scanned my memory for what to say, how to be. But there was no clear category into which the call fit. At long last, something astounding occurred to me—the caller was still on the line. She hadn't hung up, she was still talking, even though all I had been doing was making listening noises, hearing her out. What a relief. I took a risk, waded out into the water, and asked her to focus on what problem was toughest that night, what had prompted her to call, and from then on the call went reasonably well, although meandering at times, silent at times. I wouldn't say the call ended exactly, but rather that the caller felt heard, sorted out her mood a little, and could get on with her day. That was all. It was a revelation. The next caller was entirely different, and I felt the same burst of nervous insecurity, then after a while discovered once again that the caller didn't hang up. What a thrilling and scary five hours.

—

As I head home, I roll my tense, tired shoulders, and suddenly remember being thirteen, at a lakeside camp in the Poconos, where we took Red Cross courses in life saving, water safety aid, and water survival. Those courses made sense for kids who went swimming and canoeing, and they built confidence, but man, were they tough! I am a strong swimmer today because of them, and they instilled in me a lifelong ease in the water that has led to a lot of fun, kept me safe, made possible expeditions where scuba diving or snorkeling were necessary, and on one occasion allowed me to save a dear friend's life. I owe much to those camp swims. To pass the survival course, we had to tread water—fully clothed—for an hour; take our clothes off in deep water, seal and inflate an article of clothing and use it as a buoy; and be able to swim across the lake while wearing a knapsack loaded down with heavy rocks, among other equally daunting tasks. The lake always looked dark and impenetrable, with an invisible bottom and a green-brown surface that reflected the sky. Richly alive with minute plants and animals, gently churning up silt as hidden springs fed fresh cold water into it, the lake seemed mysterious and menacing, a realm of potential monsters, clutching claws, mirror worlds. Darkness bespoke danger, and a dark lake doubled the risk. Many of my fellow campers had drowning dreams that summer. I didn't understand then how clean, safe, and natural the lake really was, or how much fun it might be to study the animals whose lives it enriched. I craved its challenges, though, and by summer's end I had mastered most of them, and received a small card stamped with a Red Cross logo, which I treasured for years.

Swimming across the lake with what felt like a boulder on my back had been the toughest test—I can still remember sinking, fearing the squooshy lake bottom thirty feet below, where snapping turtles were rumored to swarm, kicking frantically toward the surface, thrashing and gasping for air, breaststroking furiously, feeling as if someone were trying to pull me over backward, sinking, kicking, swimming, then crawling out on the other shore, shaky and cold, barely able to stand until I let the knapsack fall. There, for a moment, I felt lighter than air. It was a hot August day. The sky was a dazzling blue. My face was caked with mud. A handsome counselor I had a crush on was cheering me from a nearby rowboat. Campers were watching from the other shore. A second counselor picked up the knapsack and spilled the rocks on the beach. It had seemed the heaviest burden in the world, huge and boulderlike, but as it turned out it was only a collection of rocks—many small things, not one large thing. Big stones, little stones, they all weigh the same if you're thrashing across the lake. Today at the Crisis Center there was a hodgepodge of troubles, all urgent, but none requiring the police or ambulance, yet massed together they were exhausting. No wonder my shoulders feel as if I've been lifting boulders.

So, as evening falls, I sink into the Jacuzzi in my bathroom. Both modern and pagan, it reminds me of ancient days, when hot baths were prescribed for depression, compulsiveness, mood swings, and other mental woes. Manic-depressives bathed in (and drank from) certain lithium-rich pools. Others chewed on willow bark for migraines. Steeping the flesh in hot water as if it were a bundle of tea leaves was a favorite cure for mental ills and heartbreaks alike. In the twentieth century, psychotherapy may have become the talking cure, but for centuries bathing was the water cure, and Europeans made regular pilgrimages to Bath, Baden-Baden, and a host of other spa towns to submerge in miracle waters bubbling up from the earth. The Romans before them doted on baths, and devised ingenious heating and plumbing systems, so that the bathhouse floors could be toasty, the steam rooms cleansing, and the mosaic-clad promenades a delight to bare feet. Bathhouses once offered Roman citizens an oasis—they were the perfect place for manicures, coiffures, massages, jugglers, conmen, flirtations, and gossip hounds—and an ideal spot to meditate on one's life and troubles.

We baptize with water, we purify with water, we take steam baths in small closeted clouds, we wash away the dirt and toil of the day with hot water, we dilute our food and drink with water, we stare for hypnotic hours at any abundance of water, be it aquarium or ocean, and we relax in a pool of water, especially if it has been heated to our own body temperature. We ourselves are contained estuaries, swamps, canals, and reefs. Women have monthly tides and wombs where eggs lie like roe. Small wonder the water world relaxes us. When we worship water we worship our own plumbing.

The other animals I share the yard with don't feel this way about water. Squirrels can swim, and many is the time I've seen one frantically treading water in the pool, unable to climb out until I've offered it a pole or broom to cling to. When they perch on the side of a green plastic tub to sip the fresh water I provide for them, they occasionally fall in and scramble back out again. Squirrels sometimes wash their faces with falling snowflakes. The deer drink from the stream in the woods, but they worry about deep water. The raccoons wash in shallow pools by moving their paws rapidly sideways, then they rub their faces with wet hands. I've seen a pheasant stand under a dripping tree limb to shower its feathers during a gentle rain. But by and large the animals don't wallow the way humans do.

There's the cheap and dirty wallow of a farm pond or a stream, there's the private wallow of a bath tub, and there's the high class and pricey wallow of a spa. The one that intrigues me most is at Bath in England. Although I've never submerged in its waters, I've sat beside them, plunged into them in my imagination, and often thought of the Saxon tribes who first settled the area around Bath and found the natural hot spring so astonishing that they swore a goddess produced it. Where did the water come from? It must have been an ancient rain that fell about 10,000 years ago and penetrated deep into the earth, rising when the water had been warmed by the heat of the earth's core. How miraculous hot water must have seemed to the ancients, even after the discovery of fire. It took so much fuel and labor to stoke a fire, haul water, and wait for it to boil. Hot water was rare, a luxury, and there it was day and night in flowing streams. Only a goddess could be responsible for such sensuous magic. The conquering Romans, lured by this liquid treasure, were frankly carnal about its value. But superstitious, too. The spring at Bath is full of curses—human curses. They were written on sheets of pewter and then thrown into the spring. We know many of the Roman bathers, their families, social life, and irritations only by the curses they left behind.

There are no curses or Roman mosaics in *my* bathroom, but it is a pleasuredrome dedicated to the goddess of hot water. Heavily tiled in mauve, purple, lavender, and teal, it also includes two wallpaper designs that complement each other—a pattern taken from a Persian mosque, in teal, pale green, and lavender, and a peacock-feather pattern in lavender and teal. A broad border separates the two, combining their elements—large peacocks in full-tailed display alternating with fruitful trees of life. Two white sconces glow softly like ringed planets. I love this Garden of Allah retreat with its colorful flowerpot holding shampoos and a small birdbath (complete with pottery birds) filled with aromatherapy vials. Tiled benches flank the tub, one a window seat that looks out onto a flowerbed filled in summer with phlox, in spring with bushy yellow evening primrose, and in deep summer with tall snapdragons, blue balloon flowers, spidery pink gas flowers, tussocks of yellow coreopsis, and poker-tall purple liatris, miscellaneous lobelia, nasturtiums, and dahlias. I can also see the red flag on the mailbox through the window; the mailman's visit perpetually inspires hope and surprise in a two-writer household. Or I can watch the neighbor children bike in the cul-de-sac after school.

Some of SP's callers would profit from a good long soak in a hot fragrant tub, and from time to time I recommend that after we hang up they might consider brewing a cup of herb tea and steeping themselves in a tub of lavender or pine, two good spirit lifters. If they have apple-spice tea at home, I suggest this, since some researchers have found it successful in staving off panic attacks. I don't mention that, for ages, spas have been the main escape of melancholy women, who withdrew from family and society for a spell to take stock of their lives and let others serve and nourish them for a change. I don't tell them of the long tradition of women and baths, from the sacred cleansing baths of the ancient Hebrews (menstruating women were considered dirty) to the fashionable baths of eighteenth-century French women, who sometimes entertained while in the bath. Ben Franklin reports that his lady friend Madame Brillon received guests while bathing, with a board placed over her for modesty, although I'm not sure how she concealed her breasts. Eighteenth-century etiquette required many elegancies and protocols, and lovers too were bound by ornate rules of courtesy. A woman could receive socially while in bed or bath, because she and her visitors alike were expected to hide their feelings. Madame Brillon liked to set up a chess game on her bath board so that she and Ben could play flirtatious chess while other guests drifted in and out of the room.

I don't receive guests or play chess while in the tub, but I do have a board to lay across it, since I often work there. Indeed, I do most of my serious reading while partially submerged. I usually take food and drink in with me, and also a portable phone, a pocket calendar, and a stack of good books. Two large skylights flood the room with sun and sky. Visitors often try to turn off the light, only to discover there's no light on—except the sun. Or they wonder at the dark luminosity on winter days when the skylights are covered in deep snow. But it's the twelve-inch Dynamax telescope on the tiled bench beside the tub that usually makes them twist their brows in surprise for a few moments, and then grin hugely. What better place to watch the moon and stars? The skylights turn the room into a peaceful observatory where, as Walt Whitman says:

> I open the scuttle at night and see the far-sprinkled systems,
> And all I see multiplied as high as I can cipher
>   edge but the rim of the farther systems
>
> Wider and wider they spread, expanding, always expanding,
> Outward and outward and forever outward.

Tonight, soaking in clouds of pungent jasmine-scented bubbles, I tune in the moon as it floats overhead, and sight on the changing constellations and wandering planets. The moon is full. The man in the moon has his mouth rounded—I think he may be caroling. Leo floats by with a brilliant white roar. And then a parade of glittery stars, galaxies, and nebulae fills the telescope with images of distant worlds. In the dark, it's hard to tell where that field of stars begins and ends. Watching the stars veer through tight local orders and whirlwind tumults, I cup a handful of foam, smoothing it over one shoulder, and picture suns roiling down my back, galaxies clinging to my chest and arms, molten starblood trickling from an airborne knee. Planets rise up my neck. Seething in the small of my back, a stellar nursery whorls out neutron stars, black holes, vagabond comets. Suns cascade from each wrist, where my tiny pulse dislodges a thousand worlds. I can almost hear the crackling swan song of supernovae, the mournful whistle of pulsars, the disciplined panic of the newly born. Then, drenched in immortal quiet and a sandstorm of light, I lie back, so bristling with wonder that for long granite seconds I feel calm and contented, and would not have the universe be anything it is not.

A mug of decaffeinated hazelnut-spiked coffee adds a nutty-sweet scent to the atmosphere already fragrant from perfumed soap and a bowl of fresh raspberries. I have a wonderful little book to read—*How I Learned to Ride the Bicycle,* by Frances E. Willard, a nineteenth-century feminist for whom cycling became a journey of self-discovery and a metaphor for a life well lived. A colorful Finger Lakes region map, whose creases are almost worn through, reveals a section of Seneca county between Cayuga and Seneca lakes, the planned destination for a weekend bike trip. I also have the day's mail, and, turning on a small reading light, I begin by opening a large manila envelope from a friend at the National Zoo in Washington, D.C. What I find inside shocks me wide awake: a sheaf of xeroxed articles from the Washington newspapers regarding a bizarre, horrifying event. The clippings start on Sunday, March 5 and run through Monday, March 20, with each article disposing of more rumors and adding new increasingly bizarre facts.

On Saturday, March 4, at 5:00 A.M., a woman went over a three-and-a-half foot cement barrier at the National Zoo, crossed a four-foot-wide dirt buffer, lowered herself down a nine-foot wall into a moat, swam twenty-six feet through the water, and pulled herself out onto the large stone terraces of the lion enclosure. Two African lions watched her—a 300-pound female named Asha, and Tana, a 450-pound male. Then one or both of them attacked, ripping at her jugular, tearing back her scalp, and eating her arms clear up to the shoulders. A lion keeper found her at feeding time two hours later and called the police, who spent weeks trying to figure out what had happened. She had no remaining fingerprints they could check, and there were few leads. Who was this woman? Did she die in an accident, suicide, or slaying? Had she been killed first and then dumped in the lion enclosure? When they discovered in her jacket pocket a bus pass issued in Little Rock, Arkansas, rumors flew in that most political town that her death was somehow related to the Whitewater investigation, that she was a squealer who had been "thrown to the lions." A sick thought even for Washingtonians. Each day, a new ghoulish fact appeared in print. She hadn't died immediately, but lived for several minutes while being mauled. The lions began by eating her hands, bones and all. Her scalp "had been peeled from the front and was hanging behind her neck." The woman was thirty-six, with long black hair, and wore a light jacket, T-shirt, gray cotton pants, and brown walking shoes. Police found a money order in her shoe and a business letter in her pocket. A barrette and a portable tape recorder lay near her body. The bus pass was an "honored citizens pass," a lifetime pass given to the elderly, infirm, or mentally ill. She was a twice-married, divorced mother of two, and one source said she had traveled to Washington to seek President Clinton's intervention in a child custody battle because, as she told a city clerk, "she couldn't get justice anywhere else." The clerk reported that she had tried to file a lawsuit to regain custody of her daughter, but was confused about whom she wished to sue—possibly the president—and so she went away with paperwork to fill out. She said her child had been taken from her by Arkansas authories because of her mental illness, but she seemed "focused," "attractive and well-spoken," and "calm."

At 3:00 A.M. on March 1, she checked into a cheap hotel; three days later she fed herself to the lions. A transient who lived in a veterans shelter, she had been diagnosed as a paranoid schizophrenic, but none of her therapists or caseworkers would go into much detail about her history. Social workers in Little Rock did report that she was delusional and believed she was Jesus Christ's sister, talking to and receiving messages directly from God. She had been in and out of mental hospitals. The Sony Walkman found near her body contained a tape of Amy Grant singing spirituals. In her hotel room, there were some handwritten notes "of a religious nature." The coroner ruled her death a suicide. Her name was Margaret Davis King. Had she identified in some strange way with the *Lion King* movie? In ancient Rome, Christians were thrown to the lions for practicing their faith; could she have felt punished for hers? Was she inspired by the Old Testament story of Daniel, the Judean exile, who was condemned to a lion's pit by a Babylonian king, but saved because of his belief in God? Did she imagine herself a latter-day Daniel walking into the lion's den, convinced that she would emerge unscathed? Or did she commit suicide in a most gruesome and public way?

And what of the traumatized zoo people who found her? Counseling was available to the staff, a zoo official reported, "but no one has used it."

Picking up the phone, I dial the head of public relations at the zoo, thank him for the clips, and ask how he and the staff are doing.

"Oh, there's no problem now," he says briskly. "Except for the occasional grisly dreams, everybody seems to be coping."

The occasional grisly dreams? "Yes," I say ironically, "that sounds like they're coping. Are you sure they don't need to talk to a counselor about what they're feeling?"

"They probably do," he says thoughtfully, "but I can't force them to go. If they say they're handling it okay, well..."

"How about you? You're the one who had to describe the scene over and over to the press, and make sense of the mutilation—how are *you* feeling?" I can picture him sitting at his desk as we talk: a tall, attractive man in his late forties with salt-and-pepper hair and a neatly trimmed beard. It seems impossible that he has three children, one of whom is already thirty. I have no idea how he manages a large family, his research, and all the welter of zoo publicity and politics. And now this—an atrocity on his doorstep—and millions of anxious parents to reassure that the zoo is safe.

"Okay," he says, "no problem really... well, now and then I get these flashes of that instant when she must have realized that she wasn't going to be saved, that she was going to be mauled and eaten...that things weren't going to go according to plan, but horribly, violently wrong.... That single moment when the true terror of her situation dawned on her is what gets to me," he says in the tone of voice that is usually accompanied by a cold shiver of the shoulders. "But only now and then. Otherwise, I'm okay."

I rub a wet hand over my temple, slowly shake my head. I can't tell him that I'm a counselor at SP, but I can tell him about the organization here and its sister chapter in Washington, and ask if he thinks it might help him to talk with someone. He says possibly, and files the information.

There is a code of stoicism among people who work with animals, since a certain amount of discomfort and danger is built into the job. Zoo keepers tend dangerous animals and each year a certain number of them do get mauled by tigers, drowned by killer whales, or trampled by elephants. Because zoo animals are tame, visitors assume they are timid. Not so, as handlers know only too well. On zoo expeditions to repatriate, capture, or monitor animals in the wild, life-and-death dramas sometimes unfold, but people gunnysack their feelings so that work can continue as normal, and then they unpack their feelings later, when they're safely back home, with the aid of drinks, nervous humor, and a touch of bravado.

When I hang up, I look once more at the clippings, the last of which includes a photo of the lions and notes that they seemed "high-strung and skittish" after the attack, and that the keeper had trouble coaxing them back into their cages. Only the female was hungry enough to eat the prepared lion food, so presumably it was the male that attacked Margaret Davis King. These were lions born and raised in the zoo, fed a kind of dogfood mixture at each meal. That was the only food they knew, they had never stalked and downed wild animals, but when a prey animal in the form of a human entered their enclosure, pure instinct took over. If, afterward, they were agitated and ill at ease, perhaps it was because they had done something new, something exciting and savory but wrong. Ever since they were cubs, they had been kept from mauling their human keepers, indeed had been avoided by humans, driven back or punished when they threatened humans, fed and doctored and nurtured by humans, and now they had eaten a human. As any dog or cat owner knows, it doesn't take much brainpower for an animal to understand, if only fleetingly, that it has done something wrong. Despite a public outcry, the zoo refused to kill the lions. After all, they were doing what was natural, what lions do. Should we punish them for their nature? And what of our own thinly controlled penchant for violence? We, too, have evolved into impulsive, territorial, ravenous creatures. I once heard a grim joke that was a parable for the seemingly endless conflict in the Middle East: A turtle and a scorpion sat at the edge of river, and the scorpion begged the turtle to ferry him across. "You'll sting me if I do," the turtle protested. "No I won't, I promise," the scorpion said. "After all, if I sting you, I'll drown too." "That's true," the turtle said thoughtfully, and so he agreed. The scorpion climbed onto the turtle's back and they set out across the river. In the middle, the scorpion suddenly stung the turtle. "Why did you do that?" the turtle cried in his death throes. Now we'll both drown!" "I know, but I can't help myself," the scorpion replied, "it's my nature."

Among the squirrels in my yard, tempers flare easily, violence often erupts. Male or female, they turn savage at the drop of a nut. I don't idealize them or overlook their calamities, and I don't turn a blind eye to their wicked ways. I find it remarkable that, given their violent nature they can also be peaceful, nurturing, ingenious, prudent, quirky, delicate, playful, and moody. The spectrum of their behavior intrigues me. I feel much the same about humans. No lion behavior is more bloodcurdling than soldiers can be, or gang members, or terrorists, or serial killers, or toxic parents. Humans know how to maim and kill outright, and we have learned how to wound and slowly kill the spirit. We're so addicted to violence that when we can't aim it at others we unleash it on ourselves—gouge our skin, grow depressed, commit suicide. Violence is a strong pigment on our emotional palette. No cat persecutes its prey more brutally than humans sometimes do. Cats torture for practice, to hone their hunting skills, or to teach those skills to their young. Why do we do it? A jealous husband can rage to violence of mythic proportions in which he slashes a rival's jugular and tears him limb from limb. Zealots of all stripes murder by the score. Even office politics can lead to imaginary murder. We try to control our violent impulses with laws, fear of retaliation, threat of punishment, appeals to civility (really a feared loss of face or status). We saturate our minds with symbolic violence in sports arenas. We sell murderous people and fiendish acts as entertainment on television's so-called news shows. We kill vicariously in movies, so hungry are we to sink our teeth into an enemy; indeed, we've developed a cuisine of violence, spicing up the staple elements of death and butchery in ever more horrible and ingenious ways.

Although I regret our bloodthirsty nature, I'm nevertheless a great fan of humankind. What seems astonishing to me is that, despite our ferocious heritage, we so often act so well—as virtuosos of kindness, tenderness, peacefulness, generosity, cooperation, and spirituality. We devote most of our lives to exploring the many avenues of love, not always happily or with a clear road map, I'll grant you, but what a majestic tour de force. It's remarkable how we restrain and triumph over the dark side of our genes. We are resplendent beasts. Not an easy battle, the one we wage with our brutal appetites. We carry our instincts on our backs in invisible knapsacks filled with ancient needs and cravings, we struggle under the weight, often start to sink and thrash our way back to the surface, and yet somehow we keep our heads above water, and even celebrate the world's beauty, even sing songs of praise and forgiveness, even help our kin and absolute strangers cross, too, as we swim frantically toward the far shore. We act nobly, even when to do so may fatigue or endanger us. It doesn't make sense that we should, but it is our nature.

CHAPTER 4

A Mass of Life

The forsythia, daffodils, and squat fragrant hyacinths all opened as if on cue yesterday afternoon. Only a piano flourish was missing. For a few moments, I sit with my morning coffee and watch what looks like an Impressionist painting in motion—the cascade of yellows, purples, and pinks blurring as they rock in the morning breeze, a pale yellow sun welling right out of the the earth, backlighting the forest of oaks and hickories, and the gray squirrels weaving among the flowers. Shaking my head in amazement, I crank open the garden-room window, call the squirrels, feed a few by hand and toss the rest a medley of nuts. *Cue the Snow White music,* I think, laughing to myself. Some of the grays I've given Indian names to: "Eats Standing Up," "Dark Under the Eye," "Ducks Under the Fence." It reminds me a little of mealtime in a Jewish household, and my aunt saying to her son: "Hey, *you*—mister 'Talks with His Mouth Full'—do you think you could stop eating long enough to finish a sentence?" Or: "Mister 'I Know Everything' here thinks he could run the country," and so on. Life on the reservation of one's childhood. How does that Ojibway song go? I can only remember a section of it:

> Sometimes I go about pitying myself,
> and all the time
> I am being carried on great winds across the sky.

That puts it all in perspective: the relative puniness of human sorrow compared to the gushing blast of solar wind, or the endless tumble of the Earth and Milky Way traveling through space. I picture the Earth falling into the arms of the constellation Hercules, as indeed it is, in a perpetual slow-motion swoon that will last forever. From our perspective, anyway. Planetary folk across the galaxy would be seeing things otherwise; to them, Earth might be part of a landscape, machine, or symbolic constellation that has nothing to do with romantic legends, mythic warriors, animal guides, or powerfully mysterious kings and queens. We see our parents everywhere, even in the night sky. After all, when we were little, up is where they were—bending over us to caution, praise, or judge—floating high above us in the heaven of our regard. Small wonder we think the gods live in the sky.

Two crows start violently mating on the grass. They flap together and peck, then dance and strut. It would be as if two teenagers, at a discotheque, danced for a while, had feverish sex on the floor, then danced some more. A startling red cardinal, sitting on a bushy yew, seems to be wearing a Fu Manchu mustache. A closer look reveals that it's only a long limp blade of dry grass hanging from his beak. With a slow-motion flutter of wings, he hovers for a moment then dives inside the dense branches of the yew where he and his missus are undoubtedly building a nest. Last summer, I sometimes woke to the sound of a lady cardinal hurling her feathered softness against the cold windowpane, fighting her reflection, trying desperately to enter that remote mirror world, which tormented her and left her stunned. She did not know what she looked like. When she saw herself, she saw only an enemy. Finally, her frantic thudding became more than I could bear, and I taped up a drawing of a real threat—an owl—which worked the trick. Big-taloned, sharp-beaked, with keen asymmetrical ears and a hunger for small birds, an owl was a worse adversary than any version of herself. I make a mental note to unshelve that cardboard owl, just in case she decides to punch glass again this year. I wish it were that easy with some of the callers.

I finish my coffee, put on a few layers of biking clothes, and pack a picnic lunch. Most days I try to find time for a short ride through the countryside. An hour's outing may take me to The Plantations, a beautifully groomed arboretum with a lake full of ducks, or to Sapsucker Woods, the bird sanctuary, or perhaps to a village north or east of town. Whichever route I choose leads me beside forests and along farm fields, and I love watching the seasons blend into one another; the plants green, bud, blossom, spill seed, and dry; the animals change color, call, court, mate, feed, parent, migrate, and play. As anyone setting out on a walk or bike ride knows, it's hard to empty your mind of worry and planning, analyzing and hurting, and that deadly armada of what-ifs. Your agitations seem to travel with you, and soon enough you conduct small theaters of the mind, in which you play various roles and rehearse dreaded or hoped-for conversations in half a dozen ways. But if you can give yourself a mental vacation, hold a board meeting of the psyche, and agree to leave at home all the worries, all the expectations of others and yourself, any unhappiness, any hopes, hurts and misgivings—in short, all the usual commotion of a life—then you can set off on a ride in which you are free just to enjoy the sensations of being alive. You can allow yourself the gift of being a photographic plate on which the world etches itself. The beauty of the light, the whisperings of the wind, the rustle of dry cornstalks, the squirrel calls, the birdcalls, the syrupy smell of lilac hedges, the pomander sweetness of apple trees. You can feel the wind and sun on your face, savor the air, which tastes different in every season. Even in a city, you can sit down on a bench in the park and watch a pigeon or other bird for a while, watch it carefully, affectionately, watch how it struts like a petitioner, how it preens and puffs, bobs its head, cocks its neck, flashes its eye, pecks at food. Being completely absorbed by nature in this Zenlike way is a form of active meditation that I love. It comes to me naturally, but like everyone else I do need to keep time free for it. And that I do, faithfully, winter or spring. When my jogging and aerobics days led to knee surgery, I found fitness in biking, which actually helps my knee by strengthening the muscles around it. But I never stand-pedal on hills. I'm strong enough to bike up steep hills in low gear, but I know that, if I do, I'll inflame my calves more than I can bear. On very steep grades, I get off and push the bike uphill—also good exercise—which I regard as "cross-training." I don't try to set any distance or speed records when I bike, and I don't push myself beyond the first veils of discomfort. If I did, pain would invade my rides and be a constant companion. So, I would say I'm a cautious biker, but also an addicted one.

For example, every weekend in less than bone-chilling weather, I take a longer ride with my biking buddy, Cathy. Mystery trips, these. One week she chooses the destination, the next week I do. Sometimes we follow the directions in *20 Bicycle Tours in the Finger Lakes,* by Mark Roth and Sally Walters. Other times, groping through our memories for a fact that never mattered before but now has become vital—how hilly was that road?—we invent our own tours.

Today we've decided to explore the narrow strip of land between Seneca and Cayuga lakes, and she arrives right on time, at 9:30, with her teal mountain bike secured to a bike rack cantilevered off the back of her compact car. She's wearing black leggings patterned with black roses, and a purple windbreaker, and she has tucked her shoulder-length, brownish-blonde hair behind a wide purple headband. We tether my purple bike to hers with a complex lashing of bungee cords, check our county road maps, and set off as the mist begins lifting and the sky clears to a radiant blue.

We drive north along the west side of Cayuga Lake, through villages and towns with Roman names. Occasionally the road curves to a hilltop vista and we gasp at the postcard beauty of the lake, a deep Caribbean blue between plunging mountains. Along the tops of the trees, in the umbrella of branches exposed to bare sun, buds have begun to form and give the dense forests the soft pink glow I associate with spring. Some may consult almanacs or groundhogs. Myself, I wait for the first subtle moment when the distant treetops—stark and distinct all winter—look blurred by new growth and harbor a tint of dusty rose. The weeping willow whips have already turned neon yellow. Among the dry carcasses of roadside bushes, live branches glow purple-red. Wild daylilies have started to shoot up in the culverts. Home owners have planted daffodils everywhere, and half of them are in bloom. A flock of cedar waxwings invades a hedge of wild berries, hovering hummingbird-style and flashing their yellow tail tips. It is glorious to drive along the ledge of springtime in upstate New York. A few miles north of Romulus, we find a convenient spot to park our car at the site of an Indian massacre (there are many such sites along this route), beside a paddock where two large Belgian horses graze. Their blond manes have been curled into finger waves. I doubt they are being used to pull plows; *they* are objects of strength and beauty, paragons of muscle, bodybuilders not laborers.

I really love these weekend bike trips with Cathy, during which our friendship, tentative at first, has been steadily building to a close camaraderie. Cathy and I are exactly the same age—we danced to the same rock-and-roll music as kids, wore the same felt skirts and saddle shoes, lived through the same history of space shots, Kennedy years, Vietnam War, and what was then called Women's Liberation. We're well matched athletically, which is paramount in an exercise partner, although she has much more upper body strength and far stronger back and arms (I insist it's from her years as a baton twirler in high school); unlike me, she plays tennis and racquetball each week, and goes to the gym. We crave lunch at the same time, and our energy flags at about the same point—three hours of steady pedaling. We're both latter-day hippies, which means we share a basic value system. The seventies' atmosphere of upheaval, social change, and hope had a powerful impact on both of us, as it did on so many others. Of course, some people grew older and betrayed their dreams. But I've been heartened to see how many children of the sixties and seventies have come of age, gotten into positions of influence, and kept their vision. They don't always agree on issues, but what they share is a faith in the innate goodness of people, and the determination to make a difference. At the end of Italo Calvino's *Invisible Cities,* Marco Polo says of his life that his toughest task was to try to figure out who and what in the midst of Inferno are not Inferno, and make sure they prevail. Although I didn't know it when I was eighteen, that was my quest. It continues to be. Only the forum has changed, not the underlying idealism.

For nearly a year, Cathy and I have been taking these bike trips—most of them twenty to forty miles long, always with a lake or river in view. We pack a picnic lunch, choose a road with a shoulder wide enough for us to bike two abreast, and chat about the world and our lives as we drink in the sunlight, rejoice in the scenery, and get a thigh-quivering workout. I'm fascinated by human behavior and so is she, so much so she decided to become a clinical social worker. A therapist in private practice, she has many clients—troubled children, couples, whole families in distress, college students, blue-collar workers—whom she ministers to in the course of a week. Although she has never been a crisis-line counselor, last year she served as president of SP's board of directors, and thus knows many of my concerns. We each envy the strengths of the other. But, gradually, we have both become stronger in mind and body—able to tackle longer hills, more open to occasional dabs of risk-taking. Our "sport" offers us a chance to build our friendship, and the means to improve ourselves (that great American obsession), but also an axis for our lives. Historically, women have always been praised for their softness, gentleness, vulnerability. Those are lovely qualities to possess, but I also want to feel strong and competent in the world, with the kind of mental swerve that leads you down unconsidered roads toward some ravishing vista. Passersby, examining our faces, would probably find pleasure, struggle, fatigue, and laughter alloyed there. It is not the same as watching a competitive athlete, whose whole demeanor defines concentration, skill, and power. We're not Olympians, nor do we need to be; we only need to be fitter versions of ourselves.

A mile down the road we pass a swampy pond where thousands of electronic alarm clocks are beeping. Or so it seems. The sound is immense. We park our bikes and edge carefully into the swamp.

"Frogs. Very horny frogs." I laugh, remembering the sexy discothequing crows. "Think of them as frat boys on a wild Saturday night. With the only chance at getting laid they'll ever have in their entire lives." Imagine the orgy. We can't see the frogs making so much racket because they are tiny and well-camouflaged. The sound flees before us as we advance, and then returns with a crescendo as we walk back to the road and pedal away.

When we come to a sign that says LOWER LAKE ROAD, Cathy and I exchange grins. A cardinal rule of our bike trips is: Never spurn a lake road. So we turn right and swoop down along the beautiful shore, once home to Indians who fished the waters and hunted the nearby woods. Nowadays the lake shore is largely unsettled.

"Look at those mud flats!" she says. It takes a while for us to realize that all the piers rest on stilts above the mud. Because it has been a mild winter with little snow, the lake is at one of its all-time lows. The sludgy bottom lies exposed, creating a huge beach, where people wearing hip boots tramp farther out into the lake than they've ever

dared. Stepping tentatively, they seem to be discovering the wild un-
derpinnings of the lake for the first time—that realm below the consciousness of water where ooze and small slithering creatures
combine—and one can read the puzzlement on their faces.

"I'm worried about one of my clients," Cathy says, as we bike past
a marina stranded in the air. "She's just so fragile. But, at the same
time, there's an enormous amount of rage she's trying to deal with.
When she gets depressed, she can get *very* active and disassociative.
Cut herself, threaten people, you name it."

"Wow. That must take your full attention." I can't imagine how I
would deal with an unpredictable and aggressive client.

"No foolin'. And that's just *one* of my Tuesday clients. I've got two
more who are completely chaotic thinkers. My job Tuesdays is to be
a sort of mind sheriff—you know, help them round up their thoughts
and impose some sort of order in the town. Not an easy role, I'll tell
you, especially for me."

"Hard enough to tidy up one's own life, isn't it?" Approaching a
long shallow hill, I downshift into the lowest gear, and my bike makes
a ratcheting sound seven times in succession. Cathy shifts into low,
too. We sound like old codgers gently cracking our bones.

"Hey, what *am* I going to do about my air traffic controller?"

"Oh, that's right, you've been out swing-dancing since I saw you
last. How was your date?" I ask, while keeping my eyes on the road.
Because road shoulders aren't very well paved, we have to split our
glance into several facets—the road ahead, passing cars, the uneven
ground pouring under us—always ready to swerve around broken
glass or gouged macadam. Amazing the eye can do all of that, and also
enjoy the panoramic sprawl of the lake, the piñatalike twirling of
laundry drying on a clothesline behind a small bungalow, where a
black Labrador is curled up asleep on a front porch whose second step
needs repair. In six turns of the pedals, the bungalow, the dog, the
porch, the laundry all vanish into the hinterlands of memory.

"The dancing was okay, then we went back to his place, which was also okay. But do you know how weird it is to date a man who talks like he's clearing airplanes to land?"

"Maybe you just need the right lingo to throw back at him. Let's see, there's *rotate, joystick, holding pattern, attitude, civil evening twilight...*"

"That's nice. I'll ask him about *civil evening twilight* tonight."

"You've got a date tonight?" I call as I draw up alongside her. Somehow we manage to talk intimately while not making eye contact, something people rarely do, except in confessionals, during psychoanalysis, or over the telephone. That's probably why we so often toss a glance the other's way, not really to convey anything but as a sort of punctuation.

"Call me crazy, but I invited him over for dinner."

"Want to borrow my searchlight?"

"Sure. I could nail it up on the porch when he arrives. That would make him feel at ease. Got a siren?"

"*You* can be the siren."

She pulls down her sunglasses, flashes me a don't-be-a-smart-aleck look, and sets them back in place. "How come relationships are so hard?"

"You're asking *me*? You're the one who does this for a living."

"Yeah, but it's a darned sight easier when it's somebody *else's* relationship!" She pumps the pedals hard for emphasis.

"So true," I say in a Tweetybird voice. "So true."

"But back to my client," she says, serious again, "I'm worried about her in between visits. She's not sure she can keep from fraying. I suggested she call SP." Local therapists often refer their clients to SP; we help them cope after hours, when their therapists aren't available.

A skywriter begins practicing above the lake, drawing white dashes and long steady white lines. It's hard to keep an eye on him and on the road at the same time, but, in any case, he soon darts out of sight.

"That's fine. I hope I'm on when she calls."

Turning left at Bayard Road, we climb west toward Seneca Falls, as the land tightens and fights beneath us. We become more aware of the earth's muscle when we bike, its hard steep shoulders and fistlike knolls, but also its sensuality, its fertile fields and long languorous hills. Today the hawks, vultures, and other soaring birds are out in full force, spiraling up the thermals over the lake, and in envious appreciation we exclaim whenever we spot an especially fast and swervy one. It is an ancient longing. One of the first words humans spoke, recorded in Indo-European as *pleu*, meant "It flies!" and should probably be said with our lips pursed in a silent *wow!* to capture some of the original astonishment. No doubt it was first said about birds. There is a certain abracadabra quality to birds. They have substance, but they're ghostlike, changing shape as they pirouette on high, casting daggers of glare or broad black shadows. In the Dark Ages, the devout may have seen them as flying crucifixions, as Samuel Beckett once described them. When they're motionless on the ground, the wind can still sough through them. Even their dropped feathers fly. And yet, socially, they look like shamans or courtiers, rehearsing the complex rituals and ceremonies that rule their lives. They are object lessons in cause and effect: a male performs an appeasement gesture (such as dropping a twig at a female's feet), and the female stops hoarsely braying at him and begins to burble. On the ground, they are always involved in some elaborate choreography. Aloft, they look like parts of the sky that have broken loose. In a realm alternately angelic and sinister, they slide across the blue on wings softer than skin. They remind us just how earthbound we are. Throughout the world, people speak of bird flight with wistfulness and envy, in that poignant subjunctive: "If only . . ." I remember what a pilgrimage it was for me, on assignment for *The New Yorker* a few years ago, to travel to Japan to behold flight incarnate—the short-tailed albatross, one of the rarest and most beguiling of birds. That was a tough trip, though, with many mishaps and dangers, including high seas, an active volcano, and a fall down a cliff face that resulted in three broken ribs. The pain of the sharp rock knifing into my flesh, and then the broken bones shifting inside, was pure agony. My thoughts begin to slide to Louise and the way she pictured falling onto the rocks in the gorge.

The knifelike rocks.

"I'm worried about one of my *callers,*" I say after a while. "Well, worried about myself, too."

"Oh, yeah?" Cathy says in that inflection perfected by therapists—acknowledging and leading on at the same time.

I think of Louise, wondering how best to epitomize her. "She's an accomplished and savvy woman, but also terribly fragile, prey to horrendous depressions, dangerous depressions."

"You sound really worried about her. Do you think she'll suicide?" Cathy asks. I've heard a lot of mental health people use *suicide* as a verb, referring to it frontally, not couching it in euphemisms, but I've never quite gotten use to the sound of the word. Did Cleopatra *suicide* when she knew all was lost? Somehow her death, arranged with drama and pageantry, after a life steeped in pleasure, politics, accomplishment, family, and worry, seems to require a more elaborate word. But then so does any death. *Commit suicide,* we usually say, along the lines of committing a crime or error. It's just as clinical, just as much a euphemism, but it takes longer to say. I think Sir Thomas Browne may have coined the word *suicide,* the earliest recorded mention of which appears in his book *Religio Medici,* published in 1643, where he speaks of a man becoming his own assassin, but he uses the word as a noun, referring to the "suicide of Cato." The verb form is newer, and though it is candid and precise, I still find it jarring. An intransitive verb, it hangs in the air like a leap. He died. He suicided. There is no afterward.

"Possibly. She's already doing that in small doses, sort of rehearsing the event."

"Rehearsing?"

"When she calls, I sometimes get the feeling she isn't simply struggling with a bad depression; I think she may be testing what it would be like—you know, what it would feel like, how it would affect loved ones—if she did kill herself."

"That must be scary for you, not knowing what she may do next. But you have other highly lethal callers. It sounds like she affects you differently."

"She's a sweet person…really well-read and interesting and—even though I know this must sound odd in this context—very festive about life. She's just in so much pain, and she's trying so hard to keep herself alive. I admire her courage. We would probably be friends if we met in other circumstances." Louise's story touches me because it could be the story of many people I know, the story of a lovely talented person at a time of deep distress, and all my instincts urge me to help her through her sorrows, not just by listening but more expansively, to nurture her the way one does a friend.

"That does sound like a grueling situation. But you said you were also worried about yourself…"

"Well, in one of her calls she mentioned that she goes to the Spiritualist services in Freeville on Friday nights during the summer, and I've been thinking that it would be nice just to go and see what she looks like, you know, see who she really is."

"Uh-oh," Cathy says. "Do I detect boundary problems here?"

Laughing lightly, I shake my head yes.

"What would that tell you? How would that make you feel any easier about her?"

"Did I say it would make me feel easier?"

"Right. You want to go because it *won't* make you feel easier."

"That's it, strike while the irony is hot. See if I care."

"Obviously you do care a lot," she says, brushing my joke aside. "I just wonder if it would make things easier or tougher for you, having a real face in mind—a fuller person—whenever she calls. Would you be happy just seeing her? Or would you want to talk with her? Maybe even befriend her? Do you want to get that involved with a caller? I don't know. Having any outside contact with callers is frowned upon, isn't it?"

"Totally. It would be regarded as a lapse in judgment. And heaven knows it would deny her the right to be anonymous when she calls, which, among mental health folk, as you know, is tantamount to cat-strangling."

For a few minutes more we consider what would happen if I encountered Louise. The temptation is so great, though I sense it would be a mistake. Then we let the topic melt into the scenery, to be replaced by other issues, other events recalled. In time, we map most of the week's important terrain. "Catching up," it's called. Because the route has been slightly uphill all the way, we grow tired enough after ten miles to lose our mental edge. At the outset we spoke about weighty things, such as our work problems, books we were reading, a terrorist bombing in the Midwest, a tottering relationship, a notorious trial. Fatigued, we fall silent or joke earnestly about how good a work-out we're getting.

In time, Seneca Falls flashes into view, wrapped in water like a European town of canals. We eat lunch beside an old stone church at the water's edge, then bike to the Women's Hall of Fame and the Women's National Park. Both landmarks commemorate the strength of women, women pioneers and rock climbers, women writers and pilots, women athletes and politicians. The Hall of Fame celebrates women who were larger than life. But what I like about the park museum is that it celebrates the strivings of everyday women, not only the famous. After all, strength is what we all seek, the strength to stand up to an oppressor, be it injustice, a record set, or oneself. As we become stronger and push our limits, we occupy a larger piece of the earth or sky or an idea than we did before. "Be strong," when said to women, traditionally has meant *suffer in silence. Endure your painful circumstances. Abolish hope.* "The weaker sex" is an odd way to label beings who give birth, rear children, plow fields, all of which take strong innards and mettle.

Some people seek an elemental form of strength, a desire to be strong the way the earth is strong in its skeleton of bones, to be a force of nature. The stronger we are, we secretly believe, the longer it will take the Destroyer of Delight to knock us down for the final time. Though settled and civilized, we still instinctively picture ourselves competing with animals which are powerful, fleet-footed, and healthy. It's a throwback to our cave-dwelling days—we feel an animal need to be strong lest bears and tigers devour us. The gods were never weaklings, and we pint-sized mortals yearn to be gods. One way we wrestle with our relative puniness in the face of a colossal and merciless universe is to enlarge our powers—climb the highest mountains, speed over the ground, ride dynamos that outpace storms.

Cathy and I may never be as strong as a rock face, never as dynamic as the wind, never as unstoppable as a fast-flowing river. Never as fleet as professional athletes, never as rugged and pain free as we were in our youth. Serious athletes romance pain, find ways through and around it. I share some of their chronic joint aches and muscle spasms, and think of mild pain the way heads-down racing cyclists probably do, as a sort of fog one travels through from time to time. None of that matters. Strength is relative. We dream of bike rides across the Texas hill country, through the Everglades, along the Rhode Island coast, beside the Netherlands' endless flower fields and canals. If a shuttle service to Mars started up tomorrow, we would go—but we would want to take our bikes.

After the sun sets, during the hour of gushing color and soot known to pilots as *civil evening twilight,* with a twenty-mile bike trip behind us, we drive back home, Cathy to cook a paella for her date, I to go on shift at the Crisis Center.

—

8:15 P.M. When I answer the phone, I hear a man whose voice I recognize as a frequent caller's; he recognizes mine, too. That makes it easier for me to ask what's been happening today and encourage him in what he knows I know has been a long struggle. He thinks it has been a struggle with life's harsher situations and people who don't want to accept and love him. I know it has been a struggle with mental illness and a personality disorder he may never be free from, which torments and depresses him, puts an impossible burden on whatever relationships he does make, keeps him from being able to be happy in his relationship with his children, his mate, his parents. He has a therapist, he has tried medications in the past. They cannot help him cure his terrible loneliness and longing for one truly loving soul to give him the all-consuming absolute love he craves.

"Endless Love," I jot down on the ledger.

I concentrate on the loneliness with him. He tells me he has emotional pockets that will never be filled. He understands that there is no going back, no way to reverse his past and right the wrongs. As usual, he feels he has brought his suffering on himself, because he is a bad person. He once told me that he was a practicing Mormon. Tonight I try a new tactic and talk with him about Jesus' suffering. Jesus was a perfect person who suffered terribly, I observe—suffering doesn't only happen to bad people, nor should the caller feel diminished by suffering. That touches a nerve, and he talks animatedly about God's purpose and Satan's campaign for his own "dog-eared soul." In time, he settles down into that chasm of hope-lined despair that he dwells in for much of his life. Just having another person believe in and empathize with his pain helps a little. But precious little. He does not know how he will survive until tomorrow. We concentrate on today, this afternoon, this hour.

As we're finishing, the phone rings. It is an intelligent, formal, overly elaborating, at times antique-sounding, circuitous woman who is obsessive in an unusual and rather fascinating way. As she relates her phone call with a counselor of a week before, she also studies it like a druidical text. Then she rambles and free-associates about her inheritance squabbles, brother and his lawyer assassins, slights by her children, and the in-laws, who seem to be plotting against her. Entering her verbal whirlwind is like trying to pierce a ball of string with a needle—the wadded-up strands of her obsessions continue to flow right around any question I pose or observation I make. I've a hunch her family and friends will no longer listen to her, so our taking her seriously means a great deal.

The next call is from a tense man who found our number on his answering machine. He's not sure if he should be calling us. I gently invite him to share his troubles with me.

"I don't open up to just anybody," he says defensively. "If I'm going to bleed my guts out, I want to make sure it's in the right direction." I try to explain who and what we are in a way that leaves the door open for him to call back. When I hang up I feel bad. There was a bludgeon of woe in his voice. When a tough guy's voice wavers like that he's under colossal pressure. What should I have said to make the connection easier for him?

A call comes in from an angry, sad woman who has been "depressed for a dozen years." Therapists label it this or that, but she knows she's not responsible for her upset—life has simply dealt her a lousy hand, and everyone is cruel to her. She tends to obsess about people, especially men, for long periods of time (years), is embroiled in various legal fracases—there's a restraining order against her by a chiropractor she had been seeing and was fixated on. She demands help and advice, but will listen to neither. It's a tough call of pure anger, demand, and a sense of life's impossibility.

Endless Love calls back and once again I try to enter his world. I picture him standing at a wall phone in his girlfriend's kitchen. But no, he explains, he has moved out of his place and into a small trailer park beside the stream in Forest Home. He just phoned his girlfriend, but she won't come over. She won't inspect her motives and actions the way he wants her to, and she won't provide him with the "heartful, honest, truly loving support" that he needs. And where is his daughter? His ex-wife has tarnished the girl's "pure beautiful spirit."

"It's soul murder. She should be here, helping me with her loving spirit, and enjoying the spring with me," Endless Love laments.

Blossom Day. I had forgotten about Blossom Day, which came late last year. We usually celebrate it when my friend Annie's little girl,

Alexandra, sees the first blossoms on the dogwood tree outside her window. Then Annie phones me, and the three of us "blossom sisters" gather beside the tree to perform our pagan female ritual of worshiping Mother Nature, praising the growing things of the earth, and pledging our loyalty to one another. We hold hands around the sapling, and each of us makes a little speech. Alex is thirteen now, and we began this ritual when she was seven. Each year, it starts with a solemn testimony, and then proceeds to the exchanging of small sensory presents—pretty stones, fragrant soaps, planted herbs, perhaps a vibrant scarf. After that, Alex gets to style and restyle my long hair. Last year the holiday evolved. We celebrated it late, on May 22, so that my friend Dava and her daughter Zoë could join in. Annie, Alex, and I met Dava and Zoë at the airport and we all went to a scenic restaurant on the inlet so that the girls could get acquainted. They hit it off famously, spoke the same lingo, railed at the same sorts of teachers, wore the same shade of blue jeans and T-shirts, and became instant friends. Afterward we went to Annie's and spread out beautifully wrapped presents—a symbol of Nature's bounty—on a table. But before opening them we gathered up armfuls of flowers and made a pilgrimage to the official Blossom Tree on the patio, where we held hands around the tree. I began by intoning a thanksgiving to Mother Nature. Dava followed with a little speech, then Annie added her thoughts. At this point, one of the girls said, "You guys are such hippies!" We laughed, remembering how, when we were adolescents, we too thought grown-ups were put on the earth solely for the purpose of embarrassing children. For them, the world was divided up into the "cool" and the "uncool." At this important stage in their lives, there was no way for them to say prayers aloud. So we decided to allow them leeway. For a few years, they may not wish to be the earth children they were as kids, and that's okay. The time will come when Blossom Day holds meaning for them once again, as it does for their moms and me.

We adjourned to the living room to open our presents. Once, when I asked Alex what she wanted to be when she grew up, she had answered: "President of the United States... and also a hairdresser." I promised her that if she did become president I would positively go to her to have my hair done. Now she just wants to be president which, in that household, isn't necessarily a pipe dream. Finally we went to my house for a swim in the pool, drank peppermint tea, and ate hot pecan sticky buns. We decided Paul and Carl could join us at that point, dubbing them the male auxiliary of the Blossom Sisters, the Sta-men.

This year, Alex's father is undergoing a bone marrow transplant in Seattle, and that's where the whole family will be standing vigil for the rest of the year, focused on invisible blood cells in the hollow of his bones. A blood factory. Next year, when the family returns home and the death frights are over, we'll plan Blossom Day again. Some pagan rituals feel so right—baby showers, where women gather to welcome a forthcoming life into the tribe; birthday parties, when we celebrate a loved one's mere existence on the planet; and holidays that mark the procession of the seasons.

Once, at an artist's colony on a Florida estuary where I was leading a poetry workshop, thirty of us gathered to celebrate the summer solstice with song and ritual. What a perfect setting for it. "Hammock-land" they call the odd shock of forest that sprang up in the middle of an open field in coastal Florida; long ago, a bird or other animal dropped a single seed that rooted and grew, offering shade to more seed-carting animals. First one tree takes root, swaying like a small hammock, then many animals come to rest, bringing seeds and leavings. Soon it becomes thick woods, bustling with wildlife, bearded with swamp moss. The sky curdled at 4:00 P.M. each day, as blue scarves trailed from soggy clouds, the sea-oat heads blasted apart, cascading upward, and the heavy rain sounded like falling butterscotch. A typhoon of fork-tailed swallows often maneuvered overhead, then funneled into a myrtle tree, ate the luscious berries, and swirled away. Green anoles traveled the raised boardwalk like small silent jeeps. We lived along the estuary in cottages up on stilts and connected by raised walkways, like a troupe of wild macaques nestled among the green bosoms of the trees, high above a dense forest floor which leprosy-prone armadillos shared with wild pigs, raccoons, foxes, and pine snakes. Spanish moss hung everywhere like scribbles of DNA.

Gathering outside my house to celebrate summer solstice, we each wrote a wish on a small pennant of paper then tossed the chits into the fire, where they burst into flames and danced on hot vapors into the night. Like fireflies, our unspoken hopes flashed toward heaven. I remember wondering what wish Susan, a woman sitting across the circle from me, had chosen. She was a pianist, married, in her thirties, in love with a painter, a sweet, shy man about twelve years her junior, whom she had met at the colony only weeks before. They were tight as barnacles, and snuggled blissfully beside the fire, as a professional whistler softly whistled the sprightly Shaker melody "Simple Gifts." I knew she was considering leaving her husband and starting a new family with this young man, and at the same time longing to return home to her friends and family and all that was familiar. So when she leaned over to add her scrolled-up wish to the fire, I wasn't certain if it was to ignite or to incinerate passion.

I'm sure each of us kindled an equally momentous hope of one sort or another. Looking from face to face, searching beneath the animation and jollity for a clue to the invisible realms they masked, it was impossible to read minds. Whole towns are like that sometimes, alive on several levels, with emotional riptides and currents that don't appear at first or twelfth glance. I didn't know then that I would become privy to some of my town's darker secrets, to the torments and dreams of so many of my neighbors. Seated at that solstice campfire, I watched each paper wish tremble into flame for a moment and kite higher and higher, until it joined the others in a bouquet of sparks, then mingled with the constellations and vanished into night.

CHAPTER 5

The Golden Apples
of the Sun, and Silver
Apples of the Moon

When summer arrives with its baggage of hot humid days, I discover a serious change in the squirrels. They come for nuts and sunflower seeds as before, but they're much more aggressive, challenging, growling, and leaping Ninjalike at each other, flailing with claws and teeth. Most have bite marks on their ears and claw scars on their coats. One's left ear is split in three—"Fork Ear" I name him—and he is the fiercest, driving off the others with much savagery. One squirrel has only half a tail and drags the stump behind him like a pirate with a wooden leg. And where is the Pleader? This new mob of squirrels is plump and strong. Are they adolescents? Are the Young Turks demoting and dashing the elders? Has there been a junta in which the Pleader and his kin were driven off?

Last summer I watched, amazed, as an odd war drama unfolded in my backyard. Two gangs faced each other on the pool deck and then, at a signal I couldn't detect, suddenly charged in a pitched battle. One squirrel fell in the water and struggled to climb out, others were scratched, bitten, and chased up and out of trees. I've never before or since seen them fight formally like that. What worries me, though, is that I haven't seen the Pleader for days, and I fear he may be dead, a victim of battle. Or perhaps he fell from a tree. This happens from time to time, especially if a squirrel is old or weak. Squirrels may live twenty years in captivity, and some of my well-fed yard squirrels are over three years old, but the average life span in the wild is only one year. The tattered ears on the remaining squirrels tell part of the story. When I feed them now, I'm careful to scatter the seeds over six or eight feet, because they can't seem to resist warfare if they are within pouncing distance of one another. The squirrels have different personalities all of a sudden, but so do the other animals. The forest, too, has changed in dramatic ways. Even the insects are behaving oddly.

Summer is like a new philosophy in the air, and everyone has heard about it. From atop a chestnut tree, where spiked fruits hang like sputniks, comes the sound of a bottle band and the kazooistry of birds. On the ground, a blanket of dry leaves gives sound to each motion: falling berries, scuffling voles, a skink rising from its bog. Small fence lizards do rapid push-ups as part of their territorial display. All along the weedy roadways, crickets rub shrill songs from their legs, and grasshoppers thrash and rustle in the brush. The grass has grown tall at last, and the trees offer shade for the first time in a year.

Expectant and rowdy, animals enter the green metropolis of summer through the tunnel of June, and they all have noisy errands to run. They bustle about their business of courting, warring, and dining.

Only humans fret over meaning and purpose. Animals have appointments to keep. Even the june bugs, those relatives of Egyptian scarabs clattering against the window screens—humming and buzzing, bumbling and banging—are on a mission of romance. They sometimes batter their way indoors by mistake, and then run around in a beetle-mania like wind-up metal toys. All that bugginess, glossy shell, and frenetic motion scares some people, but I like to hear june bugs clatter at the change of seasons.

Spring meant scant food, faint light, and hardship. But summer is a realm of pure growth, the living larder of the year, full of sprouting and leafing, breeding and feasting, burgeoning and blooming, hatching and flying. Nowadays the mallards are taxi dancing as they ceremonially mate, which they sometimes do on the lawn. Baby garter snakes lie like pencil leads in the grass. Wild strawberries ripen into tiny sirens of flavor that lure chipmunks, rabbits, deer, and humans alike out into the open to graze. A vast armada of insects sails into the rosebeds, and groundhogs dig among the speckle-throated lilies.

Countless birds seem to be auditioning. A bad-tempered wren will haze a rabbit across the lawn by dive-bombing straight at it, beak ready to impale. There's no way the rabbit can climb after her chicks, but wrens are pint-size scolds and highly territorial. Large glossy crows sound as if they're gagging on lengths of flannel. Blackbirds quibble nonstop from the telephone wires, where they perch like a run of eighth notes. I sometimes try to sing their melody. Because every animal has its own vocal niche (so that lovesick frogs won't drown out the hoarse threats of a pheasant barking at a dog), summer days unfold as a Charles Ives symphony does, full of the sprightly cacophony we cherish, the musical noise reassuring us that nature is going on her green evitable way and all's right with the world.

Drawn by a familiar chirp, I look out my kitchen window to see a cardinal couple feasting together on sunflower seeds. Scarlet with a black mask, the male eats first, lifting a seed, rolling it to one side of his beak, where a built-in seed-opener cracks the hull, then rolling it to the seed-opener on the other side to finish the job. Meanwhile, the dusky female stands nearby and shivers. Puffing up her feathers and squeaking, she looks helpless and cold, but actually she's inviting her mate to court. Though acting like a hungry infant bird, she is perfectly able to feed herself, and will. This dramatic appeal is the time-honored way that female cardinals (and many other birds) play house. When the young are born, the parents must feed them nonstop, so she wants a mate who knows how to respond to the plaintive signs of infant need. The male cardinal observes her display and cocks his head as if listening, but what he's really doing is looking hard. Because most birds have poor stereo vision, they see better if they look with one eye at a time. Lifting a plump seed, he pogo-hops over to her and places it carefully in her mouth.

I shake my head and sigh. I'm ashamed to admit it, but from time to time human females can act just as infantile when a male is around, and for the same reason: to mug a little kindness and nourishment from him. *See how weak and helpless I am? Doesn't a big strong man like you want to protect a poor little iddy-biddy thing like me?* Pathetic, but true. And the worst part is that it usually works. Adults of nearly all species will instinctively cosset and protect their young. We turn-of-the-century women swear we don't play that game anymore, but at some point in our romantic lives, all of us do. Even my eight-year-old neighbor—a winning little girl who is a junior naturalist and the daughter of an intelligent, down-to-earth, outgoing, successful, wholly liberated nuclear physicist mother and an equally liberated, be-all-that-you-can-be engineer father—plays games with boys in which she chooses to be the helpless damsel in distress who waits to be fought over and rescued, just as animal young rehearse courtship strategies during play. And as her mother and I both know, although the knowledge embarrasses us, men can be manipulated if we act helpless. Because it's a self-sabotaging strategy, and we want our menfolk to help us for the right reason—out of love and respect—we don't stoop to what most women would regard as bimbodom, even though we know that being a bimbo works. Nonetheless, when you're in a hardware store facing down a hundred Allen wrenches, or dealing with a car mechanic or recalcitrant civil servant, the temptation can be mighty strong. Does a human female sometimes act childlike during courtship for the same reason a lady cardinal does—to test a male's potential for parenting? It's possible. Just as the brawniest men, when they're sick, tend to become little boys, which automatically elicits nurturing from a female. Or couples talk babytalk to each other, which makes it easier to respond to someone—who after all is not a blood relative—as if he or she were one's child, that is, protectively and with unconditional love. When people grow frightened or depressed, they usually regress to a childlike state. They feel as helpless as children at such times, but appearing childlike also inspires nurturing in others exactly when it is most needed.

Back to the cardinals. What are we to make of their bickering? When a male and female finally get together, the female chases the male around, pecks him painfully, he pecks back, and they engage in a kind of spat before she accepts him. They will end up mating and rearing offspring, but why bother with the squabbling? Unless it is a way for her to test him, to make sure that he'll be a faithful and devoted father even when the going gets rough, as it's bound to once the chicks arrive. Do human lovers have spats for the same reason?

This morning, two robins are running relays to feed their squawking brood in a nest they've placed in a yew tree near the door. The chicks are all gaping mouth and yammer. How do the parents keep from feeding the same chick over and over? Do they somehow keep track of which ones have been fed? No, they don't need to. Birds have a reflex that makes them pause between swallowings. If a parent robin puts a worm into the mouth of a just-fed chick, the worm will sit there and not go down. Then the parent simply plucks it out and gives it to a different chick.

Nearby, the lavender garden is a den of thieves, as dozens of plump bees fumble the flowers. Dressed in yellow sweaters, the bees aren't stately and methodical about their work, but rather clumsy. Skidding off shuddery petals, they manage to grab a little nectar, but also get smeared with pollen as they career out of the blossoms. They hover for a moment, then dive headlong into the next flowers, and spend the day in a feast of recovered falls. One rarely notices the uncertainty of the bee, wallowing and sliding, or how flower petals are delicately balanced so that they will appear firm, but waver and flex suddenly without actually breaking off. The purpose of the design is to unsettle the bee.

The purpose of the design is to unsettle the bee, I remind myself. The bee isn't supposed to be comfortable, secure, or happy, it's supposed to get smeared with pollen—whether or not the bee suffers is irrelevant. So it goes with the evolution of anxiety, worry, grief, depression, and other states of emotional distress. Sometimes it's easy to forget that our brains evolved to solve such basic Stone Age problems as courting a mate, finding food, making kinship bonds, devising a language, cooperating with other members of the tribe, sharing food, braving the environment, and fighting to keep oneself and one's offspring alive. Problems vital to our survival. We've had to devise clever ways to deal with them: love and hate, a panoply of defenses, bluffs, and preemptive strikes, knacks of avoidance, gamesmanship, seductive innuendos, a taste for deceit, empathy to the nth, a code breaker's cunning, thoroughness to the point of compulsion, and many other basic strategies that produced the emotional weather systems we now are.

It's easy to think of evolution as a ruling secret society, whose bylaws we all abide by but never know. Variety is its pledge, *be prepared* its motto. Its single instruction—avoid what's harmful, desire what's helpful—we follow not by reason, but by instinct. Yet evolution is infinitely subtler and more complex than Carlyle's "gospel of dirt." Because we have versatile, web-spinning minds that caress ideas and abhor boredom, we like nothing better than to start with a simple melody and finesse it into a thicket of sound. Then we don't feel the reins of instinct. When, through reason, religious teachings, or stark frantic need, we boldly override the governor on those instincts, we feel giddy, boundless, galloping with "free will." One of the things I like best about human beings is that we don't like to play by the rules. We know what many of the rules are. One rule, for example, is that we're anchored to the earth, crawl the earth as infants, walk the earth as adults, bend closer and closer to earth in old age, until at last we become the earth. That fundamental law irritates and intrigues us, and so we invent ingenious ways to sidestep evolution and fly as we were not born to. Some instincts drive us against all reason, some plague us like allergies, and some we plain refuse to follow, fighting them in what feels like open warfare with ghosts.

Anxiety, dread, panic, aversion, depression. A small demonology of our age. It makes one anxious just to name them, and most people will eagerly perform any ritual, wear any amulet, intone any magic that might keep these demons at bay. But they warn us of potential dangers, so we can prepare. Indeed, the full bouquet of our cherished traits and tastes, as well as the bestiary of our negative behaviors, evolved at a time when humans lived in small bands of hunter-gatherer-scavengers. To us, their lives seem arduous and uncertain, but heaven knows what they would make of ours. The only thing is, we still navigate by their maps, still respond according to their instincts, still act like hunter-gatherers, though we grapple with problems they would not have encountered, understood, or valued.

Shedding the centuries, falling backward down a time well, I picture the small bands of humans from whom everyone on earth descended. Our terrors are their terrors, our hungers their hungers, our pleasures their pleasures, our worry their worry. We speak the same emotional language. Only the details have changed, as our vocabulary evolved to cope with everyday life, but our emotional grammar did not. We carry many of the same psychic burdens, only the satchels are different, how we fill them, and where we lay them down. We're prepared for their world, not ours, and *strain* doesn't begin to describe how emotionally off-balance, misfit, and cramped we sometimes feel, as we try to improvise with outmoded tools.

Anxiety, that masochistic terrier of one's own devising, played a life-saving role in our ancestors' lives by alerting them to potential threats so they could plan a response. "A tiger may be in that grass," one instinctive train of thought might go, "it looks like the sort of tall grass tigers hide out in. If a tiger *is* hiding there and attacks me, what would I do? Did I just see the grass move? Maybe not. On the other hand, maybe I better check again." By attacking what we value most, chronic anxiety slowly brutalizes one's sanity, burns up needed calories, interferes with work, and damages the body by flooding the tissues with cortisol, a stress hormone. Costly strategy, that. Obsessive worry about nonexistent tigers might indeed lead to an infestation of stress-related illnesses, but overlooking only one hungry tiger could result in instant death. As Nesse and Williams point out in *Why We Get Sick,* smoke detectors are a pain—they're always breaking, always going off unnecessarily when you're cooking, it's awkward checking their batteries every month, and for years they do nothing but demand attention and collect dust—but if they save your life just once they're worth all the trouble. Evolution wagers risk against advantage. Better to agonize at every opportunity about a tiger than be wrong that one lethal time. So our psyches are strewn with smoke detectors, and we are forever responding to their false alarms. The grinding down of one's spirit, hope, general health, and sense of well-being doesn't matter, only one's ability to survive long enough to launch heirs. Unfortunately, as our lives fold and refold like origami cranes, we face both profound and trivial uncertainties—the possible ill effects of fluoride, a nuclear test in the South Pacific, a rumored tax increase, deciding what to wear on a first date, worrying if the lump in your breast is cancer, making sure the garbage can lids are securely fastened so that the raccoons don't produce a mess the garbage collectors will refuse. Our penchant for anxiety doesn't sift what's important from that civilized heap. Everyday is a feast day for anxiety, with its frequent parades of pangs and twitches. Doesn't matter if the occasion is relevant or irrelevant. Anxiety kicks in even when we don't need it, want it, or know how to stop it. Even if it's a grotesque and self-destructive response to an event of little consequence. How the ancient fears haunt us. Once it made sense to fear heights, or to fear leaving home—a panic attack kept you safe. But not now, in the age of flying, skyscrapers, and bridges. Not now, when most people must leave home to forage for food, earn status and resources, engage a community, and find a suitable, equally anxious mate.

Anxiety about a relationship feels the worst of all, but ultimately it's a lifesaver. Just as physical pain warns us of potential damage to the body, emotional pain helps us avoid more complicated threats to life and limb. When you're faced with hunger, the elements, territory disputes, and wild animals, belonging to a loyal family group is your only hope. An aching need to belong becomes an instinct indisputable as rock. Not belonging is one of those things to dread and worry endlessly about. You keep checking to make sure you're wanted, won't be abandoned, won't be sacrificed if wild animals attack, won't be left to starve. Most of the time, these may be unfounded neurotic fears; but misread the situation once, overlook a warning sign, and you're dead. Thus we evolved to monitor relationships obsessively, fret about them when we don't need to, require too many gestures, promises, and reassurances, go to extremes to fit in, sadden when we feel *isolated* or *alienated,* worry ourselves senseless about attachments, sometimes worry ourselves to death.

Throughout the world, 12.4 out of every 100,000 human beings will take their own lives. In affluent countries, the rate rises to 20 out of each 100,000. That's too high a number for mere coincidence. Especially if you consider how prevalent depression and suicide are among other animals. It must confer some evolutionary advantage. Some suicides may be triggered by a real or imaginary belief that loved ones will profit (suicidal people often sound quite selfless, reasoning that their friends and family "would be better off without me"). Others may be the extreme outcome of a useful hereditary device—depression. To evolution, that great carver of psyches and cities, melancholy makes sense.

Faced with horrible adversity or nameless anxiety, the more vulnerable among us become depressed. In a sense, it's a form of temporary hibernation. The body has energy-saving strategies. Overloaded by stress, a person winds down to a low-energy state, speaks and moves very little. At night, when we sleep, we also conserve energy. Famine produces the same inert, energy-saving response. Depression also elicits concern, and nurturing, and people tend to make allowances for the depressed person who may ignore the normal give-and-take of society, not meet the same expectations, schedules, or obligations. I'm helpless as a child, the posture says, protect me, exclude me from further stress, embrace me, tell the world that I'm not available for a while.

Besides happiness, serenity, joy, excitement, thrill, and desire, it may seem that we've evolved few positive emotions, or at least a wider and subtler range of negative ones. That may be because when things are going well and the world offers nourishment and opportunity, only a few responses are needed. But imagine all the ills that can befall one: disease, predators, starvation, injury, abandonment, defeat by enemies, death of one's mate, poisonous plants, loss of territory, hazardous environments, and one's own death. To cope with those potentially dangerous tableaux, we've evolved a large variety of responses. At heart, we are optimists. It's what keeps us in rocky relationships and gets us through rough times. As long as hope persists, we can endure most anything. Hope, that small renovation of the spirit. As Martin Seligman and others have demonstrated, even learned optimism can play an important role in staving off depression. Swedish psychiatrist Emmy Gut gives that thought a twist by pointing out that a surefire scenario for depression is when one discovers that some lifelong strategy has failed, but there's no reasonable alternative. Then depression plays the important role of prompting one to pause and reconsider one's habits and goals. We think of low self-esteem as an affliction, but like all suffering it has important benefits, too. Self-esteem helps one seize opportunities, make the most of one's environment, and advance oneself. But if our ancestors had been confident in every circumstance, they would have taken too many risks—like venturing alone into the wilderness, for instance— or they might have been tempted to pick fights, challenge leaders, not bother negotiating, or create some other social havoc. Nothing was more dangerous than being an outcast, losing the safety and nourishment of the group. We still fear that isolation worse than anything. For much of our evolution, being an outsider was fatal. Small wonder loneliness frightens us as it does. Even though being excluded isn't deadly today, it still produces pain and fear, and conceals an ancient terror. The nerve it touches stretches down the arms of time to a world before humans, a world of distant relations who left us a bag of tricks we barely understand, but which we enjoy, puzzle over, and often misuse.

Otherwise, things are dandy, and we get on with tracking happiness like the elusive quarry it is. Crisis Center callers rarely mention happiness, but its loss or the possibility of it usually haunts them. How odd to live in a country whose Constitution *guarantees* us the right to pursue happiness. In a recent study of thirty-nine cultures reported in *Psychology Today*, the United States ranked twelfth in perceived happiness. Citizens of Denmark, Finland, Norway, and Sweden were the happiest, despite their gloomy weather—perhaps because they have a relatively high standard of living, good medical care and education, and a low crime rate. Luxembourg and Singapore also ranked high, whereas, surprisingly, people in France and Japan said they were among the least happy. Many cultures don't expect to be happy, though they're grateful for its state of grace, a welcome and surprising bonus to their lives. In collectivist countries such as China, an individual's wishing to be happy is thought selfish and therefore not a high priority. But we expect happiness, pursue it, feel wretched in its absence, and experience sadness as a failure. In our culture, to be unhappy is to shirk your civic responsibility. If you can be unhappy, then so can the next person and that starts to become threatening; hence the self-conscious jollity of the "happy hour," birthday parties, and other occasions. Buddhists seek happiness, too, but in a lifetime's journey aided by meditation, transcendence, and certain truths, such as that happiness is not simply enjoying as much pleasure as possible, or even achieving the absence of pain and displeasure, but a state of affectionate curiosity, in which you welcome what Jon Kabat-Zinn calls the "full catastrophe" of your life. Pessimistic as it sounds, Freud said what he really hoped from therapy was to return his patients to the "common unhappiness" most people feel. Cynically, Albert Schweitzer concluded: "Happiness? That's nothing more than a poor memory." In special moments, we sometimes do feel serene, quiet, at rest. We call such brief times *happiness,* a lovable monster of a mood as rare as it is buoyant, which we symbolize with balloons. When you're happy, the world is breaking someone else's heart. Of course, it may be nothing more than a sort of biological idle, the body being thrifty with its limited stores of energy. Negative feelings burn up precious calories, so not to be in pain or at red alert feels good, especially if we can also anticipate food, shelter, belonging, and great sex.

What continues to amaze me is how such mind-binding forces, ancient and powerful as glaciers, can be modified by choice or circumstance to produce quirky individuals living unique and unpredictable lives. However tempting it may be to think evolution stopped with us, its crowning glory, in the grand scheme of things we're newcomers. Dinosaurs roamed the earth for millions of years, yet we declare them evolutionary failures. What about us? Our evolution isn't happening fast enough to be visible in our lifetime, but it is still underway, too slow to notice, as we sleep, play, lust, worry, learn, work, dream. Heaven only knows what we will become. We live on the cusp of two worlds, the fossil and the modern; no wonder we feel off balance much of the time. I sometimes joke about this with Paul, as in: *I'm going gathering with the girls, dear; how about if you hunt down a wild peccary while I'm away? Wait a minute,* he might reply, *We had peccary yesterday. How about a freshly scavenged carcass instead? But I'll tell you,* he might say with a bogus gleam in his eye, *no one can cook rotting wildebeest the way my mother could.*

Ah, Mildred. What a remarkable lady she was, who spanned the centuries and lived well into her nineties, teaching music to every child in a small coal-mining town in the English Midlands. I still smile when I remember my visit with her in the seventies (her eighties), and how instead of a refrigerator she used a stone slab in the basement, as she had lifelong. In that medieval food cellar, Jell-O almost set, meat kept cool but not chilled. A checking account was frightening to her then, and a telephone an instrument of potential electrocution. But I must say she took it awfully well when, by mistake, thinking a pleasant classic would be a safe choice, I took her to a film version of *The Canterbury Tales* only to discover once we were seated and the movie had begun that it was Pasolini's X-rated version. *There's* a nightmare waiting to happen—meet your boyfriend's eighty-year-old mother for the first time and take her to a porn flick. I couldn't believe my eyes and at intervals I silently prayed: *Please, for God's sake, no more fellatio scenes.* But, as I say, she took it awfully well, and after the movie ended simply said with a chuckle, "I don't remember my Chaucer quite like that, dear."

———

The morning looks so luscious, I decide to bike downtown to the Crisis Center, about three miles away. Along a country road, I suddenly find myself under a squadron of goldfinches, moving at their speed as if I were part of the flock. Then I notice the tall spindly thistle by the roadside, with its spiky leaves and nectar-rich blue flowers. Thistle seed is the goldfinches' favorite. I have entered their world and am traveling through it with them. All at once they turn at a sharp angle and disappear. On another occasion some months ago, freshly fallen apples had littered the roadside, and it was like whooshing through a tunnel of pure apple. Nowadays I remember that place by the depth of smell I once found there; it is an invisible landmark. When I'm out biking in the country, I'm surrounded by sounds—the green frog that could be someone plucking a banjo string, the cicadas scraping music from their wings, the countless birds auditioning for the opera of deep summer. I can't resist adding my own birdlike sound by occasionally ringing my bike bell, *brring, brrring,* as I go.

CHAPTER 6

The Shape of Fire

Countdown, I think, as I tap the latest number code into the doorlock—9876. For security reasons, the numbers change regularly, and I devise a memory aid for each one. Some of the counselors, who flex and crunch numbers at work, find it easy enough to memorize a new code. But others, like me, need a cue to retrieve something that abstract from a largely visual memory. Before *countdown,* it was *quartet*—4444; and before that *compass rose*—four numbers located at the north, east, south, and west points of the dial; before that, *I ate two*—182; and before that, my first counselor code, *single, strike, strike, home run*—1004. At first glance, that cue might not make much sense, but I was thinking of how, when I was a little girl growing up in a suburb of Chicago, my dad drove the family all the way to Miami Beach for vacations. The drive felt endless, and to pass the time my parents devised many road games. One my brother and father played a lot was "Baseball," in which the license-plate numbers of the passing cars decreed the fate of each batter. A "1" was a single, "2" a double, "3" a triple, "4" a home run," and "0" a strike. Thus 1004 became *single, strike, strike, home run.*

As I walk in, I can hear the staff having a lunch meeting in the conference room on the first floor. Someone has finally covered the naked lightbulb on the ceiling with a cone of glass, but the place still looks like an underfunded schoolroom with its blackboard, bulletin board, and wooden tables pushed together into a single continent surrounded by mismatched chairs. Tall two-part windows let in the morning light. Hanging on the wall at the far end of the room is an enlarged color photograph of a counselor who died years ago while on a trek to Tibet. Enough time has passed since his death for someone to tuck a small photograph of a smiling newborn under the bottom of the frame, and no one finds that juxtaposition odd. Life has its exits and entrances, the impromptu altar seems to say.

One gets to the conference room by walking through the office of the director, a high-spirited, martial-arts-practicing, swing-dancing woman with long dark hair and bushels of energy. Raised by psychiatrist parents on the grounds of a mental hospital, she grew up with deeply troubled or mentally ill patients as friends, and that has gifted her with unflappable ease around every sort of person. Even extreme mental states are familiar to her and mainly nonthreatening. Among her friends are cross-dressers, schizophrenics, manic-depressives, as well as more "ordinary" people. A perfect background for directing a crisis intervention agency. She always wears earrings in the shape of Africa, where she spent important years of her life as a health worker and then as a Peace Corps volunteer, before she returned to the US to work at various jobs in the mental health field. Her office is a small museum of wood carvings from Burundi, Zaire, Rwanda, and other locales. A divorced mother of two, she loves kids and still cherishes the time she spent delivering babies on an African beach by moonlight, arranging the mothers-to-be facing downhill in the sand, as local women did, for sanitary reasons. "Works for my cat," she jokes about the inherent tidiness of the tradition.

Upstairs, Mikhail has already begun to pack up his notebooks, satchel, and lunch bag. A second-year veterinary student, he's wearing a Yankees baseball cap turned backward, a sloppy red sweatshirt with the school logo nearly worn off, a pair of high-top black-and-white sneakers with a few holes in them, and a small gold hoop in his right earlobe. Student dress code for the nineties.

"Like those sneakers," I say.

"My dad says they're more holy than righteous." He grins with mock pride.

"Don't ask him what *he* wore in school." His dad would have gone to college in the seventies—tie-dyed shirts, Nehru jackets, faceted sunglasses, bell-bottom hip-hugger jeans.

"Really," he says with an ain't-it-the-truth inflection. "Don't take any woodens." He starts down the creaky stairs.

"Wouldn't know how to," I call after him as I dump my gear on the daybed in the counselor room and sit down at the desk. Pulling a red notebook marked "Hot Sheet" from its tray, I open it to the first page. At the beginning of each shift, a counselor reads the Hot Sheet and also the Friday Letter, two notebooks in which the staff communicate directly with all the counselors. The Friday Letter concerns agency gatherings, doings, or business, and the Hot Sheet alerts everyone to possibly suicidal callers who have been in touch during the preceding week. Today, I find this note:

We have had a painful beginning to 1995. First we experienced the murder of Steve Starr and the suicide of the young man who shot him in Dryden. A few days later Fred Williams shot himself to death in Brooktondale. Last night we had news that a university student died while skiing on vacation. Many folks are hurting out there. We will most likely continue to get calls about these tragedies. Listen and reflect, reflect, reflect. Help callers to know that whatever they are experiencing is *normal,* whether it is recurring thoughts or images, guilt, sadness, sleeplessness, etc. It is hard to accept not knowing, not understanding the "why" of it all. Some call thinking they aren't *entitled* to their pain because they are too removed from the victim. Not so. Encourage all to continue to use SP to cope as often and for as long as they need. Healing can take months, years.

Wise words, from Kate most likely, the wonderful woman with platinum-blonde hair who trains new counselors. Somehow she manages to combine ebullience and big-heartedness with seriousness, which makes her fun to be around. In training, she often assumes the roles of many callers—regardless of their concern or even pathology—and becomes a convincing drunk, a plausible depressive, a believable developmentally disabled person, a scary psychopath, a truly worried parent, a persuasively hallucinating schizophrenic. It never seems like acting, more like a feat of supreme empathy. I suspect in part it comes from personal experience with such people, either as callers or in her own life, but I don't really know and I'm a little shy about prying. I do know that she has raised three children, weathered a divorce, and dealt with family illnesses, which means she has had ample opportunity to face a host of problems and characters. Under her note in the Hot Sheet someone has added a second entry:

Call from school principal at Pearson School. Suicide last week of a teacher. Wants postvention help.

How spare that telegraphic entry looks. Who was the teacher, I wonder, was the person male or female, what subject did he or she teach, was the teacher straight or gay, and, most important, what drove the teacher to suicide? Kate is right, it's hard to accept not knowing the why of it all. True in life, true in death.

The crisis line rings.

"Suicide Prevention and Crisis Service," I say as I jot down the time on a sheet of scrap paper. "Can I help you?"

"Hi, how you doing today?" a baritone voice asks. It's hard to decipher his age.

"Just fine, how are *you* doing?"

"Well, I can't be doing too well, I called you, right? What do you think?"

I think he sounds a little defensive and peeved, and I try to prepare myself for what may be a confrontational call. But what I say is, "What prompted you to call? Have you got something on your mind?"

"Yeah... the wife seems to have... exited the premises."

"You're saying that your wife has left you?" He must feel awful.

"Yeah." The silence that follows doesn't last long, but it's heavy as a steel drum. Not only are we trapped in our skin, our emotions are trapped behind the electric fence of language.

"And how are you feeling about that?"

"Well, confused, angry, feeling somewhat guilty," he says in a flat drawl. "I don't know... we've been married a fairly long time. Things seemed to have been going well. I know she was unhappy about our financial situation, but..." A long silence.

"It sounds like this came as quite a surprise."

"Yeah. Why, I came home and... you know we had an argument a couple of days ago, like we usually do, and she accused me of being silent and whatnot and not opening up and not talking about my feelings, etcetera, etcetera. She said she couldn't take it anymore as far as being with someone who didn't 'fight normally.' I mean, what the hell is that—'fight normally'?"

"What do you think she meant by that?"

"I guess in her head fighting normally means raising my voice, screaming, throwing things, quote-unquote 'showing emotion' as she puts it. But I figure there's no point in that. Why not just settle things rationally? There's no sense in letting things get out of hand."

So instead they've gotten out of house. But I can understand the caller's predicament; I don't like high-volume fights, either.

"So you had this fight a couple of days ago, and then you discovered today that she had left?"

"Umm, hmm. I mean, I assume that she's left. She's not here. I don't see her purse or coat. I assume she's gone. Of course, then again, I might be jumping to conclusions myself. For all I know she may be over at her mom's. I'm not sure."

For the first time since I answered the phone, I begin to see the caller: a man in his early thirties, medium height and build, straight brown hair thinning a little on top, square face, a habit of fidgeting his fingers as if he were rolling an invisible nickel across the knuckles.

"You sound anxious that she might leave. Are you perhaps thinking it through as a possibility? How long has she been gone?"

"Oh, the last time I saw her was yesterday noon. So it's been close to twenty-four hours. But I've been thinking about it. I just don't get it. Is it some sort of biological thing with women, that they just can't contain their emotions and fly off the handle? I mean, you're a woman, tell me, what do *you* think?"

What I think about women won't help him deal with his marriage's unique problems. What was that line Tolstoy wrote in *Anna Karenina?* "Happy families are all alike; but every unhappy family is unhappy in its own way."

"Are you asking me that because you're wondering if I can help you understand why your wife would lose her temper and get into such a rage?" I ask.

"Well, it almost seems as if she would have *me* lose *my* temper.

Although I know we're starting to cross the line into therapy, I say anyway, "You're thinking perhaps that she provoked a fight? Why do you think she might do that?"

"Well, maybe to give her an excuse to leave, you know."

A disturbing element to this conversation is how numb the caller sounds. He must be bursting inside—anybody would be—but his voice doesn't reflect his emotions. Maybe I should help him risk putting them into words. "Let me ask you something. As we've been talking, your voice has been very calm, but what you've been telling me sounds pretty serious, and it seems to be deeply troubling you. I'm just wondering what you're feeling right now, if you might be feeling a sense of loss, and maybe a little frightened?"

Voice cracking, the caller says, "... I mean, what if she's *really* gone? What will I do without her?" A brief sniffling sound.

"You're feeling frightened," I repeat.

"Yeah."

"It sounds pretty scary. It must be tough not to know what's happened, to be afraid that she's left but just not know for sure. What are your plans for today and tomorrow, while you wait to see if she returns?"

By now, the doodle of intersecting lines that I began at the start of the call has evolved into a Danish farmhouse with an overhanging roof and a garden of otherworldly flowers. Ever since I was a child, my doodles have included these lush flowers bursting with seed in a whorling cascade of dangle and bloom, and this same stylized house. For the first time, it occurs to me that my dreams almost always include a house, too. Never the same house, and never my real house. The mansions of the mind have so many rooms.

"I'm not sure. Watch TV, I guess. Work this afternoon. See if she's here when I get home. But it'll be on my mind all the time."

I don't know what sort of work he does, but that doesn't matter. He's going to need some support from friends. "Do you have a friend you might spend a little time with?

"I got a friend at work I sometimes hang out with."

"Do you think he might understand what you're going through?"

"I don't know. Maybe. How the hell could I tell him my wife left me! I couldn't do that."

"I bet he'd understand. Would you maybe like to rehearse it with me? What could you say to him to begin with?" For a few minutes, the caller tests out ways to tell his friend. He decides to call his mother-in-law's house, in case his wife went there. We discuss what he might do if and when his wife returns.

I like talking with this guy. Such callers can usually articulate their feelings; their circumstances, though awful, make sense, and they're open to problem-solving. That makes the call rewarding for the counselor—you feel you've accomplished something—even if it isn't life-changing for the caller. Mind you, counselors all have their favorites. Some love to talk with retarded people because they're so childlike, and calming their worries or helping them with small tasks can mean so much. One such call of mine was with an extremely anxious woman who spoke in a thick slurred voice. She said that she had an appointment for a "tubal litigation," but she didn't know what that meant and she was scared. Answering her long list of questions, I assured her that it was a very common operation, one you don't feel because you are unconscious while the doctors work, that it takes place in a hospital, recovery time is short, and afterward you can't have babies. She also wanted to know all the surgical details and how much pain would be involved, two issues I sidestepped, and then she remembered that she knew a woman who had had the same operation who had survived just fine and said it was a breeze. She was adamant about not wanting to have babies. Because she was panicky about where to go and when and what to do beforehand, together we made up a list of practical questions. We found her doctor's phone number and agreed that she would ask to speak with the nurse. In many ways it was a simple call, and it was so easy to help her get through the day.

Some counselors enjoy how quirky and exciting schizophrenics can be, and one strategy for dealing with such people is to reel them back to the known world if you can, ground them in reality by getting them to focus on the chair they're sitting in, the shoes they're wearing, or perhaps what they ate for lunch. The temptation (in part because it's so damned interesting) is to inquire about what their talking dog is saying to them or how many devils' faces they now see in the drapery.

Some counselors form almost family ties with repeat callers, who sometimes become chums, assume we all know their stories, and check in with us often. We all love "Saxman," a manic-depressive diabetic with a grueling life of insulin injections and other drugs, mood swings, recurrent bouts of blindness, unresolved distress about his older sister's suicide, and a host of family, love, and bureaucracy problems. His main problem is that he's sick to death of being sick all his life, and who can blame him? Sarcastic and engaging, with a slightly ghoulish sense of humor, even when he's angry or depressed, he has an indomitable spirit when it comes to women, and he always seems to be involved in some curious and complex romance. Once he called after a change of antidepressant medication, feeling good, looking forward to a jazz-club gig, able to see quite well for a couple of weeks straight, with a date that evening to go to the movies with his new girlfriend. "You sound—dare I say it?—*happy* today," I said at the time, and I remember how he had fallen silent for a moment and then said, "Yeah, I guess I am. I forgot what it was like." Most of us are fond of Saxman, and like to hear how he's getting along.

But many counselors, like me, prefer the sort of caller I just spoke with—an intelligent person functioning at a high level who, for one reason or another, is being ravaged by life—rather than someone with a thinking disorder. Mind you, I don't know where the path of this caller will lead. He seems all right at the moment, but he doesn't reveal his deepest feelings. For all I know, there may be a tempest inside, bottled up and ready to wreak havoc on the world. He may be the sort of guy who lives quietly, then one day climbs a church tower and fires a machine gun. I only hear his side of the story. He is my concern. What drove his wife away? I have no idea. Tonight he may grow depressed, or drunk, or even dangerous. I urge him to phone back if he needs support, anytime. But for this moment, at least, I have stitched him back into his routine for another few hours, temporarily stopped the furious unraveling of his life. That's really all we can do. It's never enough. I wonder if anyone ever feels what they do is enough. Does a surgeon? A teacher? A psychotherapist? A family doctor? What would *enough* be? If I had a gift for crisis counseling, wouldn't it feel like enough? Too ideal a concept, I caution myself. In America, *enough* is what the other person has.

For a few moments, I think through how best to summarize the call, then fill out a write-up sheet and file it. When the phone rings again, I hear a familiar voice. The caller sounds for all the world like Joan, someone who has been calling weekly for a couple of years. Her story is always the same—a few years ago, her thirty-year-old daughter, Mary, fell for a teenage punk named Ryan, who divides his time between robbery and selling drugs. When Mary discovered she was pregnant with twins, she moved in with Ryan, who treated her abusively and refused to let her mother visit unless he was in the room, or even telephone unless he was listening in on another phone. Once, according to Joan, he smashed a back window and broke into Joan's house, pirated her telephone charge card number, made phone calls to South America, and stole credit cards (which he sold to hoods, who ran up a hefty bill). Another time, Joan overheard Ryan planning to rob a bar, and she notified the police, who took him downtown for questioning. That infuriated him and Mary both, and they decided then and there not to have anything to do with Joan. This meant that Grandma couldn't be present when the twins were born, or even hold her granddaughters. She appealed to the county for legal help—and the county did indeed grant her visitation rights. When she tried visiting the little girls, though, Ryan stood around menacingly and threatened her, and Mary reviled her.

Usually, callers seem to improve as their predicament improves, or as they get used to their lot. But Joan has been getting progressively worse, more and more obsessive, as she feels increasingly isolated and rejected. From time to time, Ryan has attacked Mary with a shovel and a kitchen chair, but Mary has refused to call the police, and Joan has feared for her daughter's life as well as her own.

This caller sounds like Joan—same husky high voice and fast-talking, run-on sentences, same history of three children, one of whom died in a car accident, same divorce from a violent husband, same alcoholic father who abused her mother for the length of their long marriage. It has to be Joan. Those are too many coincidences. But today she has a totally different story. Today she is tormented by her "longtime boyfriend"—funny, she never mentioned a boyfriend before—who has been two-timing her with a disabled widow he met at a bar. Joan doesn't talk sequentially, and that makes listening to her a little like deciphering German. In German, the verbs often appear at the end of the sentence, and it's impossible to tell right away what's going to happen only a few words later. That grammatical felicity can lead to exquisite torment for lovers who must wait agonizing seconds to know their fate. In Joan's case, information rains down all at once, and the listener has to put it in the right order. Suddenly there is her boyfriend, Bill. He is seventy "but looks a lot younger." He told her he was a male prostitute for many years. They haven't had intercourse yet, although they have kissed and hugged a lot and they see each other often. She slit her wrist the other night because he had hurt her so badly she was simply "overwhelmed." He calls her his angel, and says he "worships the ground she walks on." When he proposed on her birthday, she refused, saying that she wasn't ready to be engaged, especially since she's convinced he is running around with other women. She didn't injure her wrist badly, she just felt overwhelmed and had to lash out. His drinking buddies suggest Bill may have many late-night drunken trysts.

One day in an excess of suspiciousness she went through his wallet and found a woman's name, Charlene, and a phone number. Bill was due to meet Joan late one night, after work, and when he didn't show up, she waited for a long while. At 1:00 A.M., on a hunch, she phoned Charlene's number and to her horror heard Bill's distinctive voice answering the phone. Joan didn't say anything, but Bill asked "Who's there?" three times and that was enough for Joan to hang up, feel creased by rejection, and want to hurt herself. Funny how the mind works. Why didn't she want to hurt *him*? He already had hurt her—why become her own torturer? Lots of psychotheories about that one. Anyway, Joan worries that if she has sex with Bill she could catch AIDS from him. She has snooped around his house, which sent him into a rage. But should it, if he has nothing to hide? she wonders. Once she secretly opened his desk drawer and discovered a lot of money and jewelry—necklaces, a wedding and an engagement ring. She confronted him with it right away, and he got mad. "Now you've ruined the surprise!" he said. "Your damn suspiciousness has ruined everything. I was going to give those to you for Christmas." Right. Should she believe his story? Joan asks me. I'm thinking, *only if you like being a patsy,* but instead I ask her if she has trouble believing it. She does. She also found suspicious letters from various women in one of his desk drawers. They sounded very lovey-dovey, but Bill said they were innocent letters from his nieces. Right. She can't trust him anymore, but she also cares for him. He's a real charmer. Handsome as the dickens. Works down at the Agway. Suddenly I picture the Agway, where I often go for squirrel and garden supplies, and one by one I survey the faces of the people who work there. Yes, I think I do know who Bill is—a tall man with thick gray hair and a self-satisfied manner. An attractive man, but no Adonis. A male prostitute? That just sounds like bragging to me. The sort of man Garrison Keillor would describe as being "a monument to the depths of a woman's need." She's confused about what to do. He tells her that her lack of trust is ruining their relationship, that it's all in her mind, and that he'll walk out if she doesn't stop policing him. She may invite him over and confront him again about Charlene, but meanwhile she sounds all in a tizzy that eases only a little by the end of the call. I invite her to call back if she needs support at this confusing time, and she thanks me.

No mention of the daughter. For over a year, I thought Joan's life was utterly consumed by obsessing about her daughter, son-in-law, and granddaughters. They seemed to invade her every waking thought. Now I discover another equally intense and complicated facet to her life, which I had known nothing about. Mentally, I file this new information in the "Will wonders never cease?" category, and I chide myself for forgetting how thick a life is, how narrow a telephone call. To understand the melody of someone's life you need all the notes. The symphonic orchestration is another matter; for that you'd need to hear the constant surf of sensations, the inner soliloquy, the heaving and sighing of emotions, the windfall of memories, the grumblings of countless hungers. But even the simplest melody is hard to hear. Sadly, I realize that even though I have come to understand so much about Joan, I know little about the full realm of her life. I thought she lived in an emotional Quonset hut, where she was forever bumping into the low, suffocating ceiling. Not so. That was the only view of her whereabouts she offered us. Maybe it was the only place in her life she felt unsafe or uncomfortable.

As I wait for the next call, I go through the logbook to see if Louise has called since I spoke with her a few weeks ago. It's something I always do on shift—check to see if Louise is still alive. Running my finger down the ledger, I backtrack through the shifts of the past week, and, sure enough, there's her name. Write-up number 104. I find it in a thick file waiting to be shredded; an additional sheet of paper, a yellow "lethality assessment," has been stapled to it. Louise was depressed, drinking some, and highly suicidal that evening. The counselor on duty wrote down few details of the call, noting only that Louise's daughter had gone to visit her ex-husband, which meant Louise was home alone with gnawing memories. Louise had lamented that her past couldn't be rewritten and her future looked bleak. She was staring at a carefully arranged row of pills, "perched on the counter like small pink rodents," she had said. That's Louise, all right. What a wonderful imagination. For over an hour, the counselor held her pain and tried to explore what resources she might have left, but when the call ended Louise sounded only fractionally less sad. "I

feel awful," the counselor wrote on the write-up sheet. "I did everything I could think of, but nothing nothing nothing seemed to work!
Very possible that this really is her 'last day on earth' as she fears it
might be. She asked me to pray for her. I'm going to worry all night."

Oh, Louise. I sigh as I return the write-up to its folder. If she had
killed herself, it would have been in the morning paper, so at least I
know she somehow scaled the Everest of that night. I can't phone her
to check on her, much as I'd like to. Looking out the window, in the
rough direction of downtown, I try to imagine her going about her
chores, fixing dinner. It's Monday night. I remember she once said
that she belongs to a woman's a capella group that meets Mondays at
the church in Trumansburg. Good. Tonight she'll have friends and
climbing harmonies; that should buoy her up a bit.

The phone rings again, and this time I hear an indignant woman's
voice shouting, "Do you know what that bastard did?"

"No," I answer. "What did he do?"

"He went up the chimney and he didn't come down!"

"He's up the chimney?" I ask, honestly surprised. Does she mean he
is upside down? Standing at the bottom? Hanging from the top? Although I can't quite figure it out, I decide not to bog her down with
questions.

"Drunk as a skunk!" the woman says. "It's the damn summer. He
gets strange as all get out and full of piss and vinegar." Stung by the
summer. He and the rest of the world of nature, I think—the squirrels, the june bugs, everyone. She doesn't sound worried, just angry
and annoyed. "There's filth all over the place!" she screams.

As it turns out, she confides, summer brings out the worst in her
husband, Joe, who gets so drunk that he does outrageous things like
pick a fight with a motorcycle gang member, jump out of a fishing
boat in the middle of the lake, or try to climb down their large chimney. It's his Irish temper. Once before he arrived at the chimney bottom "in a heap of soot with a shit-eating grin on his face," the caller
explains, "but this time the damn fool gone and got himself stuck."

Rightside up, halfway down. I can hear her husband yelling or singing—I'm not sure which—from behind the brick. Strange gargling sound, that, even over the telephone. When she moves the phone away from her mouth to yell something at him, the reception falters and I can't quite make out her words. She may be gesturing with the phone. He seems to be screaming something back, something like "Whale oil beef hooked." Then she shrieks at him. Finally she talks into the receiver again and I try to get her to calm down enough to figure out what to do. She'll call his cousin Buck, she decides, because Buck is a big strapping guy who knows how "rangy" her husband can get when he's been drinking. She'll call Buck, then she'll call me again, and we'll go from there. It turns into a very long afternoon as Buck arrives but can't seem to get Joe unstuck, Joe insists he's never coming out, his wife gets scared when Joe suddenly goes very quiet, then the fire department is summoned, Joe starts scrapping with everyone, and all I can hear for minutes at a time is the combined uproar of events. I suggest the woman might like to call me back later, but she says she needs me right then and there, and I believe she does, so I stay with her. Finally the firemen succeed in pulling Joe out onto the rug in a great cloud of soot. When Joe starts to cry uncontrollably, his wife alternately yells at and consoles him, and then she decides to "see to Santa Claus" and call us back tomorrow.

"Bizarro," I say quietly, as I begin the write-up.

"Bizarro?" a voice behind me echoes. "That sounds like an interesting call." I turn around and see Sharon, the next counselor on duty, sitting patiently on the daybed, her mouth outlined in white powdered sugar from a doughnut whose last morsel she pops into her mouth. Before I can explain, the crisis line rings. A fast glance at the clock—it's well past the end of my shift; how long has Sharon been waiting?—and I hurry out of my chair.

"It's all yours," I say. "Have a good shift." Answering the phone with one hand, she says: "Suicide Prevention and Crisis Service. May I help you?" and at the same time waves me a kiss with her free hand, then swivels around in her seat, tosses her long brown braid behind her shoulders, hunches her small body over the varnished desktop and settles into the call.

In the kitchen I find a large selection of Celestial Seasonings teas, and choose one called Bengal Spice, full of cinamon, ginger, cloves, cardamon, and other exotics. On the top of the box, a tiger lounges on a magic carpet floating across a blue, cloud-tufted sky. Just the thing for unwinding before I head home. The shift may be over, but I'm not quite ready to leave. Sometimes I need to make contact with my own sensibility again, after I've been visiting someone else's. Sometimes I need to lose my self and other selves, and just *be* among the fruits of the earth. Carrying the tea downstairs, I go out to the porch, pull up a wicker armchair, and watch the evening deepen in the field across the road. A gray squirrel gallops up the trunk of a large oak and disappears inside a bole. Where on earth is the Pleader? I wonder yet again, fearing the worst. Maybe I could ask Chris Johns to keep an eye out for him. One of *National Geographic*'s best nature photographers, Chris will be showing up at my home early tomorrow morning to start recording squirrel behavior on film. It's hard to capture furry élan vital in stills, but if anyone can do it, Chris can, I laugh to myself, remembering stories of his hanging out atop rain-forest canopies for weeks, through wind and rainstorms, to document the curious habits of the Hawaiian crow. Must remember to leave the door open for him. The weather won't matter. A promise of rain weighs down the air. Hope it gets over with by the weekend, so Cathy and I can go biking. Where will it be this time? There are those two lozenge-shaped lakes near the south end of Keuka Lake, tiny things separated by a narrow band of woods where an Indian village once stood. I bet it's less than twenty miles biking around both lakes. We could take along cheese and French bread and some hot chicory tea.

When night starts seeping through glossy dark leaves, a whippoor-will cracks the long three-stage whip of its voice, flaying the air alive. Love that sound. Whippoorwills belong to a family of birds whose

Latin name—*Caprimulgida*—means "goatsucker," because they were often seen traveling with herds of goats and were thought to milk them dry during the night. Now we know that the birds, in fact, were hunting the goat-sucking insects. But the name stuck, replacing the more common "nightjar," a better-fitting alias for a bird whose boomerang voice can jar the night right off its hinges.

Fragrant steam rises over my face as I sip the tea, and I realize that it will soon be Midsummer Eve, June 23, which falls two days after the summer solstice. Once it was said to be a witches' Sabbath, when an evil spell could dishearten the coming harvest. On that night, if a maiden put yarrow sprigs beneath her pillow, she would dream of her future husband. On that night, bathing in fern seed could make a man invisible, and walking backward with a hazel twig between his knees would lead him to treasure. Summer solstice is just a little Sabbath with the sun. Solstice, from the Latin *solstitium,* "sun standing still." For a few days, the sun will rise and set at almost the same spot on the horizon, a prelude to the longest day of the year, and then the sun will crawl south through imperceptibly shorter days, toward a still-unimaginable winter.

But for the moment it is early, spine-tingling summer. Jasmine and pine leaden the scents of evening. Spores like manna drill the sky. Pheasant eggs sneak life out of damp sod. Summer disavows any passion stronger than earth's in the sound of rain, in open field, as drizzle breaks into downpour.

CHAPTER 7

The Heart's Asylum

Of all the hungers that beset us, hunger for food is the most versatile, I decide, as I wash a few dishes at the Crisis Center before leaving. People rarely sit by themselves and eat. We like to do something else while eating, talk with someone, read a newspaper, watch actors singing about Don Quixote at a dinner theater. I smile, picturing Chris Johns wedged in the crotch of a tall hickory, cameras at the ready, as he lunches among the squirrels. There's a true dinner theater for you, an acrobatic, bushy-tailed *cirque du soleil.* Squirrels aren't what you'd call social eaters, but many animals, from gorillas to hyenas, like to dine with family and friends. Humans enrich that basic instinct in the most ingenious ways. Although our senses evolved to guide us through the hazards of nature, we are not simple, automatic creatures trapped in the emotional quicksand of our biology. We think, we dream, we feel, we hunger. We say "food" as if it were a simple thing, an absolute like rock or rain, but it's a complex realm of pleasures both physiological and emotional, and often conjures up childhood memories of safety, fun, and love. So it's not surprising that, when we search for words to describe our most intense, maniacal, analytical, or heartfelt feelings, we often refer to eating: we hunger, we crave, we devour, we develop an appetite for, we mull over, we feast on, we savor. *I'll have to chew that over a bit*, we sometimes say when considering a difficult issue, as if we could grind the problem down with our molars, moisten it with saliva, and spit it out as a relic. As if our neurons felt anything. But they are blind as mole rats, I keep reminding myself; they see nothing, hear nothing, feel nothing, smell nothing, taste nothing. The brain is silent and dark. Sensation does not occur in the brain, anymore than emotion happens in the heart. What a strange lot we are, we who live by deception, we who love by design, we who manufacture guilt, we who commit real as well as imaginary sins.

My morning shift at an end this day, I feel the need to chew something over before I head home, and so I stop for lunch at Moosewood, a local vegetarian restaurant. My passion for vegetarian fare mystifies Paul, who fears he'll get nothing at that eatery but "twigs and leaves." In fact, he swears they once served him a bowl of sand. But I love its ingenious meals. There, in a rustic setting decorated with totemic moose carvings and drawings, I enjoy ginger-miso salad and a plate of Hoppin' John (southern-style black-eyed peas on brown rice, topped with cheddar cheese, tomatoes, and scallions), while I reconsider one of the morning's calls. Melissa again. At last she has found the courage to leave her violent husband and move into a safe house (provided by the Task Force for Battered Women) with her two small children, but she was feeling a kind of vertigo. After a few years, even unhappy couples grow glued together at so many spots that it hurts brutally to rip themselves apart. It was as if she were watching someone else's life—the wrenching away from the marriage, the awkward half-lies to the children, the barrage of legal and practical chores, the new faces, the alien neighborhood, the constant fear of retaliation. She filed a restraining order against her husband, but suppose he invaded her new island of safety? Suppose he killed her and left her babies motherless? Suppose he kidnapped the children? She had seen a television show called *Unsolved Mysteries*, which urged viewers to keep an eye out for fathers who had stolen their children and fled. She pictured her children's faces on the backs of milk cartons, their rosy cheeks reduced to pools of black dots.

I knew the Task Force would help her if any of those nightmares bloomed into actuality. She was phoning SP in a philosophical mood, and that caught me off guard—before, we had only spoken when she was in acute distress—and I needed to slow up, calm down, and allow her to bask in memories, some of which were harsh. For the first time, she shared with me details of a childhood scarred by violence and neglect, which she escaped by inventing a secret life.

"It was my only salvation," she explained. "I fled into another plane of existence where no one could find me. As long as I believed I was a superhero whose value would be discovered in the fullness of time, I could ignore the horrible reality of my life. But in my household I was worthless, I was ugly, I was always *wrong* in some unexplained way that netted punishment. Only I knew about the secret self, the beautiful, exciting, powerful, lovable self."

In her fantasy life, she was leader of a team of seven men and women who traveled the world righting wrongs, working against the forces of evil, helping the downtrodden, keeping the planet from self-destructing. They belonged to a secret organization she referred to as "the Triple T"—I never asked what the letters stood for—that existed outside the politics and laws of any country, drafting the world's brightest scientists and most creative thinkers in an underground of colossal proportions. After an arranged, convincing-looking death, a scientist, humanist, or other essential person would join their ranks, knowing they could never return to the outside world. The inside world offered an ideal society of fascinating, concerned people. At times, as Melissa told me her tale, I assumed the Triple T ruled a sophisticated underground city, and at others that it was located in a beautiful but extremely remote place, possibly somewhere in the Himalayas or in Africa. She and her team were the elite part of the organization's espionage division. Although she killed deftly when necessary, could outfight anyone using martial arts, knives, or guns, and had gifts of agility matched by her cleverness and courage, she was a reluctant warrior, only killed in defense, and no sooner wounded an enemy than tried, if possible, to patch him up. Each member of her team had a specialty or two. She was superb at getting people out of places, and she was a brilliant field surgeon. In that imaginary world, where she became a combination soldier and saint, fighting like a man, finding love as a woman, and earning the respect and affection of all, she created an alternative to a home life blighted by rejection and injustice. The hardest thing for her to admit to me was that even now, as a grown woman, she sometimes retreated into that same fantasy world. But I was a stranger, a benign, faceless intimate, and I was glad she felt she could trust me not to laugh or judge. Abused children often invent secret worlds, and she was driven so far into hers, the only place where she mattered, that she was lucky to find her way out. Some don't. Had she been less imaginative, or weaker-spirited, she would doubtless have crumbled in the ruins of her family. Instead she built an escape route, self by self, created a healthier reality, and that saved her. Without realizing it, she *had* triumphed over the forces of evil, *had* saved the innocents from injustice, *had* become heroic. But she perceived her fantasies as a shameful secret.

"You know how kids pantomime locking the mouth?" she said tearfully. "I feel like I've spent my whole life making that lock more and more secure, hiding who I am so people will accept me, silencing my true self. Or, I guess I should say, selves. Sure seems like a bundle in there." Despite its urban setting, the safe house had become a sanctuary where Melissa could examine her life.

"This may sound like an adolescent thing to say," she said hesitantly, "but I really don't know who I am anymore. Half the time I feel like a stranger in familiar clothes. This morning I'm worried about what kind of mother I'll make, when I still feel guilty about things *I* did as a child, and heaven knows I feel bad about things I did as a wife. Those are my real selves, too, aren't they—legitimate parts of me? Or did those things happen to a different person?" She laughed uncomfortably. "I wonder if we are ever guilty of all the sins we imagine."

Melissa's call touched me for many reasons. So many selves make up a life, especially the early parts of one's life. Shouldn't there be a statute of limitations on guilt? "I am no longer responsible for acts committed by my previous selves" is a motto I sometimes wish we could live by. Selves will accumulate when one isn't looking, and they don't always act wisely or well. This was not what I expected when I was a child growing up in the Midwest, where the snows were shoulder high, piles of leaves could be dived into, and my life shone before me as a clear trajectory. It was the fairy tale I had been told to expect: a Knight in Shining Armor would appear suddenly to guide me and heal my life, then I would produce two children, buy a dog, work at a pleasant job, and live forever in an oasis of calm. An invisible boarder in my house, a fantasy friend became my confidante. I sometimes gossiped with her about the bohemian lives of artists; but I never dreamed that I would grow up to live such a life myself. It is only now, in my middle years, that I've begun to notice how my selves have been forming layer upon layer, translucent as skin; and, like skin, they are evolving a certain identifiable "fingerprint"—a weather system of highs and lows, loops and whirls.

Yes, I think, as I pull back the thick rind on an orange, feeling the zest release a fine spray of juice over my cheeks and nose, my caravan of selves probably began when I was little, inventing mental adventures in which I starred. My daily life was unbearable. I could have run away, I suppose, but instead I fled mentally along the Silk Road of the imagination. One continuing fantasy was that I was not human but an extraterrestrial, part of a group of itinerant artists who traveled throughout the universe. On their planet, art was deeply revered and prized, and, above all, they relished discovering the arts of various life forms, because it revealed so much about hearts and needs, values and yearnings. Each itinerant artist was born into the civilization of a planet and grew up soul-drenchingly creative, remembering nothing of the planet of origin. As one of those artists, my job was to feel. And so I felt, penetratingly, exaltingly, agonizingly. I peered for long hours into the hidden recesses of things. I trotted after thoughts to see where they led. And, in time, I created a beautiful sampler of the range of human feeling and experience. Then, toward what I naturally imagined to be the end of my life, I one day heard a voice saying to me: "Come to the window. The night air is sweet...."

Decoyed by the simple beauty of the evening, I went to the window, inhaled the scent of jasmine drifting in, and was suddenly amazed to see an alien standing there. All at once my mission became clear to me, I knew my work was done on Earth, that my destiny was to rest awhile on the small city-state of the mother ship, and then be born on a new planet, into another species, to undergo extremes of feeling and create art from that amalgam of privilege and ordeal. Learning I was not human shocked and saddened me, and I begged to be allowed to remain human. The separation was grueling. Humans were among the most emotional and volatile of all the planetarians in the universe, but human was what I knew and loved and I could not bear the thought of leaving Earth, leaving with so much still unexplored and unvoiced. "It is enough," I was assured. "There are other worlds to explore, other beings to become." And so I went with the alien to the spaceship beyond Earth's orbit, and rejoined my troupe of artists, some of whom were also between lives. That otherworldly dream haunted my early years and adolescence, and I half-expected that one day I really would be summoned to the hidden part of my destiny with a whisper: "Come to the window. The night air is sweet...."

As I grew older, what I craved was to be ten or twelve selves, each passionately committed to a different field—to be a dancer, a surgeon, a carpenter, a composer, an astronaut, a psychologist, a brain chemist, an ice skater. Some would be male, some female, and all of their sensations would feed back to one central source. Surely then I would begin to understand the huge spill of life, if I could perceive it from different viewpoints, through simultaneous lives. I had been writing creatively since I could write. If I couldn't actually live simultaneous lives, perhaps I could do so serially—by giving myself passionately, blood and bones, to what I wrote about, by becoming my subjects.

My most recent self lives in a small town of trees, waterfalls, and flowers, where most people know or at least recognize one another, and many of their stories converge. From time to time, I travel to distant places in pursuit of the marvelous. But, after all, the marvelous is a weed species; it thrives everywhere, even in yards and ditches. So I always return home to friends and loved ones. Through the many windows of a house in the woods, I watch the doings of the deer, squirrels, and birds, and the metamorphosing seasons. I think a lot about the pageant of being human—what it senses, loves, suffers, thrills to—while working silently in a small room, filling blank sheets of paper. It is a solitary mania. But there are still times when, all alone, I could be arrested for unlawful assembly.

———

A young waitress bustles by in blue-jean short shorts over black leggings, sandals, white pleated top; her straight black hair brushes five gold earings on one side and sweeps her shoulder on the other. She once told me that she's saving up to take grad school courses in zoology. As I recall, we discussed the white rhino over a bowl of goulash. Today she has a preoccupied expression, and I realize that that's what

I find most frustrating about being on the phones—not being able to see the callers. In a semaphore of muscle and glance, a face conveys information too subtle for words, and I miss that. This waitress has a heart-shaped face with one chin dimple, and small beads of perspiration have formed on her upper lip. She looks lovely. But I've been noticing lately that a great inner beauty radiates from the face of every working woman. Women laboring out of doors develop a sun-polished self-reliance borne of handling the forces of nature, and expression lines as eloquent as down-and-dirty country love songs. Women working indoors develop a strong, supple face on which the stresses and stratagems of the day play out their dramas. Sometimes you can see *resolve* standing like still water on their faces. Work tests one's spirit, helps to define one's character, and contributes heartily to that marquee of the inner life: the face. We prize young faces because we're drawn to the siren of youth, but I find few things as beautiful as an adult woman whose face brims with liveliness, personality, character, sensitivity, and feeling. "You were pretty in your twenties," I once overheard a man telling his middle-aged wife, "but you're so much prettier now that your face has character. It reflects who you are, and all you've accomplished and experienced." A face may remind us of a first love, parent, teacher, movie star, chum, or perhaps someone who frightened or double-crossed us. A face tells us how a person feels, if they're worried, mischievous, eager, or sad. Sometimes a face reveals, in its map of fine lines, a lifetime of grief, stubborness, or easy laughter. A face can be hard, welcoming, lovable, coarse...a thousand things, depending on the life and mood of its owner. It reveals a lot about her inner life, and also about the era in which she lives.

As difficult as life can be, we're lucky to live in the last half of the twentieth century, and in the West. In ancient days, women were merely arable land for the "ploughing of legitimate heirs," as the bride's father would bluntly proclaim during a Greek wedding ceremony. At long last, women have won the right to make a few choices, choices about whom to marry, if and when to have children, whether or not to worship a god, which political banner to follow, what to do with all the bustle and yearning of their lives: large white-knuckle choices that affect the heart and soul, and small daily choices that are important athletically, just to keep personal freedom alive. Women's roles have changed dramatically, and their faces reflect that change. Women have always worked with dignity and aplomb in boardrooms and department stores, in fields and restaurants, on stages and in studios, in their own and others' homes, in factories and boutiques, in hospitals and schools. But even to consider the beauty of working women is a revolutionary concept, since for much of history ideal beauty lay on the faces of the leisure class, women who didn't have to work. Or actresses, that is, women chameleons who (happily for us) could abandon their real selves and become the fantasies of others. We never asked why they yearned to be anyone but themselves, or to place their self-esteem in the applause of strangers, or why we find such quick-change artists beautiful. But we do. In the 1930s, when satin-gowned movie stars were the ideal, working women mimicked Garbo's plucked eyebrows, Dietrich's sunken cheeks, Crawford's red bow-tie mouth, Harlow's platinum hair. During World War II, when women staffed the factories, providing the materials of patriotism and victory, posters began to show working women as strong, self-confident, and stylish. Our bombers were built almost entirely by women, who riveted, cut metal, did heavy assembly, worked with blueprints, and wrote down what test pilots reported over radios. They shifted weighty metals, crafting the nacelles for the B-17 bombers in a bra factory. But they weren't depicted as unfeminine; instead, they spawned a new ideal of beauty that was available to everyone, including this young waitress at Moosewood. She seems worried about something, and her face implies a hundred thoughts as she concentrates on work or relaxes into a smile with customers.

Spreading sweet butter on an inch-thick slice of wholewheat bread, I silently bless all the world's old-fashioned bakers. Melissa had said that sharing a safe house with other women was fine, but she really missed being able to bake in her own kitchen. Wish I knew what Melissa looks like. I picture her with blondish hair parted on the left side and pulled back into a low ponytail. Or is it cut in a shag? I'd give anything for facial cues when I speak with callers, but anonymity is what they crave, and though fingerprints, voiceprints, and DNA may be more accurate, the face most defines the person. The kite of one's real identity seems to circle the face. A shy child will bury its face in its mother's skirts. When someone is ashamed, she hides her face in her hands. For one reason or another, callers suddenly find life hard to face.

———

On the way home, I stop at a neighbor's to drop off a book I think he might enjoy postoperatively, a compendium of eccentrics that two quirky British researchers have spent a lifetime compiling. Just the thing to divert a healing mind. Leaving by way of his garden steps, I stumble, lurch forward, and twist my foot hard. Pain starts bleating along the right side of the foot. Probably a pulled tendon. At home, I wrap it in an Ace bandage, ice, and elevate it. I didn't fall really, just angled my foot oddly and lunged. But by morning I discover that walking is impossible and the swollen, bruised foot hurts in an unfamiliar way, as if broken icicles were trapped under the skin. To be safe I have it x-rayed at a nearby clinic. There a doctor, who also studies and teaches honeybee science—as I said, in this town everyone has a second life—shows me a triptych of X rays and points out the awful truth: the fifth metatarsal is broken straight across. Were it broken obliquely, or in a thicker place, there might be more bone for support. No, it's just my luck that the foot fractured in a fragile spot with little circulation, a skeletal backwater. This means wearing a cast, and not a walking cast, mind you, but a nonweight-bearing one. Putting pressure on this sort of break could worsen it, and if that happened only a bone graft and screw might secure it.

I'm doomed: eight weeks of immobility. No bike trips with Cathy. No sunshine walks with Persis, my neighbor. No mousing around quaint upstate towns with Paul. No shopping on the Commons with Jeannie. No daily bike rides to the summer fields, the stream at Flat Rock, the woods across from Ludgate's roadside market where red-tailed hawks nest. It's a nightmare.

Over the next few days, as helplessness settles over me like fog, I sink under the weight of the low *d*s and become devastated, disheartened, demoralized, despondent. It's not just that I won't be able to get out to enjoy the summer, visit with friends, do the grocery shopping, run errands, and go to meetings. Handling the crisis line will surely be impossible, since there are SP's porch steps and two flights of stairs to scale. For an athletic and self-reliant person, what could be worse than suddenly becoming disabled? Trapped on the short leash of your infirmity, you discover how much of the world is out of reach. Imagine yourself sitting on a couch, growing chilly, and not being able to close the door, which is on the other side of the room. Imagine not being able to reach food or supplies, not being able to maneuver into the bathroom or take a bath. The terror of paralysis hits me hard, and soon I worry that my friends will tire of my predicament and abandon me. Two days after the fall, trapped in a wheelchair on the living-room rug whose pile is too deep for me to muscle my way across, I start to cry. All I want is to get to the screen door so that I can inhale the summer air and drink in a little sunlight, but I can't travel four yards. I can't see the cardinals nesting in the cushion yew. I can't feed the squirrels, whose lives have begun to intertwine with mine. I can't go to the Farmers' Market on Saturday mornings and see the glorious produce the local farmers have raised. I can't walk barefoot through the basil patch. I can't swim while feeling hot starbreath on my back. But, worst of all, I can't go biking with Cathy. I hadn't realized how symbolic those trips have become. Biking has meant freedom, discovery, friendship, and self-reliance. At last I know how desperate some handicapped callers must feel, how exempt from normal life, how impotent and alone. They say so, and I try to empathize, but now I know. If I didn't work at the Center, I would be calling in with what for me is a dreadful crisis.

Because I can't visit the fenced-in rose garden at the bottom of the backyard, Paul picks two purple-red "Othello"s, and my favorite this year—a large, pink-yellow-coral "Abraham Darby," whose dense petals are tight as a crepe-de-chine ruffle. He arranges them in a terracotta vase. Adorning the tiled bathroom vanity with color, the roses reflect in the large mirror and gush scent. Suddenly a combination cook and bellhop, Paul runs the house errands, hitches a ride to the supermarket with a neighbor and does a colossal job of shopping, fetching things, making dinner, washing up, and tending me. He bemoans adding my chores to his. I hate being an invalid, hate being a passenger.

Despite the fears, my dear friends gather round. Jeannie and Steve ferry me to and from the hospital. Cathy arrives Saturday afternoon, without her bike this time, to present me with a kindred spirit: a tiny brass mermaid resting on her bottom with tail flukes gracefully lifted in the air. Her pose shows off a large bosom, her hair flows down her back, and her face is tilted up in a combination of pleasure and resolve. A mermaid. The very thing. What an insightful gift. Then Cathy pushes me half a mile in my wheelchair to a deli, where we eat large freshly baked mocha-chip cookies. Soon we're gabbing and laughing as usual, and I can't resist sharing with her a recent discovery—how many zoo animals are on Prozac.

"No!" she says, her mouth dropping open. "Which ones?"

"Well, there's Gus, the polar bear in the Central Park Zoo who was depressed..."

"Wait a minute," she interrupts, "How did they know the polar bear was depressed?" She eats a bite of cookie and sips a diet Coke. *Doing and undoing* it's called.

"For one thing, he kept swimming all day long."

"Obsessive compulsive behavior," she says, nodding in Freudian parody. "Go on."

A nice surprise: my iced tea has been spiked with peach juice. Didn't notice that when I ordered it. "And then there was this weird trick he started playing on children," I explain between sips. "Whenever he'd see kids pressing their faces to the window he'd charge straight at them with claws out, in a sudden harrowing attack, which he'd stop right before he hit the glass. Scared the shit out of them."

"Unbelievable!" She laughs.

"When he wasn't compulsively swimming, he seemed listless, or he paced a lot, or did other neurotic things like chew on his enclosure, bob his head, become overly sexual, play with his excrement, hurt himself on purpose—you know, the same stuff severely troubled people do.... So they gave him some Prozac."

"Didn't they try talk therapy first?" she asks wryly.

At the thought of a polar bear engaged in talk therapy—a huge white bear seated in a black leather Scandinavian chair, gesticulating with one paw as he talks about his cubdom—we both start laughing so hard that people turn to stare. What could a wheelchair-bound woman be howling about?

The principle, though, is a serious one. Captive animals often become neurotic, anxious, depressed. They suffer some of the same pains of confinement, boredom, stress, loss, grief, and anxiety we do. And when bears that normally roam many square miles are jammed together like city dwellers, or doomed to solitary confinement for years on end, should we wonder at their plunging spirits? Nuns may "fret not at their convent's narrow rooms," when they have spiritual kingdoms in mind, as Wordsworth claims. But there isn't much difference between a horse in a small stall chewing on the wooden slats ("cribbing" it's called) or swaying back and forth all day as if to an inaudible samba, and a stressed-out co-ed compulsively picking at her cuticles or automatically twisting and pulling strands of her own mane all day. All animals endure crises, some unique to their species, some only too familiar to humans. When their instincts tell them one thing and their captors (or the invisible captors of society) another, they have the added stress of an identity crisis. So I'm not surprised that many vets are prescribing antidepressants for animal patients, nor that a growing number of animal therapists, whose job is to analyze neurotic behavior, compare the animal's living conditions with what would be normal for that animal in the wild, and try to devise a cure, given the restrictions, attitudes, and preferences of human society. House pets often must live on human schedules of light and dark, food and fasting, when and where they may move their bowels. Remove a monkey or a dolphin from nature, and it loses its bearings, it grows disconsolate. And there is no wilderness consulate where it can go to defect.

Safe and dry in our clean and well-lit homes, at arm's length from the weedy chaos outside, no longer prey to weather and wild, we can also lose our inner compass. The hardest thing about my injury is how it separates me from nature, whose green anthem stirs me, whose moods fascinate me, whose rocks and birds help define my sense of belonging. Even if I'm feeling low, I can always find solace in nature, a restorative when dealing with pain. Wonder heals through an alchemy of mind. But, exiled from paradise, where can I turn? Once knitted into nature, I feel myself slowly unraveling. Standing upright may be our hallmark, and a towering success, but sometimes bone, joint, and spine can't live up to the challenge and act subversive. A house of bones, the Elizabethans called the body. Imprisoned by my need to heal, I crave the outdoors. To heal I must rest, lie low, shelve things, restrict myself, be willing to sacrifice pleasure for recovery.

Delayed gratification, it's called. A uniquely human idea, some argue, an example of our superior gift for planning and restraint. But I've noticed a red squirrel in my yard who does the same thing. He appears at breakfast with the grays each morning, but doesn't stop to feed his raging hunger as the grays do. Instead he grabs a nut, races away a hundred yards across the backyard and up his pine tree (where I lose sight of him in the woods). He stockpiles. He postpones pleasure. It's only recently that the world of nuts-out-of-season has been open to him. I'm sure he's as hungry as the grays are, this vivid red banker. Only when his account seems full does he rest, grab one of the grays' leftover hazelnuts, and noisily gnaw at its hull. Like many animals (though not the grays), the red makes a loud *Holy cow! I found food!* sound over and over while he eats. I'm sure the last thing he wants is to share anything with rivals, but he cannot control the mechanism that alerts them to the whereabouts of food. Sneezing, farting, and chirping at the same time, he's loud as the dickens, a real temper-monger. I've named him Red Rodney after the trumpeter who traveled with Charlie Parker's band, a man who never had much of a voice, but could belt out an excited song in an odd sort of warble.

The grays seem almost placid by comparison, lumbering giants. They still joust and challenge one another for social reasons, but they avoid warfare with the reds. They suffer the chipmunks, who silently steal their food. They steer clear of the crows, who also steer clear of them. They ignore the blue jays. But the reds are in-your-face squirrels, and Red Rodney tries his damnedest to terrorize all comers by standing on a stone rise and pelting them with abuse. There is nothing quite like the chattering hysteria of the red squirrels, who go off like alarm clocks when frightened. They tremble, rock, hop, shake, and scream all at the same time, and always attack in anticipation of being attacked.

I can tell by the grays' response—twitching as they shuffle away from the reds' screams—that they find reds truly annoying. But they prefer not to tackle Red Rodney. He's tiny and toothy and fast, and he talks big. If threats foretold size, he'd be a platoon of trouble. He risks the back window when the gray squirrels are feeding there. Sometimes he bumps into one, rears up to expose stilettolike claws, and a brawl ensues, with Red Rodney darting away before he's hurt. His favorite tactic is to dash in with guns blazing, making loud *Don't you mess with me! I'm a tough guy!* noises. During the Korean War, enemy soldiers would attack screaming and wailing such bloodcurdling abuse that American soldiers, who were silent fighters, became terrified. Was the noise a scare tactic, or to strengthen the nerve by blotting out fear in an avalanche of violent sound? This strategy works well for Red Rodney among the grays. But the grays rarely attack chipmunks either. Feed and let feed seems to be their motto—except with one another.

Then food isn't all that's at stake—they could lose face, possessions, and other wordless things.

A mature female red squirrel I've named "Bangs" because of her mocha-colored widow's peak, and a shy young female I've named "Youngun" act a little more reserved. If there's no one at the nuts, they rush in silently and grab walnuts, which they struggle to pick up, since a walnut is almost the size of a red squirrel's head. Somehow they manage to carry nuts away, holding them a quarter inch above the ground. When grays are about, though, even these females come in strafing, making a machine-gunlike, scratchy, high-pitched, attack racket that gets higher and faster by the second. Sometimes the reds sit with a walnut, mewling in delight—a soft, catlike sound—as they spin the nut, looking for a spot to pierce it. Or they burble or chatter to themselves. They're real motormouths. A blue jay may land, eager for a peanut, and a red will scare it away with a rooster cackle.

But Red Rodney is belligerent even for a red squirrel. It's all bluff, of course, the sergeant major how-dare-you-backtalk-me stream of invective, but it does work. When a few grays are feeding and won't shove off, he stands in their midst and pivots like a weather vane, viciously barking at each one in turn. Once, to see what would happen, Paul put out a shallow box of nuts, and sure enough the grays approached it carefully, took one nut a time and moved away to feed. When Red Rodney arrived, he leapt into the box, started screaming at the grays and became so obsessed with defending his treasure that he didn't pause to eat. Ultimately, the grays dislodged him and he retreated without a single nut. But it took half an hour, many assaults, used up a ton of energy, and netted him nothing. It was more vital to possess the nuts than to eat them. Lashing out at others became more important than nourishment. Most of the time his violent nature allows him to prevail in a harsh world of giants. But this time his violence became an end in itself and only he suffered. Red Rodney may be a little loudmouth Napoleon, but, as I say, red squirrels are natural orators, and they're as beautiful as a Rubens.

Related to the grays, red squirrels glow in shades of burgundy, mahogany, and rust, with a clear white ring around each eye. They are small squirrels, shy of humans, and occasionally mingle with their enemies, the grays. For me, it is like watching two early species of upright apes, closely related but strangers, wary of each other. Because the reds are rare, few in this yard, and brave to risk a feeding frenzy of grays, I sometimes lob a walnut so that it lands right at a red's feet. The heaven-sent manna surprises her; she looks at it without moving for a split second, then grabs it up and darts away with it. As she runs, her feet stretch wider than the grays'; and she looks like a nineteenth-century painting of galloping horses. Before the invention of the camera, horses were painted with legs splayed wide. It was only when the camera's fast shutter stopped motion that people saw, to their amazement, how a horse's four hooves strike the ground one at a time and underneath it's body. The rhythm of the gallop is a little like that of a gambler throwing dice, or a baseball pitcher releasing a pitch, except, of course, that what's being released is not an object but motion itself.

Five times this morning Youngun hot-rodded across the yard and five times I hurled her a walnut, then watched her carry it across the grass, through or around the rose garden, up a rock, up the chainlink fence pole, down a willow sapling, and right to the base of a tall pale red pine in the woods at the southwestern perimeter of the property. Then she waited awhile, to eat a nut or two, I imagine, before she began her shuttle run once again, a quest which took her into the frightening world of the muscular grays and the mythic world of the huge primates. I've seen the three reds out all at once, but I know the family is larger. Bangs's nipples have grown prominent, and the fur around them is pressed flat—a sure sign she has nursing babies at home. I pray they survive. Even with my leg in a cast, I limp to the garden-room window each morning by using a row of chairs as an archipelago, to feed and watch the squirrels briefly, then leave them to their world, families, and squabbles.

—

After a few days of shock and denial, I decide to take charge of my fate and rent walkers and an electric scooter. "Tom Swift and His Electric Runabout," I tell friends, when they ask what I'm up to. One morning Persis and I go walking on our habitual route, up and down the hill, past the Catholic church, and around a small sweet woodlands. Pushing me in my wheelchair, she doesn't seem burdened by the workout, and I'm relieved when she says buoyantly at the finish, "This was easy. Thank heavens, we can take our summer walks." On our outing the following week, I use the electric scooter, which makes it even easier. Sometimes I chug over to the grocery store, half a mile and twelve minutes away; the improved mobility, however slight, does much to lift my spirits. I know I must have seemed quite an apparition one day as I rode home through a light drizzle wearing a long flowing summer dress, holding an umbrella. Mary Poppins? a friend offered. Paul said: A geisha floating under a parasol? Bewildered, neighborhood dogs fell silent as Aztecs beholding Cortés on horseback for the first time—where did the human stop and the other creature begin? But the many children on the street—used to seeing me biking in cold weather in what looks like a Ninja suit—took it all in stride. At least I can journey outside the house now and savor the light.

Occasionally I "stroll" awhile in the sun, then park under a tree in the garden. Few things are as delicious, on a sweltering summer day, as dunking oneself in a pool of shade. Shade beneath a tree is especially refreshing; you can sprawl on the cool, damp ground and savor each fidget of breeze as if it were an Arctic blast. And, of course, shade is the traditional haunt of summer lovers, who turn the dullest thicket or grungiest corner into an oasis. A mother sometimes uses her own body to shade the face of her easily burned and overheating child. In the Amazon, striated herons stand with their backs to the sun, so they can see the world more clearly and hunt in their own shade. We call a ghost a shade because it lives in a shadow world, is miragelike and but a semblance of a person. We put shades on our windows so that we can close them like eyelids. Shade is a precious commodity. It can be minute (the shadow cast by a wintergreen leaf), or gigantic (night on earth). Shade feels like a cool compress on the brow of a summer day. At resorts, vendors often sell shade—umbrellas or cabanas. In Josephine Jacobsen's poem "The Shade Seller," men sell shade to tourists on a scorching Mexican beach. One day she hears them say *No hay sombre* and realizes to her horror that they're fresh out of shade.

What would life be like without its small, cool, temporary asylums? Or warm, damp ones. The sensual and erotic nineteenth-century French writer Pierre Louÿs describes the pudendum as "the humid cave, the ever warm shelter, the asylum where man rests on his way to death." There are so many forms of asylum, from the shade of a large hosta leaf, beneath which a gray squirrel may cool itself on a hot day, to the political asylum Holland offered Jews during World War II, which was a double asylum, one obvious, the other microscopic, because the Dutch were protecting the lives not only of individuals but of a gene pool. The very word *asylum* fills one with a sense of relief, and can make a lovely antidote to a stale metaphor. I like these, for instance: *the asylum of your regard, the asylum of a glance, the asylum of the bourgeois family, love is the heart's asylum, how safe she felt in the asylum of his arms.* A shy child can find asylum in the folds of his mother's skirts. In this world of earthquakes, heartaches, rivalries, drive-by shootings, how we treasure the idea of a safe place. A place like a hideout, but public. A pool of mental and emotional shade. We seek asylum.

And yet how ironic it is that some people still call psychiatric hospitals *insane asylums.* They do protect their residents from the weathers of the world, give them a kind of amnesty, allow them to retreat from life while they heal. But our prejudice about mental illness, and our fear of it, taints the word with horror. *You belong in an asylum!* a man might yell in anger. *They dragged him off to an asylum,* a woman whispers to a friend. The word has lost its fundamental calm and dignity. Originally, it meant a church or other sacred place that was inviolable, where one could not be seized by outsiders. And what have we replaced it with? "Psychiatric institution?" The brain is a psychiatric institution, a small parliament of cells. "Mental ward?" An overly dependent child is a mental ward. The euphemism we use with SP callers is "hospital." Do you think that you might feel safer in a hospital? we might ask a suicidal caller. We could not say asylum, or the caller would picture rat-infested cells where prisoners squirm in straitjackets. Asylum is a fine rich word that even sounds protective, like a sanctuary with thick stone walls. If only people wouldn't attach *lunatic,* or *insane* to it.

———

Paul has to leave on business for a week, so a girlfriend flies in from Long Island, staying a few days that are a godsend. On the eclipse cruise, where Frank Drake told me of his SP years, we spent an unforgettable week at sea, relishing a natural phenomenon that terrified our ancestors and often changed the course of history. In the Orient and Middle East, and in medieval England, people swore they saw a dragon devouring the sun; in Germany, wolves were the sun-ravaging beasts; in the East Indies, it took a monster, part-eagle, part-lion, to rip the heartlight from the sun. Some cultures thought the Sun and Moon were mates having violent sex. Ancient priests knew about the eclipse cycle, but they usually kept that arcane truth a secret. One year, they would predict a mad catastrophe of the sun, after which the crops and herds would die and darkness reign forever—unless the people did as they were told to appease the gods. The Chinese scared the dragon away with ferocious dances accompanied by loud drums and gongs. The Japanese covered their wells lest the water be fouled. The Inuits turned their cooking pots upside down to keep the evil drippings out. But priests also issued more compelling demands: incantations, sacrificing animals (sometimes humans), small fortunes, promises of fealty, war or peace. To the ancient mind, no celestial fireball was being quenched but a god or goddess, and no doubt they pictured that downfall in horrific, blood-curdling detail. After all, they hunted and slaughtered animals themselves, they knew how wolves and lions ripped their prey limb from limb. Feeling its hot breath on their bodies each day, the ancients relied on the sun as a paramount deity, a lifegiving, crop-raising, time-telling source of growth and light. A deity that blinds. Eclipse watchers who don't protect their eyes can get crescent-shaped scars on their retinas. It's hard to imagine how frighteningly real the imminent murder of that deity must have seemed, or the putrid gore they thought would spill at its death. As we stood on deck watching the sky curdle, the air grow loose and damp, and a sepulchral gloom settle over the ocean, it was easy to understand how people could swear, sacrifice, pay, relinquish, condone anything to bring back the light. Both of us were on assignment—*Travel Holiday* had commissioned my friend to write an article about the eclipse, and me to write a poem about it—the two ran side by side in the magazine. In the poem, I tried to capture some of the fear, magic, and savagery of the eclipse, the desperation people must have felt to bring back the sun; but it was also a poem about emotional eclipse, how brutal depression can be and the relief of returning to a brighter mood in a sunlit world.

ECLIPSE

The black dogs of hell
are chasing down the sun
whose horns pour light,
hooves cut sparks,
eyes weep the clement sap
rippling through our veins
that keeps the heart limber
and the seasons sane.

The runner stumbles.

The air stiffens like a tomb.
Butchered light staggers
across the sea. Then day fails,
time eases its grip
and, thrashing, the world reels
upside down.
Stars pant on the horizon
like a regiment of wolves.

The runner stumbles.

Darkness falls at noon.
The cold fabrics of night
cascade through skies
fantastic and grim.
A cloud cortège struts
above the ancient ruins,
where planets appear
like silent drumbeats.

The runner stumbles.

A door opens to the ghost towns
of our past, and we pray
that nothing will phase the sun
undulating
through our crops,
tethering our clocks,
sweeping the nightmares
from our dreams.

The runner stumbles.

We would sacrifice anything—
our wealth, our limbs,
our power, our kin—

> to ransom that hot-blooded
> infernal mate, so rash
> and unruly, immense as life,
> that sweet cheat, that savage light.
>
> The runner resumes.

Despite the bleakness of the poem, written from bone-chilling memory, the trip was a sea idyll full of fun and discovery. In my study I have a framed photo taken on that cruise—the two of us standing arm in arm on deck, clothed in black eclipse T-shirts and white pants, wearing shiny pink and silver "eclipse glasses" to protect our eyes from the sun—on our faces grins only ten-year-olds can usually muster.

Her flying in now acts as a tonic, as she knew it would. Tossing my wheelchair into the trunk of the car, she bundles me off downtown to the bird sanctuary to see the Canada geese chicks—all fluff and waddle with bones delicate as twigs—and for meandering drives through the blossoming countryside.

CHAPTER 8

The Darkness of Our Days

July days begin early, with a soft light that insinuates itself among the trees and ferns, picking out the pink of wild geraniums, the drooping jester-hats of columbine. Not the sharp light of fall or the faint light of winter, but a soft, swampy, fertile glow. The often-humid sky is thick with pollen and midges and other flying things. We can see them, touch them; we breathe them in, along with the same molecules once inhaled by Shakespeare, Colette, Leonardo. The earth wastes nothing, neither its water nor its air. Life gallops through all living things, presses flowers up upon their roots, makes bellies swell. Every breathing being opens wide, stretches out, feels a rush in its veins, welcomes risk. The long days of July feed our hunger for light, saturate the small pineal gland located in the forehead, and we feel healthy and livelier than ever. *Breed,* the silent voice in the cell bids us, *do it now.*

The clamor of an insane blacksmith has been filling the air for days, and the neighbors have been complaining to one another about some tactless early rising remodeler, so I track the sound to see what it's about. To my delight, right at the edge of the front yard I find a scarlet-headed, diamond-shaped woodpecker frantically using a metal stop sign as a sounding board for his mating songs. The bird version of a rock star using an electric guitar. Two squirrels galloping loudly across the roof remind me to serve breakfast. Putting away my binoculars, I hobble into the garden room, open the window, and toss out peanuts and sunflower seeds. Ten squirrels appear as if conjured into being and feed quietly side by side. A shudder of leaves and bushes catches my eye and I see a battered, frightened squirrel staring tentatively at the nuts. A large patch of fur is missing from his back and head, where raw skin shows. Seeing his ear mark, my heart sinks and soars at the same time. It is the Pleader, woefully subdued, all the spirit knocked out of him. I open the window. He doesn't come. It is painful to see him so broken and ill. Even if he builds up his strength on the nuts and seeds, will he dare the yard where the others rule?

At last the Pleader drags in after most of the other squirrels have fed. I toss nuts out to him and he eats a few, patiently, slowly, in a kind of trance. The others growl at him, one attacks and he leaps onto a sapling. Then he returns, eats a nut, and leaves. The wound on his back reveals angry flesh; and his eyes are lusterless, not glossy and alert. The change in personality is startling. For a while, there weren't enough nuts in the world to eat or store. He wanted all of them, endlessly, and could drive away any squirrel who bothered him. Now he seems lethargic, tentative, and frail, with little appetite. When other squirrels threaten him, he cringes. Slowly he climbs up a large hickory and lies down on a branch, looking tired and weak, while the others feed below. A human in that condition we would call depressed.

The volunteer fire department's horn blows and, almost simultaneously, lesser horns resound in the distance like retreating ripples. Although I know the sounds are horns, the cinema in my mind's eye plays a film of seals barking to one another from their rocks in the Falkland Islands. I smile. That was years ago, on the way back from the Antarctic. A sheep farmer in the Falklands told me that local rats fish in the surf by facing away from the ocean, dragging their tails in the water, and waiting for a bite. I half believed him, and ever after asked every rodent specialist I met (I've met a lot) if they'd heard of such a thing. None had, but they thought long and hard about it. It flitted along the fine edge of possibility. Rats are clever and adaptive, and, unlike us, they can't vomit up poisonous foods, which means they have to pay close attention when others are eating, and take lifelong risks to survive. They would watch the squirrels dine on pumpkin and sunflower seeds, see none keel over, and judge the fare safe. For all I know a cautious rat may be watching now.

All I want is to go from one end of the house to the other, not something I usually think about, a trip of minutes. But my cumbersome, graceless, slow-motion efforts have changed time. Time has fractured. Showers are elaborate, lengthy juggling acts. On my crutches I hop like a flightless bird. I have to plan each excursion around the house, think economically, allow extra commuting time. After a fifteen-minute travel odyssey using wheelchair and walker, surmounting small steps, and hobbling through a spring-loaded fire door to the garage, I climb at last onto the scooter and set off next door to say hello to Persis. Her freckle-nosed, curly haired four-year-old, Joseph, meets me first and pantomimes what's supposed to be a hair-raising Power Rangers attack. His sandals are decorated with Power Ranger Shields, and even the patch on his pant knee is, as he puts it, "a special secret Power Ranger patch." Ah, yes, one of the young obsessed.

"Do you *morph?*" I ask soberly, referring to the Power Ranger gift for changing shape.

"No," he says, but explains that, like all Power Rangers, he travels in disguise and fights the forces of evil. Since he's little-boy-fascinated by all vehicles (watching bulldozers sends him into raptures), I show him how my scooter works and let him press the horn, which makes a half-hearted *beep.*

"How fast can it go?" he asks hopefully. Full-throttle sends me creeping along, which leaves him mightily disappointed. His face brightens. "You need to say"—he does a spinning leaping fist-punching-the-air jump—"GO GO POWER RANGERS!" How Power Rangers travel at the speed of light.

"GO GO POWER RANGERS!" I cry to Joseph's delight, and Persis and I set off down the street at 1.6 mph.

I'm not surprised by Joseph's mania. A fantasy for every generation of children seems to be the secret avenger, righter of wrongs, messenger of good. Small and relatively helpless in the world, aware of family limits but not yet of nature's, children dream shatterproof dreams of grandeur. These almost always include impossible feats of prowess—flying, becoming invisible, battling a horde single-handed, deflecting bullets. Imprisoned in our bodies, cursed and blessed with minds that crave omnipotent extremes, we compete with one another toward those extremes, which for some reason we call perfection, we fantasize about besting the best, breaking free from the bonds of our flesh and becoming something other than we are, something more noble, we think, something more talented, something unlike our humdrum and tarnished selves, something that doesn't pollute its body with food or evacuate the filth from its bowels, something that doesn't catch cold or go haywire, something us but not us, beings who could defy time and drill a knothole in death. Every child rediscovers that craving, to be magic emperor in an imperial world, where his birth matters, his desires are met, and his extreme neediness is masked by his ability to dispense rewards. In that costume drama of fantasy and desire, we champion the good, obliterate the bad, become the whole world's favored son, and pin accolades to the garments of our self-esteem. Not only children confuse the real with the unreal; it's just that children are allowed to. Ironic, isn't it, that the one time we condone grandiosity is in the minds of the smallest and weakest among us? I've always found it a curious paradox that, in general, the taller a man is the better he'll succeed, but when it comes to true greatness—in art, philosophy, politics—heroes quite often tend to be short, as short as children who have not outgrown their grandiose dreams.

During wartime, evil wears a familiar face; there are Nazis or barbarians to fight. In peacetime, in the absence of concrete enemies, there are Satanic forces to invent, infidels to subdue. But the struggle always pits good against evil, us against them, our wholesome sunlit ways versus the putrified souls of night denizens. Why, I wonder, do we endlessly stage this cockfight of good and evil? Why value kindness, altruism, honesty, justice, fairness, loyalty? When you page through a family album, it's easy to see from whom you inherited your cowlick, your small waist, your square chin. Not so easy to compile a family album of personality traits, although relatives are bound to point out that you're hot-tempered just like your father or outgoing just like your mother or have your uncle's sense of humor. But where is the family album into which all humans can peer to understand the swirling riptides of their nature? I'm lucky to live in an age when people have begun asking such questions. *Evolve? From monkeys? Our moods and personalities?* Only a century ago, that line of thought was heresy. Now we're aiming for a detailed cartography of the brain's mysterious shores.

When we return from the walk, Persis heads indoors to nurse one-year-old Rose. I wonder if it really is true, as Melanie Klein argued, that our emotional hungers go back to a memory of "the good breast," a phantom we search for throughout our lives. Over the past eight years, I've often seen Persis nursing one of her three children. Do they store away powerful memories of that never-again-to-be-found bliss? As she walks into the house, I look at her closely, the pretty brown eyes, small nose, large forehead filled with brains. To have that much power. I remember what an Interplast surgeon in Honduras answered when I asked if he thought of the child he was operating on during the operation itself. "My God," he said, suddenly alarmed, "if I did that, I'd be petrified."

———

Home again, I no sooner settle down in a chair than I hear the most god-awful scream, a high-pitched throbbing shriek. When I look out the kitchen window, I see a crow with some small furry creature in its claws. Suddenly the crow flies off to Persis's yard to dispatch its prey. Mouse? Its ears are longer. Maybe a kangaroo mouse? I return to the chair. But within minutes I hear the same bloodcurdling scream. Once again I hobble over to the kitchen window. To my utter amazement, I see a baby rabbit with a chipmunk of equal size attached to its neck. A chipmunk trying to kill a baby rabbit! By now the rabbit's screams are ear-piercing. Hobbling outside as fast as I can, I chase the chipmunk away, and then approach the rabbit, which sits frozen like a statue, shocked and trembling.

"Run away," I gently urge it. But it remains stupefied. When I nudge it with the rubber tip of my crutch, it hops under the broad leaves of a caladium. Maybe it will wait out the day there, get its energy back, and have a brighter future tomorrow. I go back indoors.

Minutes later, I hear the same death screams and know what carnage to expect. Sure enough, when I rush to the front door I find the chipmunk has the bunny by the neck again. I scare the chipmunk away as I limp out after the rabbit. This time I try to chase it across the driveway and into the neighbor's yard, out of the chipmunk's territory, but the rabbit is too young to understand how to flee. It runs toward me instead of away from me, and when it encounters a wall it swiftly grows confused. Limping back inside, I grab a large plastic bowl from the kitchen, and head outside once more, where I find the bunny half exposed under the caladium leaves. I nudge it into the bowl with the tip of a crutch. Then I lay a crutch across the top of the bowl as a sort of grille, and hobble toward the neighbors' yard just as young Cornelia comes running, her pigtails flapping.

"Don't chase the bunnies into the open!" she cries, her voice tense with worry. "The crows are eating them!"

Her eyes widen as I show her what I have in my hands: a bowlful of frightened bunny.

"I'm not chasing them," I explain, and tell her about the carnivorous chipmunk and the newborn bunny. "Could you take it across your lawn and turn it loose?"

"The crows will get it," she says, anguished. Then her face brightens. "I'll take it home," she says. "Maybe I can keep it."

"Good plan." I give her the bunny, a breathtakingly adorable quiver of grayish-brown fur with small pointed ears. It is so new and alone, so confused and frightened. No wonder rabbits have many offspring; the attrition rate among bunnies must be colossal. But carnivorous chipmunks? I had no idea they were meat-eaters. Nor that they hunt down bunnies the way Serengeti lions do their prey, sinking sharp teeth into the animal's neck and dragging it down.

Again I return indoors. But soon Cornelia reappears, this time accompanied by two neighbor girls. Cornelia's dad, who builds synchrotons by day, has built a temporary cardboard house for the bunny, and her mom has given it some lettuce. Cornelia's plan is to call the SPCA tomorrow and ask if they'd like to place the bunny in a good home, or if there is a safe place to turn it loose. She promises to look after the bunny, and to let me know its fate.

Even a bunny needs luck, I think as I go indoors. Those death screams resounded throughout the neighborhood. Sometimes at night I hear similar screams from the woods, and I've always assumed a raccoon was throttling a small mammal. Now I know it was the sound of a rabbit in its death throes. I suppose that nerve-shredding screech is intended to be the final sound the animal makes, a last-ditch effort to scare its attacker or to summon help. A desperate long-shot. This time it worked in an unexpected way and brought compassionate humans running.

—

After such excitement, I decide to spend a quiet afternoon on the patio behind the house, an aerodrome for moths and dragonflies, and am rewarded with visits from half a dozen hummingbirds, which I am going to write about for *The New York Times Magazine.* That forces me to throw open the doors of my senses and attend nature's one-room schoolhouse. I would have attended anyway, but you always try harder when there's a test in the offing. One of my favorite birds, manic and beautiful, the hummingbird reminds me of creativity's hidden costs, something I decide not to say in the essay. Despite their joy and beauty, they lead secret lives of passionate danger. And there is one truth about hummingbirds that continues to astonish me.

A lot of hummingbirds die in their sleep. Like a small fury of iridescence, a hummingbird spends the day at high speed, darting and swiveling among thousands of nectar-rich blossoms. Hummingbirds have huge hearts, and need colossal amounts of energy to fuel their flights, so they live in a perpetual mania to find food. They tend to prefer red trumpet-shaped flowers, from which nectar thickly oozes, and they must eat every fifteen minutes. A hummingbird drinks with a W-shaped tongue, licking nectar up as a cat might (but faster). Like a tiny drumroll, its heart beats at 500 times a minute. Frighten a hummingbird, and its heart will race to over 1,200 times a minute. Feasting and flying, courting and dueling, hummingbirds consume life at a fever pitch. No warm-blooded animal on earth uses more energy. But that puts them at great peril. By day's end, wrung-out and exhausted, a hummingbird rests near collapse.

Then, in the dark night of the hummingbird, as it sinks into a zombielike state of torpor, its breathing grows shallow, and its wild heart slows to only thirty-six beats a minute. When dawn breaks on the fuchsia and columbine, hummingbirds must jump-start their hearts, raise their body temperature, and fire up their flight muscles for another all-or-nothing day. That demands a colossal effort, which some can't manage. So a lot of hummingbirds die in their sleep.

But most do bestir themselves. This is why, in American Indian myths and legends, hummingbirds are often depicted as resurrection birds, which seem to die and be reborn on another day or in another season. The Aztec god of war was named Huitzilopochtli, a compound word meaning "shining one with weapon like cactus thorn," and "sorcerer that spits fire." Aztec warriors fought knowing that if they fell in battle they would be reincarnated as glittery, thuglike hummingbirds. The male birds were lionized for their ferocity in war. And their feathers flashed in the sun like jewel-encrusted shields. Aztec rulers donned ceremonial robes of hummingbird feathers. As they walked, colors danced across their shoulders and bathed them in a supernatural light show.

While most birds are busy singing an operetta of who and what and where, hummingbirds are mute. Such small voices wouldn't carry very far, so they don't bother much with song. If they can't serenade a mate, or yell war cries at a rival, how can they perform the essential dramas of their lives? They dance. They spell out their intentions and moods with body language, just as bees, fireflies, or hula dancers do. For hummingbirds, that means elaborate aerial ballets, in which males twirl, joust, sideswipe, and somersault. Brazen and fierce, they will take on large adversaries—even cats, dogs, or humans.

Persis once told me how she'd been needled by hummingbirds. When she lived in San Francisco, hummingbirds often attacked her outside her apartment building. From their perspective, she was on *their* property, not the other way round, and they flew circles around her to vex her away. My encounters with hummingbirds have been altogether more benign. Whenever I've walked through South American rain forests, my hair braided and secured by a red ribbon, hummingbirds have assumed my ribbon to be a succulent flower, and probed my hair repeatedly, searching for nectar. Their touch was as delicate as a sweat bee's. But it was their purring by my ear that made me twitch. In time, they would leave unfed, but for a while I felt like a character in a *Lil' Abner* cartoon named something like "Hummer." In Portuguese, the word for hummingbird (*beija-flor*) means "flower-kisser." Most languages identify them as "flying jewels." It was the practical, industrious American colonists who first imagined the birds humming as they went about their chores.

Last summer, my friend Jeanne had an intimate encounter with a female hummingbird. Over the years, Jeanne winced to see her cat, Beltaine, drag in voles, birds, and even baby rabbits. Few things can compete with the blood lust of a tabby cat. But one day Beltaine dragged in something rare and shimmery—a struggling humming-bird. The feathers were ruffled, there was a bit of blood on the breast, but the bird still looked perky and alive. So Jeanne fashioned a nest for it out of a small wire basket lined in gauze, and fed it sugar water from an eyedropper at regular intervals. To her amazement, as she watched, it miscarried a little pearl. Hummingbird eggs are the size of coffee beans, and females usually carry two. So Jeanne knew one might still be safe inside. After a quiet night, the hummingbird seemed stronger, and when she set the basket outside at dawn, the tiny accident victim flew away.

It was a ruby-throated hummingbird that Jeanne nursed, the only one native to the East Coast. In the winter, they migrate thousands of miles over mountains and open water to Mexico and South America. She may well have been visited by a species known to the Aztecs. Altogether, there are sixteen species of hummingbirds in North America, and many dozens in South America, especially near the equator, where they can feed on a buffet of blossoms. The tiniest—the Cuban bee hummingbird—is the smallest warm-blooded animal in the world. Only two-and-half inches long from beak to tail, it's smaller than the toe of an eagle, and its eggs are like seeds. No hummingbirds live in the rest of the world. They are a New World phenomenon. So, too, is vanilla, and their stories are linked. When the early explorers returned home with the riches of the West, to their deep frustration, they found it impossible to grow vanilla beans elsewhere. It took ages before they discovered why—that hummingbirds were key pollinators of vanilla orchids—and devised beaklike splinters of bamboo to do the work of birds.

Now that summer has come at last, I spend lucky days watching the antics of hummingbirds. I find the best way to behold them is to stand with the light behind me, so that the bird faces the sun. The trembling colors aren't true pigments, but the result of light staggering through clear cells that act as prisms. *Iridesce,* another of those startlingly intransitive verbs like *suicide.* Hummingbirds iridesce for the same reason soap bubbles do. Each feather contains tiny air bubbles separated by empty spaces. Light bounces off the air bubbles at different angles, and that makes blazing colors seem to swarm and leap. All is vanity in the end. The male's shimmer draws a female to mate. But that doesn't matter much to us gardeners, watching hummingbirds patrol the impatiens as if the northern lights had suddenly fallen to earth.

—

After dinner, I take a taxi downtown to the Crisis Center, and maneuver up the porch stairs by using my walker as a lever, then up the two interior flights, pushing off from the dock of each step and hopping on one foot to the next one. Muscles trembling, I stop to rest halfway. Sitting on the landing, looking down at a flight of stairs and up at a flight of stairs, I could be in the middle of an Escher drawing. No use calling to the counselor on duty; I can hear him talking quietly on the phone. The next flight goes a little faster, and when at last I shoulder the door open and hobble into the counselor room, sweating and flushed, with my knapsack on my back, a heavyset man with glasses turns around in his chair and smiles. For a moment his face quarrels about what to do. The caller needs help, but his fellow counselor also seems to need help. His body tenses to rise and I think he plans some-how to stay on the phone while helping me sit down, so I pantomime that I'm okay. He nods and says into the phone, "Let me see if I un-derstand this right, you've discovered that your ex-wife has been tap-ing your phone calls and editing and retaping them to say something else? And she holds a mini tape recorder whenever she talks with you...uh-huh...she can splice them together that well?...What does she have you saying?...Oh, boy, I can see why you're wor-ried...I don't know if it would hold up in family court; you'll need to ask a lawyer...How do you feel when she stands there talking to you with a tape recorder going?"

Sounds like an interesting call. Settling myself into a nearby chair, I read the Hot Sheet and Friday Letter and check the bulletin board. A postcard from Jamaica says: "At last a place I can sleep undisturbed. Tropical greetings to all, Jack." That would be Jack Smythe, a coun-selor I've only heard about. One day, a few years ago, Jack was on overnight shift despite a feverish flu, and when he lay down to nap awhile he tumbled into the world of cement sleep. During the night, a frequent caller, Hank, phoned and grew concerned when no one an-swered. Possibly he had dialed the wrong number. He phoned back. Still no answer. How could that be at a twenty-four-hour hotline? Hank had been calling for years, he regarded the SP counselors as friends, and as the night advanced he grew more and more worried. At last, panicky, he notified the police, who contacted Marian van Soest, who in turn phoned SP and, when she got no answer, summoned the police to meet her at SP. Racing upstairs, they found the door locked. No amount of banging fetched a response. Rushing back downstairs, the two policemen parked their car beneath a second-story window, climbed onto the car roof and let themselves in through an office win-dow. Then they unlocked the upstairs door and let Marian in, and all three began shouting and banging on the locked counselor-room door. Silence. Had the counselor had a heart attack? Rummaging through a desk drawer in one of the offices, Marian found the key to the counselor room. Fearing the worst, she and the policemen walked in to find Jack sound asleep on the couch. When Marian lightly touched his leg, he snapped to attention and said automatically: "Suicide Prevention and Crisis Service. May I help you?"

When Jim finishes his call, I stand up in my walker and inch forward. "I feel so wild tonight, I brought my own cage," I explain.

Laughing, Jim helps me into position at the desk. "How on earth did you do that?" he asks. For a moment I'm tempted to spin a good yarn, tell him I was sexing alligators when one complained, or that I was fulfilling a lifelong ambition to be a rope dancer in a circus. Instead I offer the bland truth—a few shallow stairs, and then anything but shallow tears. A kindhearted, divorced, middle-aged lawyer, Jim often takes shifts on Christmas Eve, Thanksgiving, New Year's Eve or Day. There is a patient goodness about Jim, and what I suspect is a tough daily battle with loneliness. I tend to phone on holidays, knowing that he'll be on duty, just to say hello and wish him good cheer.

"Your stairs or someone else's?" he asks in a mock professional tone.

"Forget it!"

He throws up his hands in a gesture of *Okay, I won't touch it with a ten-foot subpoena,* and gives me a sympathetic pat on the shoulder as he leaves.

My first call of the evening comes from a twenty-year-old woman who wants to discuss her being a prostitute. Matter-of-fact and uninhibited, with a light Spanish accent, she explains that she's been divorced for less than a year from a thirty-four-year-old internist. She describes herself as a tall, bosomy, heavily freckled redhead. In August she met a woman at a restaurant who recruited her into a call-girl service, and most of her johns are doctors. As her story unfolds—how the madam recruited her, the sort of men who hire her—I find my mouth hanging wide open in surprise. A call-girl service specializing in local doctors? I had no idea! Quickly I shuffle through faces in my memory—could *he* have employed her services? how about *him?* or *him?* She talks in some detail about how prostituting makes her feel more and more feminine, more whole. And then I realize that I haven't been paying close attention; instead I've been shocked and fascinated by the facts. The facts are irrelevant; they just feed my prurient curiosity. The caller is what matters. At that point, I slide back into step with her, and try to understand why something many women would find degrading has the opposite effect on her, making her feel more feminine, more whole. Her new boyfriend, Edgar, fills her body, and she says they have a satisfying sex life. Why do the lusty attentions of a parade of strange men make her feel better about herself? It's a puzzle. Mind you, being a high-class call girl is a frequent fantasy for women, hence the popularity of such movies as *Belle de Jour* with Catherine Deneuve playing the role of a bored housewife who turns tricks by day when her husband is at work.

My caller is scared to death her young son will find out, hates betraying him, judges herself harshly, and needs "to resolve the situation." She says she prefers big, burly johns and describes her first experience with one, how lying on the bed with her legs spread as he was about to enter her she felt a sense that something poetic was going to happen in her life, a momentous change. In a casual tone of voice, using frank anatomical language, she describes the scene. The john had a large penis and threatened to split her open with his thrusts, told her over and over he was going to kill her with it. She describes how exciting his violent language was, how she felt when he shoved inside her, how deliciously sore she felt afterward. Instantly I picture the scene, imagining it from several perspectives—hers, the john's, a voyeur's. Have I fallen into a film noir? Sensing the man's heat, smelling the man's sweat, imagining his hard thrusts, I say nothing, ask nothing. I don't believe the caller means this to be an obscene phone call. I take her at her word. It's just so damn sexy.

From there, we explore a few issues she might want to think about and pursue with a therapist. Is she trying to sabotage her future? Did she get married too young? What part does being submissive (to the woman who acts as her madam and to the johns) play in prostitution's appeal? Why does she feel "nourished," "more feminine," and "whole" when she is being "done by" man after man at a boozy party? I suspect she felt somewhat faceless as the young at-home wife of an older doctor, and that her double life gives her power over her ex-husband and other men. I suspect her past is complicated and sad. But these are so clearly therapy issues that I urge her to call the Mental Health Association to find a counselor to work with, since she's keen to understand her motives, and wants to change a behavior she's become addicted to. Ending the call, I encourage her to phone back to talk, and she thanks me, asking when I will next be on duty. Because I'm not allowed to tell her that, I assure her she'll find the other counselors equally concerned. The truth is that some will be more so than others, and she'll feel safer talking with some than with others, but no one will judge her. They might wish to have her problem, or date her, but they won't judge her.

"I need a cold shower," I say out loud to no one, after the call ends and I start my write-up.

Fifteen minutes later, a low-energy, rambly man calls in a mournful mood. His dearest and most frustrating wish is to be able to experience pregnancy. When he goes into a department store, he's drawn to the baby clothes—"it's the peaked caps and footies that break my heart"—and although he sometimes babysits for his sister's two children, he yearns to carry a new life inside him, feel its kicking, joyfully give birth, hold his baby in his arms, nurse it from his breasts. Nursing, especially, appeals to him. The good breast again. Persis would understand. In many ways a tender and poignant call, it could as easily have come from a woman as a man, so I treat it genderlessly. I do not know if he is gay, but it doesn't matter. Women without children sometimes also have such yearnings, which can strike like sheets of lightning across the soul and make the world temporarily a sadder and emptier place. For some while, he pours out his secret disappointment, which he feels deeply but can tell no one. Women routinely talk about these things among themselves, but men don't. Who would understand? In time, he says all he can tonight, and we hang up. He called because he felt lonely and out of step with life, which is reason enough.

As I set the telephone receiver back in its cradle, it rings at once. A woman is worried about her medication, which has worked well as an antidepressant for the past month but this week has prompted terrible migraines. Her psychiatrist works at the Mental Health Clinic, closed tonight, and she feels alone and frightened. I offer to find him—or someone knowledgeable—for her, try to calm her, reassure her that antidepressants can sometimes have frightening and confusing side effects which are not life-threatening. I call MHC, but get a recording. Her doctor isn't listed in the phone book. So I phone an emergency after-hours consulting therapist, who advises me that Paxol can indeed produce migraines. She can stop taking it for today without harm, he advises, then call her doctor tomorrow. I phone her back, talk it through with her, and she sounds relieved. Few things are as frightening as being on a medication that seems to be causing dangerous reactions, with no one to call, and no idea what's "normal" for the drug.

Paxol, like Prozac and other relatives are SSRIs, Serotonin Selective Reuptake Inhibitors, drugs that fight depression by increasing the amount of serotonin available in the brain. Many people believe that depression strikes most often when the brain's serotonin level drops. Indeed, researchers studying the brains of suicide victims, discovered a much lower than normal level of serotonin. The question is what comes first, the depression or the drop in serotonin? When something devastating happens, we may well become depressed—the event shocks our system and the serotonin level drops, among other physiological changes. Or does a low serotonin level lead to our finding otherwise bearable situations devastating?

How the SSRIs work intrigues me. In the brain, information travels from one neuron to another, and I picture the place where they meet as the coastline of two countries. In my mind's eye, they're northern European port cities during the Renaissance, with a river flowing between them, across which cargo must sail. Serotonin waits in ware-houses on the east coast, and at a signal the boats are loaded and they cross the river. At the other side, locals rejoice to see so much serotonin arriving. Their mood brightens even at the sight of such riches. At that point the serotonin's job is finished. Shippers carry it back to the east coast, where it's once again stored in warehouses to await another order to cross the river. In this metaphor, the river is a *synaptic junction*. The cargo contains serotonin, a *neurotransmitter*. Returning to the east coast and putting the serotonin back into the warehouses is how *reuptake* happens. SSRIs work by "inhibiting the reuptake." In terms of our metaphor, the docks suddenly close and the ships filled with serotonin end up waiting in the middle of the river. From the perspective of people on the west coast, it's a bonanza—a large supply of serotonin within easy reach.

When I tried Prozac about five years ago, it lifted my mood as planned—if anything, it made me feel a little better than well—but the most extraordinary thing happened. To my surprise, it temporarily altered how I could think. For the first time in my life, I became a linear thinker. I could arrange, structure, plan, analyze, explain, be practical and efficient to my heart's content. Had I been a linear thinker beforehand, this would have amplified my natural abilities and given my work a real boost. But, through the mysteries of mind and matter, I was born with a poet's sensibility, and Prozac made it impossible for me to do what comes naturally—think metaphorically, allusively, exploring the hidden connections between seemingly unrelated things. An iron cage fell over my imagination. Effervescent thoughts decanted to still wine. This occurred in such a mechanical way that it didn't alarm me, because there was no question about what had happened. It didn't feel like a writer's block, for instance, or that eager but fretsome, anxiously spellbound period before starting a new book, during which I'm mainly letting the well fill up. This was neither of those natural states. It felt as if someone had walked into the ballroom of the imagination in the middle of a festive New Year's Eve party and turned the lights off. All the dancers and musicians stayed in place, but they stopped playing and dancing.

On Prozac I could write straightforward sentences such as this one. But the minute I reached for the tongs of a metaphor to grasp a shadowy piece of life and drag it into view, nothing happened. It was like standing on a precipice and reaching into thin air... as opposed to reaching into that same air and grabbing a falcon out of it. If you know the falcons are there, know you can grab them, but now find the air empty, it's bewildering. Of course, it was truly fascinating to glimpse a little of how a sensibility works. But I couldn't lead my normal life like that, so I stopped taking Prozac and the minute I did, the ballroom came to life again as suddenly and mechanically as it had been stilled, the air thronged with falcons, and I was back in a familiar world.

Years later, I was sharing this memory with a neuroscientist friend, who nodded knowingly and said, "I think I know why that might have happened. One of the things Prozac does is to raise the threshhold for the neurotransmitter dopamine in the brain. For some creative people that could be an obstacle." To continue using the metaphor of the two Renaissance port cities: it would be as if supplies of dopamine were also sitting in dockside warehouses, ready to be loaded up and ferried across the river, when a new law went into effect. Instead of ships leaving when they had one ton of cargo, they would have to wait until they had five tons. Dopamine would still journey across the river, but it would take a lot more before that could happen. Why is dopamine important? It seems to be associated with processing novel information. As with all the neurotransmitters, too much of it is as bad as too little. Some argue that schizophrenics seem to have too much, and become flooded with more novel information than is useful.* Some sci-

---

* There are many schools of thought about what causes schizophrenia, a calamitous illness that afflicts 2.3 million people in the United States alone. Most researchers believe that an abnormality in fetal brain development is the main culprit. As the infant's brain is forming, important nerve cells migrate to the wrong place. Miswired,

entists believe that too little dopamine may underly what we regard as great eccentricity. According to this argument, eccentrics aren't able to process such basic information as how to function in society. Many eccentrics are happy and charming and beloved by appreciative friends, who cherish their uniqueness and sense of humor. But other eccentrics complain of feeling lonely and low, perpetual outsiders. When they're given amphetamines, which increases dopamine in the brain, they're better able to decipher the subtle rules of being personable, which allows them finally to fit in. Fascinating studies such as these imply volumes about personality, and also show us how supple and trainable the mind is. In principle, depression, anxiety, paranoia, and other uncomfortable mental states could be eased by tampering with someone's neurotransmitters. Then even the "Black Dog," as Winston Churchill called his lifelong horror of depression, would return to its kennel. But depression can spring from many sources.

In a postmortem study of people who committed suicide, researchers discovered a host of biochemical abnormalities. As I said, they had much lower than normal levels of serotonin, a condition not only associated with depression but also with heightened impulsiveness. You feel dreadful, and you act on it. Equally intriguing, their brain cells controlling pleasure and pain were different. Lying on the surface of some brain cells, opioid receptors respond to opiumlike chemicals produced naturally by the body, and play a vital role in our sense of pleasure, pain, or well-being. We require a basic level of feeling comfortable, content, and pain-free to believe life enjoyable and worth living. Without that minimum happiness, people would not wish to survive, so over the millennia it became selected for and added to the overflowing attic trunk of a human being's personality.

---

the brain then develops the altered reality of schizophrenia. But what causes neurons to move out of place? Some think the ultimate cause is genetic; others say it's environmental, caused by a mother catching a virus during critical months of pregnancy.

But the brains of suicide victims, who presumably were horribly depressed, contained 100 to 800 percent more of one type of opioid receptor, and only 50 percent of another opioid receptor. Because their brains were wired differently, life became a desert where thirst could swell to unbearable abstract proportions. "I can't stand the pain any longer," depressed people almost always lament, referring to a deep fracture of the spirit, a pain that seems to hurt all over the body but in no place they can point to. It is not a physical entity, but a ghost in their neurons, like phantom limb pain. If, at that moment, they could process pleasure and pain differently they would not be depressed. Many depressed people also suffer from chronic physical pain (there's a link, for example, between depression and migraine or lower back pain). Something going haywire in the opioid system, perhaps in people predisposed to it, may well trigger depression. I find it suspicious how often depressed people describe their suffering as "pain." They feel helpless and hopeless, but they perceive this as raw pain. Why does it register that way in the brain?

That's just the sort of naively devastating question that led me to college in the first place. I remember the exact moment such thoughts began to tantalize me. I was sixteen, school was out for the summer, and there were not yet any warnings about skin cancer. Rock-and-roll beach movies kept us sunning and singing, and it became the fashion to spell out your boyfriend's name in masking tape on your back, then lie in the sun for hours until you wore his brand. I was sunbathing one day in the parkway near our house, reading the newspaper, when I stumbled on a brief report that schizophrenics' sweat smells different. Thunderstruck, I found the implications thrilling. What felt like spiders of ice crept over my neck. Could all mental illness be a quirk of chemistry? Or perhaps a virus? How about creativity, belligerence, optimism, moodiness? Then what exactly is a *self*, and how does the brain become the mind?

When I was a freshman at Boston University, I intended to major in what was then called physiological psychology, and look for answers to some of those intriguing questions. For various reasons, in my sophomore year I transferred to Penn State, whose computer mistakenly placed me in English, and since I had been writing shyly but enthusiastically all my life, I considered it fate. But I've always kept my original fascination with human nature, a fascination often rewarded these days, as biopsychologists turn up provocative hints and insights. For example, about 8 percent of people who are hospitalized for psychiatric reasons, or who commit suicide, have a "Wolfram" gene that may predispose them to sadness. People with the gene (about 1 percent of the population—over a million people) are eight times more likely to need such hospitalization or to commit suicide. There's also a "BDV" virus carried by some horses that's been associated with mental illness in humans. People with low cholesterol have twice the suicide rate as those whose cholesterol is higher. A real curiosity, that. Scientists wonder if low cholesterol may be slowing down the transmission of serotonin. When people were connected to PET scans and asked to think sad thoughts—which they did on command, some even bursting into tears—the orbital frontal cortex of the brain became active. In men, though, only the left side of the brain grew aroused; in the women both sides of the brain participated. We know from experiments that women are better at recognizing sadness on the faces of both men and women. When some women complain that their men are insensitive to their feelings, they may be right, but not because the men don't care about them. Men, in general, are a little colorblind to expressions of sadness.

So, do women become sad differently or more often than men do? More women report being vulnerable to depression, and there are certainly good social reasons for it. Women have been helpless more often, had fewer opportunities, swallowed more injustice and inhumane treatment. But there may be biological reasons, too. Faced with stress, men, who were the hunters and fighters, had to be able to respond fast, in ways that led to action, even if it meant wasting energy in a fight with animal or man, and even if it meant risking death. As nurturers, women had to stay alive to bear and nurse the children, so when *they* were faced with stress they would have profited more from energy-saving strategies, ones that made them more sensitive to how others were feeling, so that they could avoid danger whenever possible.

Also, women tend to put up with relationships both painful and degrading, which sometimes become masochistic. Many of our callers are women in abusive marriages they can't fight their way out of, or walk away from. The reasons they can't are manifold, but men walk away from bad relationships much more often than women do. Stalkers, physical abusers, and other dangerous spouses are almost always male. This is in part because, thanks to their evolution, males express themselves and solve problems more violently than females do, and in part because females value attachment and dependency more than males do. That doesn't make it any easier when a distraught woman phones. It wouldn't help to tell her that part of her distress is fossil, that her heritage is betraying her. Freud once said that when a couple meet there are always six people in the room—the couple and their invisible parents. More than that, I reckon. Countless ancestors mill about, too, making mischief, even in a twentieth-century lake town.

———

As an hour passes without calls, I idly wonder about the last caller. I hope her migraines stop, but, especially, that she makes peace with her medication and her fears subside. Who wouldn't be frightened? We think of the body with fascination and horror, fascination at its complex subtlety, and horror that our consciousness hangs onto life by such coarse yet fragile threads. Waiting for the phone to ring, I lean out the window and look up at the sky. A cloud-strewn night. The perfect time for Joseph's Power Rangers to strike. In the fight of good against evil, the bad guys usually scurry in shadows like rats and commit heinous deeds under cover of darkness.

The Pleiades, an open star cluster, sparkles in the constellation Taurus. I locate it by looking for a group of flies on the bull's rump.

Although I can't see it with the naked eye, I know a "brown dwarf" lives there, a faint denizen of deep space too large to be a planet but too tiny to be a star. Brown dwarfs, which form from a collapsing cloud of gas and dust, are suns that for some reason didn't ignite into leaping infernos. Frigid at the core, not bright enough to see, they're only detectable because of their abundant lithium. Lithium, the chemical manic-depressives take to stabilize their moods. I bet manic-depressives would enjoy knowing they share an elemental chemistry with huge objects in the far reaches of space, wondrous objects located and defined by their use of lithium. In stars like our sun, lithium boils down into a nuclear furnace where it's destroyed. Because brown dwarfs are too cool to churn and boil, lithium stays on the surface, and that becomes their signature. If I stare hard, I can count only six of the Pleiades tonight. Looking through binoculars, I've been rewarded by dozens of blue white stars in a tantalizing beehive I know contains as many as two thousand stars, or "a swarm of fireflies tangled in a single braid," as Alfred, Lord Tennyson, wrote in *Locksley Hall*. Viewable by 80 percent of the world's population, the Pleiades have been worshiped, mythologized, or celebrated by the Egyptians, Chinese, Persians, Mayans, Australian aborigines, Greeks, and Japanese among many other cultures. "Subaru" the ancient Japanese named the Pleiades, and when six companies joined forces in 1953 to produce cars, they used a stylized star cluster as their logo. Among Paul's collection of Hopi kachinas (the painted, decorated cottonwood dolls Hopi carve to teach their children about the world), stands a black-and-white figure named "Mastop." It is the kachina of the sky, with a white handprint on its forehead to symbolize the human imprint on the universe. On one side of its face, eleven white speckles represent the Pleiades. For some reason, seven of the Pleiades' brightest stars have always been considered female—the Seven Sisters, a Hen with Her Chickens, an alter ego of the goddess Isis, the Virgins, or the Maidens. I wonder what's so female about that gaggle of stars in a smoky veil. Do people find it vulvalike? Or wide, flowing, and fertile, like a woman's torso? The very thing to consider on a hot summer day, while sitting in a pool of shade. Our ancients admired the Pleiades, but its stars aren't particularly ancient. As the blue color reveals, they're most likely young, hot unstable stars, twitching, in a frenzy, whirling and spouting, surrounded by gas. The dinosaurs are older than they are, humans roughly the same age. Alas, their short, dark companion who uses lithium is invisible. If I stare hard enough, my straining eyes might seem to glimpse it nonetheless. I guess it shouldn't surprise us to find ourselves linked to the stars. Every atom of gold or silver jewelry was created in supernovas. The water we drink, the air we breathe, the ground we walk, the complicated pouch of fluids and salts and minerals and bones we are—all were forged in some early chaos of our sun. I think it was the astrophysicist John Wheeler who remarked that we are the sun's way of thinking about itself.

Wish Frank Drake were here to share that thought with as I drink in the starlight. Forty years ago, Frank did his doctoral dissertation on the Pleiades, which he observed from Oak Ridge Observatory outside of Boston. There he aimed a sixty-foot radio telescope into the heart of the Pleides and listened. It was like cupping a large metal hand toward the heavens, listening, listening, through the longest night we can imagine, the night that stretches between the life and times of stars. He ached to hear the urgent whisperings of the cosmos, other planetarians calling from their distant outposts. Every night he went through the same routine of preparing the machinery and eagerly listening. Then one night the miraculous happened: he heard a signal, an intelligent signal both regular and repeating. Imagine his excitement, at twenty-six, to be the first person on earth to detect alien lifeforms, to eavesdrop on otherworldly minds. He was breathless, shaken, sweating, in a cold thrill, on the eve of what he knew would mean a vast change in human history, and *he* was the only person on earth who knew about it. According to Frank, it was in that heart-pounding moment that his hair suddenly started to turn prematurely white, a process completed before he was thirty. The signal kept coming in along the hydrogen band, a logical choice for an alien civilization, since hydrogen is abundant throughout the universe. As part of a normal sequence of tagging the signal, he shifted his telescope off the Pleiades cluster, and the most shocking thing happened: the signal went with him. Heartsick, he realized in a flash that it was not an alien message after all, but merely interference of some sort, probably from the military. It was not extraterrestrial in origin, not a voice from the Pleiades. Hope crumbled to disappointment in his fingers. Talk about a rollercoaster from manic to depressive—in a few minutes he soared to unparalleled heights and sank to the bottom of a well. Frank was always a good listener, of people and of the stars, patiently attuned, listening in darkness for other voices, other realities, able to sift meaning from noise. Two Fridays a month he overnighted at SP. Who better than a radio astronomer to take the night watch, a time of day that puzzles or scares most people?

I love the night world, land of moonscapes and shadows, patrolled by the flickering eyes of night creatures, overhung with a bustier of stars. But I know I'm unusual in this. Most people associate the night with mischief, or with the combination repair shop and cinema known as sleep. What odd creatures we are, who lie down in darkness for a third of each day. In sleep, the body seems calm, a pitcher from which the ale of consciousness has been poured. But all the while the brain travels, tells tales, grows frantic, doodles with strong emotions, wallows in the ghost-studded night. What we call "night" is the time we spend facing the secret reaches of space where other solar systems and, perhaps, other night-fearing beings dwell. The only shadows we see at night are cast by the moon, or by artificial light, but night itself is a shadow.

Because it bedevils our senses, the night world both tantalizes and spooks us. By day, our senses warn, charm, and guide us. But at night they struggle, and we become vulnerable as prey. Other creatures master that world—bats, snakes, rats, insects, lions. Things that live by night live outside the realm of normal time, and so suggest living out-side the realm of good and evil. We come to associate night-dwellers with people up to no good, people who have the jump on the rest of us and are defying Nature, defying their circadian rhythms. If we had to exist in the rain forest and protect ourselves against night-roaming predators, we would live partly in terror, as our ancestors did. As even now we sometimes do at night in our poorly lit concrete jungles. Even waking, we picture monsters moving through a dreamtime in which reality is warped. Thinking of bats and other beasts being masters of the night threatens the safety we take for granted each day. Anything living outside the usual rules we suspect to be an outlaw, a ghoul. No matter that beautiful and benign hawkmoths steal through the shad-ows of the rain forest by night. We're not awake to see them. They are mainly rumor to most of us, and if we did see them, in the twilight or the moonlight, they would look strange, hard to focus on clearly, per-haps magical. In monster movies, savage Wolfen or Aliens stalk us by night. Clearly, we aren't comfortable yet at the top of the food chain; night still reminds us of our delectable frailities. Remember, to make Hell seem all the more loathsome, theologians depicted it as a world lit only by the flickering confusion of flames. Unable to construe the spreading inkblot of the night, we personalize it with our own private monsters. To stifle the fear we transform the night, turning it into an event complete with discotheques, all-night diners, amusement parks, gambling casinos, and whole cities like Las Vegas, with their sand-storms of light.

Severed from the sensory spill of daytime, with work done, no one to see, no place to go, people seem to grow most alone at night. They drink until they fill their minds with darkness, or fantasize about be-coming part of the darkness forever. People who call SP from the mansions of the night often sound as if they've strayed beyond time, lost their map and compass, and are wandering outside the huge pen-dulum of night and day. They have the predawn crazies. As F. Scott

Fitzgerald wrote in *The Crack-Up,* "In the real dark night of the soul it is always three o'clock in the morning." If they can just get through till daybreak, the gloom may lift a little, and familiar people and routines offer hope. Better if they could find a starlit path back home, but in the nightworld crevasses lie everywhere.

CHAPTER 9

So Glory Descends

Shifts aren't always eventful, even night shifts. During the lulls, it's easy to grow bored and hope for a call to break my isolation, something novel and dramatic. I watch the phone, alert for the first sounds of unrest. Then I feel guilty, because it means, in effect, wishing someone to be in trouble. "Have a good shift," a departing counselor usually says to the next person on duty, and I think we mean *May the telephone ring often and may you rise to every occasion, so that you feel your time here was worthwhile.* But we keep it vague, because what we should mean is *May no one suffer today and need you.* Unlike a big-city crisis center, which might receive hundreds of calls a day (as San Francisco's does), at SP it's a bustling and busy day if thirty people call. And yet I've often been on shift when five or six people phoned per hour.

To pass the time, I read through past Hot Sheets, some of which have news clippings attached. Three events recently required SP's involvement, two suicides and a murder. The murder was also a self-destructive act, because a twenty-four-year-old killed the new boyfriend of his ex-girlfriend, dooming himself to a lifetime of imprisonment. One suicide, a sixteen-year-old boy, shot himself in a car. The teenage father of a handicapped baby, he had felt unable to support his family and handle the sudden spate of responsibilities. This was the second suicide in his high school in the past year, and part of SP's ongoing job is to find ways to handle the subject in the school, which his brother still attends. We want the students aware enough that they can call SP, but not cause so much commotion that the surviving brother might be stigmatized. SP's postvention crew has gathered the family together and talked with them, because after a suicide family members often blame themselves, and think they should have gone to thus and such an event that the boy wanted, or not said something or other, or have given him something he asked for, or listened better when he spoke. They get snagged at an "if only" stage, and can't get on with the necessary ordeal of grieving. On this occasion, the family was in denial, and couldn't fathom why the boy killed himself. But an investigation turned up clear motives: he was a teenager burdened by marriage and fatherhood, finishing school, trying to support his new family, and he was abusing alcohol and drugs. A psychological autopsy, it's called. When I first began to work for SP, a new friend of mine confided that he had been a counselor at the Los Angeles branch of Suicide Prevention when Marilyn Monroe died, and became part of the psychological autopsy team in that controversial case. Imagine attending the mysterious death of a naked icon. Although the circumstances of her death were confusing, and rumors circulated that she had perhaps been murdered, my friend felt convinced that she had indeed taken her own life.

More clippings. Only a few months ago, a twenty-two-year-old woman shot herself in the driveway of her boyfriend's house after he broke up with her. As young as she was, the future seemed intolerable without him. Her family was beside itself with shock and loss. A few months before that, a thirty-year-old man had a fight with his girl-friend, went out to his truck, took a hunting rifle and shot himself. She ran after him, but got there too late. Finding the body horrified her, as it would anyone, and she needed considerable counseling.

Postvention counselors, working with the survivors, try to elicit memories of the physical facts rather than the emotions, draw out the sensory details that make an event unforgettable, because that's how traumatic memories are stored in the brain—evocatively. Incidental things may become obstacles. For example, if a woman cooking pasta received a call about her sister's suicide, making pasta might always tinge her with sadness, though she may not understand why. There's a technical term for this phenomenon—*state dependency.* If something is learned in a specific setting, then it will be remembered when a similar setting occurs. Especially trauma. If a similar state isn't encountered for a long while, the memory may lie dormant, an unexploded landmine.

Still the phone sits quietly on the desk. *Don't want it to ring,* I caution myself, as I consider a pile of magazines. Paging through an issue of *New Scientist,* I stumble across an article that makes me smile. Researchers gave women T-shirts worn by men for two nights, then asked the women to choose which appealed to them. The women consistently chose shirts from males with immune systems different from their own. There was one exception—women on the birth control pill chose men with similar immune systems. Why would we evolve to be attracted to mates by unconscious cues such as smell? Because if you marry someone with a different immune system, your offspring have a better chance of inheriting strengths from both parents and surviving. But pregnant women have special needs—rather than a new mate, help from related males who will care for and protect the baby. Of course. One more piece of the jigsaw puzzle. One more snapshot for the human family album. If I put together enough shards of behavior, will I at last be able to see the panoramic whole? Turning down the corner of the page, I lay the magazine on the couch, so that I won't forget to copy the article before leaving. Now what?

Ring, I command the telephone. *Nothing mortal. Something solvable.* Silence, yards and yards of silence.

A glass jar on the desk shimmers with silver foil. Reaching into it, I remove a handful of Hershey's chocolate kisses, each one perfectly breast-shaped, the ultimate essence of suck. I bet it took a committee of post-Freudian marketeers to design.

From my knapsack, I pull a yellowing, dog-eared copy of Walt Whitman's *Leaves of Grass,* and browse among familiar passages, stopping at some favorite lines:

"Of life immense in passion, pulse and power"... "We also ascend dazzling and tremendous as the sun"... "A tenor large and fresh as Creation fills me"... "Where the alligator in his tough pimples sleeps by the bayou"... "Stretch'd and still lies the midnight"... "the flag of my disposition, out of hopeful green stuff woven"... "Long have you timidly waded holding a plank to the shore"... "Let your soul stand cool and composed before a million universes"... "Through me many long dumb voices"... "the drench of my passions"... "Life... the leavings of many deaths"...

Leaning back in the chair, glancing at the cracks in the ceiling, I remember visiting the house where Whitman was born, surprised to find it loafing on a quiet street in Huntington, Long Island, like an oasis tucked into the desert of suburban sprawl. It must have been a large rambling farmhouse in 1810, covered with natural cedar shakes that undulated and swelled and cracked as they dried to the color of stale blood. Whitman's father, a carpenter, had built the house himself, and it bears many of his stylistic quirks, like the Dutch doors, corbeled chimneys, and especially the battalion of extravagant windows, recklessly uneconomical, through which sunlight gushes.

Inside, the house erupts with motion, from the oak stairs on which knots are carefully arranged right at the lip, to the blueberry stain trimming the whitewashed walls as well as the mantels and doorways and the doors themselves. A house that outside wears the twisted wood of trees inside breathes with sunlight and the colors of the nearby ocean—a froth of white walls and the pounded, gunmetal blue of the sea. The oak-plank floors are studded with blacksmithed nails, but the attic beams are pegged. In Whitman's day, settlers sometimes went so far as to burn down their homes and collect the nails when they moved. Timber was plentiful, handwrought metal rare as radium.

I discovered that most rooms have two or three tall windows, with twelve handblown panes of glass over eight, each pane quarto-size, as was Whitman's first edition of *Leaves of Grass.* The original panes are delicately flawed and lenslike; they gave off a visual vapor when I peered through them, imagining how he had cooled his head there in summer.

When I stood outside, looking into the soul of the house through its windows, all was blackness. There was no Whitman anywhere, not the fresh lonely boy who collected eels and gull eggs by the shore, not the sensitive lonely man who, in his notebooks, kept a tally of his lovers, noting their facial features, ages, and interests, as if he feared there might come a time in his life when he would forget that he had loved and been loved. Not the free-thinking hothead who held dozens of jobs as teacher, printer, and reporter, and who founded newspapers himself. Not the omnivorous reader and poet blessed with passion who, years before Darwin's *Origin of Species,* wrote about evolution, as well as "the ancestor-continents away group'd together." Not the health fanatic, who took cold-water plunges everyday. Not the Civil War nurse, who traveled among battlefield hospitals and became one of the finest war correspondents who ever lived, while caring for the sick and dying with a saint's conviction. But when I looked *out* through the same windows, the world quivered into focus, became a pageant of color, vitality, and detail, as it was for Whitman. It was much easier to look out of the house than into it, knowing so little about the man, but caring deeply for his vision.

America had many poets before Walt Whitman, but there was never an *American* poet before he held the country in the sea-to-sea embrace of his imagination, named its wonders like a latter-day Adam, proclaimed its common men and women to have lives of beauty and dignity, blessed it as good, and then revealed it to itself in all its bustling, fidgeting, trailblazing, huckstering, big, booming, melting-pot panorama. He especially loved America's social "turbulence," which was its lifeblood and the perfect parallel to its wild unbridled landscapes. Whitman's portrait of America was rich with sensations and unnervingly complex, but he also saw it whole, as one democratic fabric, where a great personal deed had room to grow.

Because there was a new breed of American surfacing in the fast waters of the nineteenth century, Whitman decided to invent a radically new poetic language, translating the revved-up mosaic of the daily newspaper into a poetry full of street talk and everyday events, a poetry so plural it sought to sum up America, a poetry aggressively intimate that buttonholes the reader, cries with the reader, woos the reader, a poetry written in a breathless, ecstatic style, through which flows the electric of his vast athletic vision, a poetry that celebrates the human body in frank sexual detail, a poetry of catalogues and parading images, a poetry that drastically changed the idiom of poetry by bringing into it all sorts of untraditional things like astronomy, Egyptology, carpentry, opera, Hindu epics, census reports: the whole big buzzing confusion of life.

Whitman was the first American poet that the Universe didn't scare. He took it literally—as one *verse*—and wanted to touch and be touched by and leave his mark on all of it. Voluptuously in love with life, his mind was unquenchable and nomadic, always pitching the tent of its curiosity someplace new. He believed the poet's duty was to change people's lives by teaching them how to see, by throwing a bucketful of light onto the commonest things. And he believed that perfecting his own life was essential to perfecting his art. Indeed, he became the embodiment of the nineteenth century's ideal, the "self-made man," and was self-reliant, robust, obsessed with the physical; *Leaves of Grass* is, among other things, a journey of self-discovery whose message is that you can change your personality, change your fate, invent the self you want.

The central event in Whitman's life was the Civil War. In 1863, he visited his wounded brother in a makeshift hospital, and the first sight he saw was a heap of amputated limbs. Rigid with horror but boldly compassionate, he began his work of visiting war hospitals every day, to tend the young soldiers as they died. "I have never before had my feelings so thoroughly and permanently absorbed," he once wrote, "as by these huge swarms of dear, wounded, sick, dying boys." At night, he would migrate from bed to bed, writing letters for them, or giving them spoonfuls of stewed fruit or jam. But most of all he brought his extraordinary presence: a large, healthy, magnetic man charged with energy, white-bearded like the God of the Old Testament. He held their hands and kissed them. Sometimes he told a dying boy that he, Walt, was Death incarnate, and not to be afraid. What an extraordinary act of mercy, to make death physical and kind for the dying. Yes, I think, letting my eyes follow the ceiling cracks to where they gather like lines in a palm, waiting to be read, that's where he really got to know the America that figured in his poems, through the mainly adolescent boys torn out of their hometowns to fight one another. For a while, he was a hospice worker, a death's-door counselor.

Working on the crisis line sometimes feels like a battlefield, too, with callers caught up in their own civil wars. They often create a kind of poetry in their calls, dramatic monologues spoken heart to heart. They do not mean to be poetic, do not try to be exquisitely, heartbreakingly human. They cannot help themselves. What they've taught me is bound to influence the poems I will write, even the poems not about them, and has already widened my sense of suffering, courage, and nobility.

Whitman really only wrote one poem, although he added to it life-long, and sometimes made separate books of it. It was a great poem of being, a great epic of life in America in the nineteenth century, in the solar system, in the Milky Way, in the infinite reaches of space. He began with an eye like a microscope, focused on the beauty of the lowliest miracle, say a leaf of grass, and then stretched his eye out to the beauty of the farthest nebulae. He was not a churchgoer, but deeply religious. If there is no choired Heaven in his poems, there is also no death: "I bequeath myself to the dirt to grow from the grass I love, / If you want me again look for me under your bootsoles." He taught his contemporaries, and latter-day children such as Loren Eiseley and me, a new way of prayer.

A shocker in his day, when Victorian prudery gagged at his evangelism of the body and his sensuous relationship with the Universe, he electrified the country's notion of its humdrum self. Not long after his death, schoolchildren were given *Leaves of Grass* to read as a sacred American text about the essential goodness of people, the dignity of the common person, the holiness of the human body viewed naked and up close, the need to forge one's own destiny, and the duty of all to discover the world anew, by living in a state of rampant amazement at the endless pocket-sized miracles one encounters every day. He reminded us that "A mouse is miracle enough to stagger sextillions of infidels." Even now, Whitman's vision is one children are taught in schools, one we cherish as a great opera of American life. Taking the coastlines and canyons and mountain ranges and farmlands and cities, he stitched them together into one sweeping vista that begins and ends with the self. What must it be like, I wonder, to create a mental landscape in which your neighbors, fellow countrymen, and even future generations feel *expressed* and at home?

How sad that he felt obliged to change the sex of his lovers when he wrote about them in his diaries, writing "he" only to erase it and replace it with "she," erasing that, reinstating "he," then "she," and so on. If he lived here in town, he might well be one of our callers, many of whom grapple with sexual identity issues. Married men afraid to reveal that they're bisexual, single men afraid they might lose their jobs if people knew they were gay, men and women confused about the first stirrings of homosexuality, or how best to deal with their families, and a long list of relationship problems of miscellaneous sorts. If he called with the problem of his diaries, which clearly worried him, feeling ambivalent or unsafe about his homosexuality, how would I regard him? If I recognized his voice or his story, would I need to keep in mind that he was Walt Whitman, because you can't disentangle an artist from his life? Or would being his admirer make it harder for me to help him? How could he feel understood, appreciated, taken seriously, if I didn't convey my powerful faith in his unique talent and vision? Or would that be a mistake, because the heart wears no label or costume, and a lonely banker is just as lonely as a lonely poet? Should I think of his creativity as a job like any other job, important to the journeyman but, during a call, irrelevant to his grief? If I ignored his creativity, would he at last be the Everyman he personified and loved? An artist hides much of his private self beneath his public self by trade, which can lead to a sense of fakery, a self-doubting, "if-only-they-knew-the-truth-about-me" feeling, a belief that he's composed of disjointed selves, one public and admirable, one private and deplorable. So, shouldn't I regard the whole man, the creative core and the knotted bundle of turmoil, as a single, authentic, troubled yet triumphant, thickly woven universe of mind and matter?

In a town filled with artists, artisans, and performers, we often hear from creative people, and those callers sometimes pose special problems for me. I can't reveal how intimately I understand their struggles, or how fascinating I might find their minds. When writers call, it's tempting to advise them, though of course I mustn't. For example, a college freshman phoned whose parents were hounding him to go into medicine, but he loved writing and wanted somehow to work in the arts and sciences simultaneously, but wasn't sure if that was even possible. A frustrating call, that. Of course, I wanted to say, *I believe Diane Ackerman lives in town. Why don't you phone her and ask her advice?* After all, I could share my own experiences with him, make suggestions for courses to take and interdisciplinary paths to explore. It was hard to resist guiding him. But he wasn't calling for my professional advice, he was calling because he felt dread, shame, and anxiety, among other emotions. He was calling to vent his frustrations, sadness, and fears, and so we talked about how it felt letting his parents down, and the best way to handle their upcoming visit and the inevitable confrontation. Although I did finally steer him gently toward an interdisciplinary department at his college, when we hung up I felt thwarted. All the knowledge and experience I couldn't share with him! It's astonishing how solidly one's ego can get in the way. I remember Nina Miller (first director of the agency, and also a fiction-writer) advising counselors in training that "There are times when you talk to somebody, and the connection is so pure that it's hard not to feel, *Oh, is this person lucky I happen to be on shift now, because look how we're connecting.* I once was in the middle of that kind of call," she admitted, "being terribly self-congratulatory with this very articulate, literary type, and he quoted a line of poetry and before I could censor myself, I said, 'Oh, that's Keats,' or something like that. And I lost the call. He stopped talking about what he called for, what he painfully needed to talk about, because of my own ego need. That's why you have to be very leery about sharing any kind of personal information. A caller is not calling to find out about the counselor."

It has taken me a long while to appreciate what Nina meant. A natural urge to connect, to prove that you understand, can tempt you to reveal experiences you've had that are similar to a caller's. Then the identity you've managed so successfully to shelve starts to slide off the shelf like the slippery fabric it is. Let go for an instant and it tumbles all over the floor—an untidy and distracting heap of color and folds. Best to resist and keep your own life in the margins. But it's tough when you touch voices with a kindred spirit.

One morning a young poet called who was depressed, desperate, and lamenting that she couldn't bear the intensity which she also craved. I understood exactly what she meant by that paradox. I felt the same way in my twenties, when the sun was always at noon. Useful creatively, but impossible emotionally, it was a renegade state both glorious and hellish. Here is a journal entry written when I was twenty-four:

These days I'm like a nettle under my own skin. If only I could pull a sheet up over my life and lie quietly, let go. The yard is infinitely distracting. A troupe of fat crows is picnicking in a bush, dragging the limbs down like shiny black fruits. I've begun to feel alien again, go through long spells of control, then these shorter ones of such helplessness, paralysis, unworth. My hallucinatory sensibility I adore, feast on, but cannot live with... I hear the whistle of some bird, like a rusty gate closing, see the separate leaves flickering like coins in the sunlight, the sky white as paper. Two blue jays have taken to the sycamore. There are huge shadows in the trees, made angular by vagaries of light and relief. The air fills with the toots, crackles, and songs of a kindergarten band: sandblock, kazoo, chime, sticks, recorder. Heat shimmers on the window pane... I've let everything slide: letters, work, house. Life seems intractable, like sludge. Surely there's a trick of perspective, a coping mode, a callousness, a remove, a way of holding oneself within the fire but without the burning. I have not found it. Today I will not die like a fly or a swallow. There is so much light in the woods the yellowgreen leaves look painfully raw. I cannot seem to live in half-doses, to shake my heart calm enough to work. The treetops look like African masks, burning bushes, weather balloons. Birds carry the motion of the leaves across the frame like an electronic signal. Sunlight in the woods gives an air of lucidity, as if, could I but squint harder, the far side of the teeming leafage would appear. I squint hard, but nothing budges, comes forth, silently opens to view. What is life that it should include this torment, as well as that parley of birds in the ever-green? ... I have not the wherewithal to do my chores, eat, phone the electrician, renew my library book, get dressed, even sleep. I am losing weight recklessly. I read somewhere that solar deprivation makes one ail, so I've stripped down and gone out back to bask in the sun. The rays feel like liquid vitamins I took once when little. Mother tilted my head back like a baby bird's and poured the syrupy gold straight down ... My filing cabinet is woefully backlogged and chaotic. I've let it all slide, all slide. ... The trees now are dark as Goyas. An occasional spore floats across the sky. I'm growing seasick from watching a leaf twist on its tender petiole, turn and turn about. I can hear the urgent weathering of the paint. A handsome red dragonfly, whose slim body pikes like a diver in midair, has been sitting on the chaise for long minutes now. He spreads his double wings like a biplane and, as I pray my dirged spirit will, soars.

I don't recall writing that paragraph, whose unbroken cascade of images and soul-ache, tumbling out with no shift in mood or gears, alarms me a little even in retrospect. But, oh Lord, do I remember how exhausting those days felt, when the same emotional charge applied to everything. I also hear in that passage a persistent and, though I didn't know it then, healthy effort to ground myself in the real world, to steady myself with the familiar handholds of leaf, bird, and sky, desperate to anchor them in words. Dragging myself back to dramas fascinating and external, I must have instinctively understood the redemptive power of bathing in nature at its most radiant, an act that excites the mind while it cools the blood. Only oxymorons begin to describe how nature stirs me: an alert and stimulating calm, a sedative thrill.

Fortunately, that stage of sublimely unlivable intensity sometimes passes as young poets get to know and control their creativity better, and also as the chemistry of their growing bodies levels out. Today I perceive the world much the same as I did in my teens and twenties. Looking upon nature, I'm just as likely to record some of those images now. But I process the world differently. The steep sensations don't frighten me. The intensity hasn't changed, but it has become familiar and manageable, I don't feel so much in its thrall, and at times I can summon or ignore it. But there's no doubt the teens and twenties test your mettle. If you can survive the first rapids of discovering you have a terrifyingly intimate relationship with the world, then you'll get used to it, treasure it, and life may eventually calm down. Unfortunately, for some artists that tempestuous stage lasts until an early death. Such was the case of Sylvia Plath, an immensely gifted and subversively angry poet addicted to ritualized resurrection. Throughout a tumultous marriage, and despite her two young children, she kept trying to kill herself until she finally succeeded. But what an adorer of the world she was, one of life's keenest observers and celebrants. Her precise, surprising imagery takes my breath away. When I was in graduate school at Cornell, women poets obsessed about her. If life could overwhelm someone with that gift and passion, what hope had they? Many wrote her epistolary poems. Some romanticized her *because* she killed herself, finding something enviable in a passion so intense it led to death. I was visiting the Rare Books Room of Penn State Library one day when the curator walked up with a book in his hand. "Here's something you might find interesting," he said casually. It was a translation of Goethe's *Faust,* a standard college edition. When I opened the front cover, my heart leapt. It had been Sylvia Plath's copy. I quickly discovered with a smile that she had gone through, daring to improve the language, tightening up images, turning woolly lines into memorable phrases. She also underlined sections dealing with death, destruction, and torment—a theme that visibly obsessed her. It gave me a chill to see warning signs of her suicide, so clear in retrospect. Later I wrote her the following poem:

ON LOOKING INTO SYLVIA PLATH'S
COPY OF GOETHE'S *FAUST*

You underlined the "jugglery of flame"
with ink sinewy and black as an ocelot.
Pensive about ash, you ran to detail,
you ran the mad sweetshop of the soul,
keen for Faust's appetite, not Helen's beauty.
No stranger to scalpel or garden,
you collected bees, knew how to cook,
dressed simply, and undressed the flesh
in word mirrors. Armed and dangerous
with the nightstick of desire,
you became the doll of insight we knew
to whom nearly all lady poets write,
a morbid Santa Claus who could die on cue.
You had the gift of rage, and a savage wistfulness.
You wanted life to derange you,
to sample its real muscle, you wanted
to be a word on the lips of the abyss.
You wanted to unlock the weathersystem
in your cells, and one day you did.

I never loved the pain you wore as a shroud,
but your keen naturalist's eye,
avid and roaming, your nomad curiosity,
and the cautionless ease with which your mind
slid into the soft flesh of an idea.
I thought you found serenity in the plunge
of a hot image into cool words.
I thought you took the pledge
that sunlight makes to living things,
and could be startled to joy
by the green epaulets of a lily.
But you were your own demonology,
balancing terror's knife on one finger,
until you numbed, and the edge fell free.

Still later, on shift at SP when the young poet called, I knew only too well the danger she faced. How my maternal side longed to take her under my wing, reassure and comfort her. Alas, I could only listen and empathize; together we tried to plumb her resources. But, as an SP counselor, I couldn't confide or teach. Revealing myself might be temporarily more helpful to her, but how about in the short hours before dawn, when the ingots of dread start weighing heavily, or when an inevitable rejection punches her down? An artist's life is always acceptance or rejection, surfeit or famine. What then? My job was to help her find solace whenever she phoned the agency, to allow the agency to become her lifeline, not me. She needed to be able to spill emotion, somewhere to someone, anonymously, whenever the demons struck, regardless of who was on shift.

Suppose someone breathtakingly talented calls when I'm on shift, someone like Plath or Whitman? For all I know, he or she may be one of our callers. The thing about Whitman is that, for all his gift, success, and competence in the world, he was troubled by relationships of usual sorts; exposed to much war trauma; and, at times, some would say in flights of hallucination or megalomania, became delusional enough to depict himself as Death incarnate. Though inseparable, his bright and dark sides were rarely viewable together. For the most part, his ecstasy was public and his tumult private. I must try to keep that in mind when furiously depressed people call. The part of their selves I don't hear from may be the scintillating, resilient, and powerful part that will write *Leaves of Grass*. This is so hard to remember when someone calls in despair, especially if it's a long, lingering death-bound despair. Hard to remember that part of them may be indomitable, self-glorifying, pure acrobat. It's a therapist's job to help them come clean, and integrate their bleak, agile, and dynamic sides. In that sense, I suppose therapy is related to the ancient religious cleansing and purgation that was part of a "soul journey." Our job, on the other hand, is far simpler, though it can feel elaborate. We strive to bind a caller to the present for a short while, a very short while, one more hour, one more day. It may seem a long cool drink in the wilderness of their suffering, or a breather only a few heartbeats long. "What will you do today?" I once asked Louise as we were ending an agonizing call. "It's not the days that worry me," she had said. "It's the hours."

The phone rings and I'm so startled I flinch. My heart sprints a moment. I collect myself, clear my throat, answer on the third ring. "Suicide Prevention and Crisis Service," I say. "May I help you?" A loud click. Reaching for the logbook, I jot down: Hang-Up. "Rats," I say to no one in particular, and tap my fingers on the desk. Maybe they'll call back. My heart returns to idle.

Waiting for the phone to ring—a familiar discomfort, something humans do. How often I have anxiously waited for a loved one to call. I laugh when I think of teenage girls and their telekinesis vision, staring at a quiet phone, trying to whammy it into action. Then there are those late-night calls, when you lie in bed, the phone's cool cheek cradled against yours, as you drowsily talk with a sweetheart. It is not surprising that several clergymen should be among the founders of SP. With its tiny perforations, the mouthpiece of a telephone looks like the screen in a confessional. In church, people enter a telephone-booth-shaped place and anonymously call upon the priest for help. Many of SP's clients are calling from phone booths. In both anonymous acts, where life and death may be at stake, and sometimes heaven and hell, two people touch voices through a thin screen. The telephone's is smaller, that's all. The voices pass through those tiny holes as if they were wisps of nothing, and yet they carry large dramas. We pour our hearts out into the small confessionals of telephones. But where are all the aching hearts tonight?

As I push back the chair and grab my walker, a sharp pain stabs my left little toe and I wince. Three days ago was a real scorcher, so I took off my shoes and socks for a short spell while I worked in my study. Reaching for a book, swiveling the wheelchair with my good foot, I somehow managed to roll a front wheel over my little toe, breaking it. Now I have a broken fifth metatarsal on the right foot and a broken little toe on the left foot. If it weren't so painful, my predicament would be laughable, a carnival of disasters. The human foot has twenty-six bones, thirty-three joints, a hundred ligaments. That's a lot of scaffolding. Break a few of its girders or lashings, and the whole contraption collapses. All my weight now has to rest on the center and heel of my left foot, and that makes even hopping a trial, the wheelchair and scooter harder than ever to mount, the stairs at SP a military exercise. Nonetheless, I've been swimming on my back for half an hour each day, held afloat by a Styrofoam vest, while I kick gently (though only in the vertical plane). If I'm lucky, both injuries will mend at about the same time.

Most mornings, I sling a net marketing bag across my body, stash a plastic vase and shears in it, hobble outside using my walker, and cut flowers to arrange. Sometimes I feel melancholy, looking up at a vase on a shelf I can't reach, but sober up fast when I remind myself that children, the elderly, and many handicapped people live with countless such frustrations every day. Thank heavens my limits are temporary. I no longer fret over how long simple tasks take; I've recalibrated my mental scales and clocks, as well as my physical goals. Now that I've discovered how to override the governor on the electric scooter, I can dash to the grocery at 2.5 mph instead of 1.6, which translates into twelve minutes instead of eighteen. I've developed a comfortable boldness in asking strangers to help me open doors or cross streets. Amazing how many people offer help, unbidden. Complicated thoughts fill their faces when they do, and it's clear that they're trying to assess my handicap (people with broken bones usually use crutches, not scooters or wheelchairs). They never ask about the injury. Making an effort to be cheerful, they try not to be condescending, but rather to strike a delicate balance between sympathy and pity. I find that touching. Some of SP's callers are disabled, too, and live with all the frustrations and dependency of wheelchair life. Many of them have been the object of ridicule and scorn, not compassion. On outings with friends, I've been appalled to discover how few shops, restaurants, movie theaters, public buildings, and even doctors' offices are truly wheelchair accessible. Some have ramps that are too steep to maneuver solo, others have ramps into the building but steps to the bathrooms. My injuries have given me a clearer understanding of what the handicapped face. Of course, some callers are stricken with invisible disabilities that restrict them, often without anyone noticing, and that must be tougher still.

In the Center's kitchen, I add water to a cup of corn chowder soup and pop it into the microwave. Someone has taped a panorama-shaped poster on the wall, containing a list of names set in many elegant and stylish typefaces: *Abraham Lincoln, Virginia Woolf, Lionel Aldridge, Eugene O'Neill, Ludwig van Beethoven, Gaetano Donizetti, Robert Schumann, Leo Tolstoy, Vaslav Nijinsky, John Keats, Edgar Allan Poe, Vincent van Gogh, Isaac Newton, Ernest Hemingway, Sylvia Plath, Michelangelo, Winston Churchill, Vivien Leigh, Emperor Norton I, Jimmy Piersall, Patty Duke, Michael Faraday.* Beneath that rollcall runs a banner in red:

PEOPLE WITH MENTAL ILLNESS ENRICH OUR LIVES

Below that, a long red line, then a footnote:

These people have experienced one of the major mental illnesses of Schizophrenia and/or Manic-Depressive Disorders. For more information: 1-800-950-FACT. Alliance for the Mentally Ill of New York State.

An eyecatching poster, it's remarkable for all the equally afflicted and brilliantly creative artists and scientists it doesn't include: Hieronymus Bosch, Wassily Kandinsky, Albrecht Dürer, Johannes Kepler, Tycho Brahe, Hugo Wolf, Camille Saint-Saëns, August Strindberg, Arthur Rimbaud, Charles Lamb, Guy de Maupassant, Theodore Roethke, T. S. Eliot, Hart Crane, John Berryman, Robert Lowell, Anne Sexton, Jonathan Swift, Serge Rachmaninoff, Lewis Carroll (Charles Dodgson), William Blake, Martin Luther, Rod

Steiger, Dick Cavett, Joni Mitchell, Beatrix Potter, Charles Baudelaire, Edvard Grieg, Arthur Schopenhauer, Randall Jarrell, Delmore Schwartz, Lawrence Ferlinghetti, William Styron, Tennessee Williams, and Friedrich Nietzsche, to name only a few. Indeed, it's hard to think of many artists whose lives weren't troubled by alcoholism and/or mental illness. Can it be, as Aristotle insisted, "No great genius was without a mixture of insanity"? Plagued by suicidal lows and stratospheric highs, did nineteenth-century composer Robert Schumann require his emotionally gruelling bouts of manic-depression to produce masterpieces? Schumannolgists have discovered from his letters and medical records that he wrote most of his music in his manic periods. For example, in 1839, a time of deep depression, he created four works; the next year, riding a freshet of mania, he created twenty-five. An important aspect to his genius is that it produced equally triumphant music in both states. Although he composed more during his manic years, he wrote much ordinary work and some brilliant work in pretty much the same ratio as he did when depressed. The only difference was output. The mania gave him more energy—not more insight, passion, or sensitivity.

Artistic genius requires heightened sensitivity, risk-taking, impulsiveness, a belief that the world waits for you to add your vision to the sum of Creation, the faith that you can stain the willows with a glance. Not all creative people struggle with depression, manic-depression, or psychosis. But studies of artists conducted in three countries show a much higher incidence of alcoholism, schizophrenia, and depression. What would be the evolutionary point of that? Why on earth would an artist such as Van Gogh find creativity and mental illness in his genetic suit? Surely it has no survival value if it leads to suicide at an early age. Moderate doses of creativity may be fine for finding new ways to hunt and gather, organize people, attract mates, anticipate and revise in the face of danger. To our ancestors it would have been a useful, even life-saving, quality. Intense creativity, though it may produce magnificent art, wouldn't be as useful. So the tendency toward alcoholism and psychic distress may be just an unfortunate side effect of the gene for creativity, not a worry in people who are moderately creative, but intensified in those people for whom the creativity is intensified. Even so, the large majority of artists don't suffer from these ills. If you look closely at a family, you can often see creativity expressing itself in different doses. In my family, for instance, my mother's side includes her immigrant father, who was a spare-time inventor (of the backless vest and other items), taught himself five languages, and acted as a translator for the gypsies for many years; two uncles who are extremely clever electronics inventors; an aunt who writes songs and, at eighty-five, continues to be a performing belly dancer; my mother, who always wanted to be an architect and has spent her life crafting and designing things. I know little about *her* mother except that, in Europe, she made a living by embroidering vests (only the fronts), and selling sugar cubes to men who drank coffee as they played dominoes. My father's side of the family is altogether more practical, good at numbers, and less artistic. I turned out a poet, my brother a businessman.

On the other hand, artists are people who tend to have two or three jobs, face rejection and indifference, often live in poverty, don't keep the same hours or schedules most people do, don't fit into the norms of a workaday life, are more introspective than their neighbors, entertain unusual ideas or points of view for a living, feel deeply as a profession, and usually find little understanding or respect unless they become famous, in which case they're constantly being judged— every work has to be as good as the previous one, and good in the same way. That doesn't sound like an inherently stable lifestyle. "Solitide gives birth to the original in us, to beauty unfamiliar and perilous—to poetry," Thomas Mann wrote in *Death in Venice*. Artists may require solitude to work, but where does solitude end and loneliness begin? Add to that the way artists sometimes romanticize extremes of consciousness. For some, creativity is a moody art, relying on a cynical outlook and many subtle rituals of despair. For me, it is most often a form of celebration, inquiry, and prayer, but I believe I am unusual in this. Many artists spring from troubled childhoods, and create art as an act of personal salvation. Georges Simenon swore that "Writing is not a profession, but a vocation of unhappiness." There are few artists who haven't been hurt into art. So I haven't decided in favor of nature or nurture as being the great persuader in a creative person's life. It may be a pas de deux, in which at times nature leads, at times nurture. I picture the two outer planets, Neptune and Pluto, whose orbits overlap in such a way that they trade places from time to time. At the moment, Pluto happens to be the farthest out, but not long ago Neptune was. Given the raw materials of personality and talent, who can say where they will lead? Given the gravity of family life, who can say what it will shape?

I am convinced, though, that the part of the artist that becomes depressed, schizophrenic, addicted, or mentally ill is separate from the part that creates. It waits through the drunkenness, sadness, mania, hallucination, narcosis, for a return to relative clarity and stability, a still point in which to create. It creates alongside the psychic distress. Others may disagree, but I believe even the most disturbed artists create out of health and strength. William Faulkner wrote novels despite his alcoholism, at times of partial or (occasionally) complete sobriety. Indeed, as his drinking grew heavier and heavier, he was rarely able to write at all, until alcohol finally replaced ink as the main fluid in his life. The same is true for Eugene O'Neill, John Steinbeck, Dylan Thomas, Lillian Hellman, Tennessee Williams, Ernest Hemingway, Victor Hugo, Malcolm Lowry, F. Scott Fitzgerald, Stephen Crane, Jack London, O. Henry, Truman Capote, and so many other alcoholic writers whose gifts didn't flow from the bottle but around it, and who would have written even more and better without it. Running away from the ghost of depression can also be a tonic. Frightened of being immobilized by despair, depressives often fling themselves into frantic activity. Hoping to keep gloom at bay, they work until they drop, seem to have inhuman stores of energy, and create art nonstop. They can't afford to stop. If they slow down, the missile of depression might catch up with them.

———

Stirring the hot, thick, corn-sweet soup, I hobble back into the counselor room and carefully arrange myself at the desk, one foot on the hassock, the other on a chair seat. Of all the names on that poster in the kitchen, Churchill's may be the biggest surprise. For most of his life, he crumbled under the repeat blows of a depression so familiar, loud, and unshakable, that he called it his "Black Dog"—I suppose because it hounded him. It had its own life and demands, was uncompromisingly brutal, and became a monstrous family member to be reckoned with. It seems to have been an affliction he shared with a number of his ancestors, including his father, who suffered from what was described as "melancholia." A small, feeble boy, bullied at school and neglected by his remote, glamourous, high-society parents, Churchill grew into a dynamo of a man packed with energy, assertiveness, bravery to the point of recklessness, a tough attitude, extreme ambition, plentiful ideas, willfulness, aggression alternating with compassion, artistic tastes, egomania, and a yen for daring adventures. The deprivation he felt as a child may well have fueled his ambitions, but, having no innate sense of value, he was easy prey for the armies of depression that plagued him throughout his life.

Carrying a burden as heavy, unpredictable, and frightening as that, how on earth did Churchill raise children, rise in politics, paint beautifully, write with wit and confidence, and lead a nation through war? In psychiatrist Anthony Storr's fascinating character study of Churchill, he argues that in 1940, when all the odds were against Britain, it took a bold conviction for Churchill to rally the British people, but "it was because all his life, he had conducted a battle with his own despair that he could convey to others that despair can be overcome." Storr sees in Churchill's story a classic relationship between depression and hostility, in which an emotionally deprived child resents his deprivers but can't risk showing any anger or upset, since he desperately needs the very people who are torturing him. Depression results from turning that hostility against oneself. Sometimes such people aim at opponents in the outside world. As Storr observes, "It is a great relief to find an enemy on whom it is justifiable to lavish wrath." In Churchill's case, "fighting enemies had a strong emotional appeal for him ... and when he was finally confronted by an enemy whom he felt to be wholly evil, it was a release which gave him enormous vitality."

For the last five years of his long life, Churchill sat in a chair staring at a fire, partly paralyzed by a stroke, wholly demoralized by depression. He stopped reading, rarely spoke. The Black Dog finally caught up with him and pounced, flattening him under its rough weight. But what a dynamo he had been, so inventive, so courageous, so resilient. A history-making, difficult life. Yes, I think, that's what we all lead, in smaller arenas perhaps, lives sometimes gleaming, sometimes difficult, that change history for many of the people with whom we come in contact. Isn't it odd that one big-brained animal can change the course of another's life, change what the other sees when it looks at its reflection in a mirror, or in the mind's mirror? What sort of beings are we who set off on symbolic pilgrimages, pause at mental towns, encounter others who—sometimes without knowing it— can divert or redirect us for years? What unlikely and magical creatures. Who could know them in a lifetime? When I start thinking like this, wonder shoots its rivets into my bones, I feel lit by a sense of grace, and all my thoughts turn to praise.

Still no calls. The telephones look plastered to the desk. Maybe if I use one the other will get the idea.

Will Cathy be home tonight? This might be a good time to plan a future bike trip. While the weather holds, we could take a stab at the Sodus Point ride—forty miles along the shores of Lake Ontario. 20

Bike Rides in the Fingerlakes describes it as mainly level terrain strewn with fragrant orchards of plums, peaches, apples, and pears.

Dialing Cathy's number, I get a busy signal.

Forty miles is more than we've ever tackled, but level miles float under you like steam. They'd be a snap. Well, maybe a long slow sweaty perfectly fatiguing snap. Could we drive there and back and bike forty miles in one day? I don't think so. We'll have to stay over at a bed and breakfast. A smile creeps across my face. The last time we overnighted with our bikes was last August, when we drove to Cooperstown, biked some that afternoon, slept at a bed and breakfast, and the next day biked twenty-two hilly miles through old forest, rich farmlands, lake resorts, and continuous natural beauty. Recalling the serene mysticism of that ride, I ease it through my memory as one luscious spill of sensations:

In the lavender hours after daybreak, before the sun leapt onto the blue stage of the sky to begin its light opera of soul-searing heat, we set out on our bikes to circumnavigate Otsego Lake, which, encircled by dense forest, lay flat as pounded metal, thickly gray-purple with a light mist rising, yet wavering clear like an ancient mirror—the lake the Indians named "Glimmer glass"—and pedaled hard up a long steep incline, as the temperature of our bodies and the day rose together, and within the aubergine drapery of the forest, twigs crackled, a confetti of light fell through the leaves, small quick beings darted among the tree trunks, and an occasional loud crunch or scuffling led our eyes back a million years through several tunnels of instinct to shadows we automatically interrogated for bear or mountain lion or highwayman or warrior, as a mixed chorus of insects and birds sang out, oblivious to our cycles, but mystified perhaps by our talk and laughter, or by the sight of a woman with blonde hair riding upon a teal green bike, wearing black shorts with purple chevrons the color of a mallard duck's underfeathers, and behind her the same thing but different—a woman with black hair riding upon a plum-colored bike—following a road dusted with loose gravel spread in winters past, weaving along undulating mountains that roll the way a dancer rolls her hips as she sprawls, while shadows staggered like eighth notes through the woods, the lake grew calm as cold wax, but the sun yellowed and swelled, and water began to seep from our faces, so we drank long gulps of clear warm water from bottles, not the lake water, deepening to black orchid whenever a castle-sized cloud drifted over, not the mirage of water shivering on baked macadam up ahead, not the salt water plumping up our cells that gives us shape and flow and spirits the mind through soul journeys, but water captured from a spring in Vermont we had never seen, filtered by rocks, as we are filtered by the sights we see, especially the majestic indigo of the lake, the lavender air, and the night-purple convalescing in the forest, as we pedaled into the open where rich growing fields surrender to the sky their perfectly ordered rows of corn, with leaves like ironed green collars and tassels shaking glitter in the uproaring sun—sights we sometimes savored with little comment and a few delicate sips of mind, while at other times wolfing down whole vistas—but we both knew the tonic value of the journey, which fell somewhere between pleasure and hardship, though we are not the sort of people who picnic on pain, or calibrate fun, but we reveled in working ourselves through the landscape, which we discovered tree by tree, farm mile by farm mile, with chicory and Queen Anne's lace bunching in the culverts, pedaling hard though we were steeped in pure exhaustion, pure exhilaration, leading us through the hinterlands where all emotional battles meet and become one tenderness, knowing that faraway behind us in the village of Cooperstown, shops would soon be lifting their awnings, museum doors yawning wide, and the great ladle of enterprise slowly stirring, as the sun rose higher and the town thrummed with a million colorful intrigues, but we were panting and pushing and pedaling and steadily pulling the day up behind us, changing gears, as sunballs of blinding neon raced over the lake, more violet than wet, and we biked toward noon, not thinking of showers, or rest, or grilled orange roughy served on a lakeside veranda where we would later stare in amazement at the lake we'd circled, stretching bright as a spill of mercury under the steadfast sun, but happily lost in a long serenade of mauve water, and the what-will-be somewhere around the bend.

CHAPTER 10

The Orators of August

At the Spiritualists' campground in Freeville, New York, wooden lodges nestle along meandering dirt roadways that lead down to a small chapel in front of a pond. Driving past the Office and the Séance Hall, past a girl riding alone on a bicycle built for two, I park my car by the chapel. Above the door to the white wooden church the words THE TEMPLE OF TRUTH appear in bold letters. Inside, fourteen wooden pews flank a center aisle, their varnished wood shaped into gothic shields at the end of each row. The chapel could hold about forty people, three to each pew, but the twenty present seem ample to fill the room with talk and laughter. Because of the low ceiling and the rows of brown pinstripes running up the cream walls, it feels a little like entering a hatbox, or one of the rooms in a dollhouse. I take a seat at the back, on the aisle, by the door. Two fans turn slowly overhead. On a small stage at the front of the room, next to the wooden pulpit, sits a low table with a glass vase full of carnations, baby's breath, and fern leaves. Store bought, not picked from someone's garden. Also on-stage are two pedal organs and an American flag with a traditional brass eagle atop its pole. A row of half clamshells etched into the glass of two torchère lamps looks more Floridian than New York State. A large painting of Jesus oversees everything from the wall behind the stage. Wearing a pale green toga, he floats against a kingdom of golden clouds. Would he have worn a perfectly folded green toga? A dress code in heaven? I think of Christ as a barefoot preacher. The evening's director—a middle-aged blonde woman—sits in one of two upholstered chairs, chatting with the visiting minister, Reverend Wilson, who leans toward her from the other chair. A white-haired man in his sixties, he has a kind, open face, a squarish jaw, and fair skin that's sunburned from the past week of hot, humid weather.

But where is Louise? I wonder, as I quickly scout the room, starting in the first row and fumbling everyone with my eyes. It's hard to tell much about people from the rear, glimpsing a turned face, catching a piece of conversation, searching someone's body language. Still, I suspect the two young women up front are college students—something about their clothes and gestures. Too young to be Louise, who is in her mid-thirties. Next to them, a chatty seventyish man and woman. Two middle-aged women friends, one of whom looks sad. Could that be Louise? I make a mental note, and go on. A single woman, in her sixties I'd say, joking with an older man and woman. Two middle-aged women seated together, talking intimately about something. One has a round face, her braided hair ends in a white bow near the bottom of her neck, and her eyes flash urgently as she whispers to the other woman, who is auburn-haired with an angular face. I've always pictured Louise with curly, shoulder-length brown hair. Think hard—

did she ever mention her hair color? I don't think so. It might be one of those women. I make another mental note, and go on. An elderly woman wearing glasses. A woman with her middle-aged daughter? For some reason most of the people are wearing either lavender or vivid pink shirts or blouses. Most of the women are heavyset. What size is Louise? When large women get depressed, they usually lament their weight, but I don't recall Louise ever referring to her figure or a diet. A woman in her twenties walks in and sits down beside a mother with a grown, handicapped daughter. At precisely seven o'clock, with twenty people in the pews, the doors close and the service begins. We stand and sing from the hymnal: "He will take care of you, God will take care of you," in a cheerful melody swaying like a porch swing.

Then the minister offers a benediction, inviting "loved ones in the spirit plane to come close to us, that they can bring us words of comfort and joy from their higher realms of existence, spirit teachers to bring words of inspiration, and the unseen healing current which is forever present to touch each and every one of us." The Lord's Prayer follows. Next the director leads the congregation in a recitation of The Declaration of Principles, a pledge of allegiance to Spiritualist precepts. Number five states: "We affirm that communication with the so-called dead is a fact, scientifically proven by the phenomena of Spiritualism." When she sits down, the minister returns, asking us to bow our heads and close our eyes for his guided meditation. In a steady, comforting voice, he says: "Slowly, the unseen healing current will enter our systems, starting at the feet. Feel it flowing into the body, up the legs, along the arms and shoulders... and as we feel the spirit moving up through our neck and head, we know that we are being healed. We *are* being healed. We *are* being healed. We *are* being healed. And each of us has the ability to send forth this healing to others, knowing that *all* things are possible. Send it forth to the person sitting in front of you, who may need your healing this day, to the person on your left who may need spirit this day, to the person behind you who may need physical healing, to the person to the right of you who may need the spirit for reassurance. We send these healing forces forth, knowing that those people are being healed. They *are* being healed. They *are* being healed. And as this healing force gathers inside us, in peace and harmony, we feel it grow stronger, and we send it forth to those who are in institutions, on battlegrounds, in their homes—wherever their need takes us—and we know that *all* things are possible.

"And as I pause for a moment, each of you place into the ether the names of your loved ones who are in need of that healing touch..."

My mother is going in for a medical test on Tuesday. I place her name in the ether. And Paul, trying a new heart medication. And my counselor friend, Ruth, who is getting a biopsy next week. And George, who is starting radiation treatment soon. As well as these dear ones, Louise and SP's callers. I'm not sure I can picture them all at the same time as individuals. Maybe something more abstract. A city of lights? That doesn't work either, so I simplify the image. Back to Mom, Paul, George, Ruth. Trying to hold them simultaneously in my mind's eye, I end up grouping them like statuary. The moment I put in a new figure, I lose sight of one of the others. Concentrating hard, I try again to keep all four clearly in focus at the same time. That just doesn't work, so I picture them one by one instead.

"...and as you send it forth visualize them whole and well, knowing all things are possible. We know that they are being touched by the Holy Spirit and that they are being healed. They *are* being healed. They *are* being healed."

As each person flashes into mind, I see the ill places on their bodies glowing red, and picture a healing yellow light encircling them. What was it that that masseur pictured flowing down his arms into the muscles of his clients? Oh, yes, a green force strengthening them. Nature at its most tonic.

"And finally we send forth our healing throughout the country..."

My friends vanish like holograms.

"...especially to our own beloved United States of America, and as we reach all its individuals they will be touched by this healing current, and the world will be led to peace in our time. And, dear spirit, we ask for a healing of Mother Earth, for we know that all things are possible, *all* things are possible." Possible that politicians will vote to protect the soul of the wilderness instead of the money-making interests of their financial backers? Doubtful. Better to concentrate on healing in the abstract—clean lakes, clean air, rich oceans, deserts where bats and roadrunners thrive, temperate northern woods that look gift-wrapped each autumn, sense-drenching jungles.

"Now as the spirit slowly leaves our body again, flowing down the neck, down the shoulders and arms, down the legs and out the feet, we know that we've been truly touched by the divine force. And let each of us realize in the days to come, if we're in need of a healing touch, we but need to ask and we will receive, for we know that *all* things are possible. This is our healing prayer, in the name of Jesus, the Christ. Amen."

Scanning the room again, I still don't see anyone who might be Louise. While I was on shift this afternoon, she called, and at the sound of her voice I felt worry pour like marbles down my spine and the telephone begin to get sweaty in my hand. She burned with an unbearable psychic pain, and there was no use problem-solving. I just sat and held her suffering for a while, relieved to hear her voice, that she could still speak, still reach out. I want her to call for help, no matter how pitiable or ashamed she may feel, and sometimes, when she hates herself for calling about her self-hatred, I don't know where to enter her emotional house of mirrors. This afternoon she was grave and anguished, a tangle of depression and self-loathing, as her words tumbled out colorfully at times, but also thin as dried leaves. Between her calls, I sometimes forget to worry about her. One of life's castaways, she has survived emotional hurricanes in the past, reinvented herself a hundred times. But the moment we speak, I realize anew how perishable she is.

Is she here tonight? Perhaps she didn't feel up to getting dressed, driving out, staging a public face. Sneaking glances around the room,

I feel uncomfortable; I'd make a lousy spy. Shouldn't I have phoned Cathy and let her talk me out of coming? I'm much too curious and worried to stay away. If I could just *see* Louise, examine the face that harbors the tormented voice, maybe then I could figure out how best to help her. Taking out the hymnal, I turn again to the the Declaration of Principles and reread number four: "We affirm that the existence and personal identity of the individual continue after the change called death." It's always about identity, isn't it? Our callers become their mood, sometimes their history. But not a face, not a stance, not the whole budget of their lives. In Henrik Ibsen's *Peer Gynt,* a man in Purgatory is offered the chance to hover there, a painfree and anonymous soul, avoiding the flames of perdition. But he chooses Hell instead, because there at least he would be able to keep his identity. He'd suffer eternal torture, true, but it would be his own personal torture. For most people, a distinct sense of self is worth any Hell, and longing to keep one's identity forever enhances Spiritualism's appeal. It's hard to believe our dead ones become anonymous dust motes, shards of energy, sifting into the universe at its most elemental level, becoming the leaves of grass, as Whitman imagined, becoming the air we breathe. Some religions take comfort in that ultimate democracy of belonging everywhere to everyone. But Samuel Beckett is right, we're born astride a grave. We own nothing but a name; everything else in our lives we borrow, even hearts. The narrow word "I" is our sole possession, and we guard it fiercely. We prefer to think of the dead with personalities intact, people we can holler to, fight with, or confide in, still nameable on another plane of existence.

Crisis counselors willingly forgo their identity, precious as it is. The letting go is precious, too. Selflessness brings relief from the exhaustions of identity. For a short while, you close up the summer house of the self, toss sheets over the accomplishments, draw the drapes on self-esteem, lock the doors to the relationships, and leave sorrow on the doorstep. Speaking like spirits across the ether, counselors are disembodied voices, invisible guides. Selflessness. Paradise, the goal of several Asiatic religions, may only be reached by way of selflessness, and the abandonment of hope, worry, objects, desires, attachments, a clearly defined self. Not by becoming inert, as in death, but by being alert without striving.

The balm of religion, that great soother of souls, how does it help Louise? I wonder. When depressed, she becomes afflicted with herself. Through guided meditation and prayer, can she achieve a temporary death of the self and some of the pain piercing it? Or is it the opposite—does she believe in the vividly imagined, personal healing Spiritualism promises? For that matter, how much support does Spiritualism provide Louise? Not enough, I think at first, and then correct myself. For all I know, it may be what stands between her and death. Or SP may be. Or her children may be. Or her work. Or her friends. Or her music. Or her garden. Or all of them. I keep forgetting there are no simple answers. Actually, I never forget that, I just keep hoping it might not be true.

The congregation rises to sing "Count Your Blessings." Then Reverend Wilson begins his sermon, "We all have many blessings in our lives..." His is the voice of a down-home southern minister minus the twang, an incantatory, heartfelt, onrushing voice.

"Sometimes we're not sure of those blessings. Sometimes we're a little ill, or things aren't going the way we want them to go, or there are problems in the family, or discouragement in our jobs. Sometimes we do not see the many blessings that we all have in our lives. Today, here on the grounds, I was thinking back over my own life, all the many things that have happened to me, all the really truly blessings that I have truly had. Some of them in the beginning were sad, some of them I couldn't accept or understand at that particular time in my life. But there were times when I was able to find a doorway through which I gained new knowledge and understanding, and I was able to accept conditions and things that happened, and out of that chaos came many good things. It gave me new directions, a new form of life."

My eyes fall on a youngish woman wearing a black cloche hat in the fourth row. I missed her on the first scan of the congregation. If she turns her head, I'll have a better guess at her age. Also a gray-haired woman wearing a string of glass beads. You'd think the minister would be hot in his suit and tie. A navy blue suit, and a cheerful tie splotched with red and blue. A tall man, he grips the front of the pulpit with one hand as he talks, leaning forward as he speaks, loudly, but also intimately.

"Someone who knows me very well asked me one day: How can you say that life is a blessing? Because people who know me know many tragedies in my life—a daughter who is in spirit; a young lady, whom I loved very much, who, two days before we were to be married, was killed in an accident. I know tragedy."

His fianceé died two days before the wedding? How awful. It must have been a gut-wrenching trauma, and yet he speaks of it so calmly. Maybe it was years ago and he has finished mourning. Still. As I think about it, Jack Lewis handles life's tragedies in a similar way, with a combination of candor, deep emotion, and total acceptance. I'm not the only person who finds Jack saintly. I suppose it's easier to embrace life's blows if you believe in a well-meaning God with a plan. Add the word *purpose* to a job description and everything changes.

"But I know that in some way somehow I was able to see a light," the minister continues. "I was able to move toward that light of truth and understand, pick myself up, brush off the dirt, and walk again. Was there a blessing there? I think so in many ways, because I learned to have more compassion for people, I was able to understand people better than ever before. My life was never the same, it's true, but out of tragedy I learned, and I accepted certain conditions—as we all have to going through life. But as I have traveled on that road, I have found the biggest blessing of all has been my religion, my belief in the continuity of life."

Continuity. I say the word slowly in my mind, trying to understand what it must feel like to believe in a heaven where people wear clothes and use up-to-date turns of speech; to believe you are headed for that lifelike place, an invisible village, from which you watch your descendents go about their chores, fall in love, mourn your passing.

Who are Louise's spirits, I wonder. She rarely talks about relatives or friends, but I think both her parents are dead. She wishes her ex-husband were. No siblings. Does she heed the spirits? Does her common sense speak to her in that way, as advice she can attribute to others?

"Spiritualism teaches that healing is forever present.... We can eliminate all the headache pills.... Why not sit down and meditate, and ask for the healing touch to come you? Take a few minutes each day to meditate. You'll be surprised how much better you'll feel...."

Can't go wrong urging people to meditate. Anything that stills the nerves and quiets the radio station in the brain for a while. Especially if the mental airways are filled with complaints from coworkers, appeals from friends, demands from family members, and the miscellaneous static of what if..., if only..., and should have been.

"Look around yourself at the beauty of nature. Take time. Smell the flowers. Because nature, if you watch it closely, has so many answers. Think of the Native Americans, who believe in, who work with nature..."

Oh, dear, not the happy noble savage routine again. Native Americans must get tired of being stereotyped in that way.

"...If we as individuals could follow in their footsteps, we too could have a much more abundant life." Does he really think all of them are leading abundant lives? A lucky few may indeed feel nourished by their relationship with nature, but many are prey to poverty, illness, prejudice, and other civilized miseries.

With that, he holds the congregation's attention for a moment longer, then steps back and sits down, to be replaced at the pulpit by the director, who says, "And now we give thanks to the minister." A man passes around a plate into which people lay dollar bills, nesting them together, while the organ music gently pours. Most seem to be giving between one and five dollars. Not much of a living for an itinerant preacher. The director leads us in "Sweetly Falls the Spirit's Message," a hymn about those on the other side. Then the minister returns to the pulpit.

"Tonight we're going to use flowers for our message service," he says, gesturing to the vase of carnations. "I'm still going to need the sound of your voices so that I can feel the vibrations between the two worlds."

Flowers? Of all the mediums in the country, leave it to me to find one who reads flowers instead of crystal balls. Flowers from the earth with messages from the dead who are blooming in heaven. Strange that they're store-bought flowers, though. In upstate New York, in high summer, the gardens gush with blooms. Wouldn't that make it more interesting, to be reading evening primrose, dahlias, phlox, coriopsis, and hollyhocks—instead of assembly-line carnations?

The minister picks a multiflowered stem from the vase. "I want to go right here," he says, gesturing with his open hand held sideways, so that all the fingers point toward a woman with short curly white hair in the second row.

"God bless you," she says.

Caressing the flower, running his hand along its stem, he says, "I like this flower, the color yellow, as I'm touching here with you, I feel a lot of things. I want to go back a generation and bring a grandmother vibration to you. But I see her as a photograph, I don't think you knew her well on the earthplane. Do you understand that, please?"

"Yes," she says, nodding.

He pinches the stem with thumb and forefinger. "Here I see a little bud, just starting to open, I feel as though that might be a very small baby that wants to come, a miscarriage or stillborn perhaps, but this child is growing on the spirit side of life."

The woman doesn't respond.

"If you can't place the child, that's all right, because spirit sometimes chooses children to send because children are happy people, and spirit wants to bring joy to your vibration." He continues stroking the flower, seeming to touch every cell of it. "And as I'm touching here, your spirit is showing me over on this other side here, see this little opening—I almost feel as though you've been going through a difficult time when things haven't been going along as easy as you'd like, if you understand that. There seems to be a little stumbling block. Do you understand that, without my going into details?"

"Yes, I do," she says, smiling.

"See, there's a new shoot here and everything will be fine. Just be positive. You have a tendency to be negative. I want you to always look on the positive side. The spirit is there and wants to bring comfort and wants to bring change from the spirit side of life. The flowers here along the top are very bright, are very beautiful, and they're very big, and they're already starting to open up for you, which means to me that the cycle of your life is starting to change and you're moving into a much better direction." He pauses a moment, considers the top blossoms. "But you know I have three big flowers up here and I feel as though in the spirit world there are three people who are very close to you on the spirit side of life, who would like to bring greetings to you.

"Yes," she says knowingly.

"I like the color yellow, because yellow is a good spiritual color, and I feel as though you are looking for a more spiritual life, you understand, and if you continue seeking you will find."

"God bless you," she says, as he hands the flower to a helper who delivers it to her to keep.

Picking another flower stem from the vase, he considers it for a moment, then, without looking over the congregation, lifts his eyes suddenly and points with an open hand at the same time.

"I want to go all the way into the back," he says, "that lady there, may I have your voice please?" Is he gesturing to me? He is. What if Louise *is* here and she recognizes my voice? Unlikely. She won't be expecting me.

"Good evening," I say cheerfully in a strong voice. Not the quiet, receptive voice with which I answer the phones.

"Yes, he says," stroking and fumbling the stem, and running his hand over the single flower, "I'm very conscious that a gentleman is coming to us from the world of spirit and this gentleman is moving in a particular vibration—I have two—but the first gentleman I feel I want to be in a grandfatherly way here to you. And the other is a younger man I feel may have lost his life in some sort of mishap."

My heart pounds. I only know two people who have died—my grandfather, and my friend Martin, a pilot who crashed when he was twenty-four. Even though I don't believe in spirits, thinking of Martin makes my eyes water.

"He sends you greetings from the spirit side of life and brings you love," the minister continues, "...and he has a beautiful spiritual growth, he's growing well on the spirit side."

That's what we want, isn't it, to believe loved ones are still vital enough to grow? Growth is the opposite of decay. Hard as it is to think of our loved ones helplessly corrupted, becoming the earth, it's harder still to imagine our own crumbling end. If we don't acknowledge it, maybe it won't be true. If it isn't true for my relatives and friends then it won't have to be true for me. Don't ask, don't tell. "How can I die when I've collected all these beautiful things?" my mother once said wistfully when she was younger. It was horrifying to think of a lifetime spent collecting things—family, friends, wisdom, travel experiences, honors, money, a home, pastimes—all of which simply disappeared. If life just stopped, then what was the point of working so hard, worrying so much, *wanting, needing, wishing, hoping?* In the futuristic film *Blade Runner,* a humanoid goes on a quest to meet his creator and learn the date of his preordained death. While dying, he laments that all the wonders he has seen, the sensations he has felt, the rich life he has lived—all of it will be lost. Such is the tragedy of our existence, we beings who crave life, cherish life, acquire life, spend life. We cling tooth and nail to life, and yet we are a species that dies.

Nothing can resolve that paradox. It's one of the cruel jokes evolution has played on us, right up there with having brains that can imagine states of perfection they cannot achieve. Little can bridge such vast chasms, but we are brave and imaginative, and so we invent a million strategies, defenses, and balms. Sculpture gardens. Family reunions. Courtrooms. Hot air balloons. Wall Street. Proms. Mind-altering drugs. Religions. In-ground swimming pools. Rickety bridges that fail in the end, they lead us on, giving the illusion of safety for a while, especially when we're young. But if the dead are thriving in a parallel world, there's nothing to worry about, and nothing really changes, not even relationships. People who talk openly about death we call "morbid." Life loves life, and it's an erotic affair; to think bluntly about death is considered odd, even ghoulish. Despite that taboo, Sherwin Nuland's book about death, *How We Die,* recently became a bestseller. We love life inexhaustibly, and some of us are inexhaustibly curious about all of it, even its end. How much easier if the borders of life and death are blurred, and an emissary in the form of a medium crosses them for you. That's not much different really from the ancient Greeks believing in Charon, a boatman who crosses the River Styx from life to death, where individuals change shape but continue existing. I don't know why we're so addicted to opposites, why every orthodoxy requires a sense of heresy, and all our finales cry for new beginnings.

"But you know when I look at this stem," he says, "there's a little new growth right here, and I feel that at this particular period in time you are starting on a new venture, in your work or business, you understand that?"

"Yes," I say. There is the new venture of this book.

"I know you're worried about it, but you shouldn't be because look how straight this stem is here..." He holds up the flower with its clear straight stem. "...it branches up here, and there seems to be a new ladder, a new growth for you. And I feel very comfortable with you, because although it's just starting, look how beautifully formed it already is." While stroking the stem lightly but fast, as if to polish the tips of his fingers, he says: "... and I feel that you're interested in spiritual things but you keep the material world important in your life also. You keep that balance within your life."

Turning, stroking, staring at the flower, he seems wholly entranced by it.

"But before I leave your specific vibration, along in here I feel this little bend in this particular flower here." He stops at something I can't see from my pew. "I feel that somebody here on the earthplane is having a little difficulty down through this area here." He gestures across his lower back, the location of the unbearable pain that I had only managed to stop recently by changing a lifelong habit of sleeping on my stomach. It took about six months, and only succeeded because wearing a cast pretty much anchored me to one position, and when I finally taught myself to sleep on my side, the pain stopped.

"... you know who it is—all right. I wish they would do something about that condition..."

It was worth breaking my foot to cure the back pain. Well, maybe not. Must remember to call the chiropractor, once my foot heals, and learn those back exercises he mentioned that involve stretching across a large inflated Swedish ball.

Reverend Wilson relaxes, as if he has finished, then swings into action again. "I see down here on the stem a blip—there seems to have been a little bit of a misunderstanding between you and someone else—do you understand that?—sooner or later that fence will come down and I can't say that the relationship will be the same, but it will be better than it is right now. And I think you should send a force out for healing in this particular area. And God bless you."

"Thank you," I say. His helper brings me the flower, a small yellow carnation tinged with a ruffle of rose-purple. It would be beautiful growing in my garden. I never think to grow carnations; they seem so ordinary. Maybe that's why he has chosen them and not foxglove, monkshood, or some other unusual bloom. Stare at the extraordinary and it bewitches you. Stare at the ordinary and it offers a universe of possibilities. Humans appear alike, just as carnations do, until you look at them closely. Then you discover that one has a certain bend down low, another one a branching out up high, yet another one a curious node right in the middle. They're alike enough to have much in common, but just different enough to keep life interesting. I change my mind: It was a good choice, those store-bought carnations.

Picking another stem out of the vase, he looks immediately at a woman sitting in the third row and to his right. "Two women are coming to you from the spirit world," he says in a conversational trance. "Mom is one of them. But do you know a Lil or a Lilian?"

"Oh, yes, God bless you!" the woman says. She pushes her round glasses up her nose with one finger, as if she might be able to see the spirits better that way.

The minister continues: "She says 'I'm here and I want to be recognized.' She wants to send you greetings from the spirit side of life. I have a gentleman who touches here with you, too, from the world of spirit. I don't know who he is, but I keep hearing 'Claude, Claude's here.'"

The woman smiles and shakes her head, much gladdened and moved.

"...and he wants to send you greetings and say he loves you from the spirit side of life." Turning the flower stem around in his hand, flexing it, holding it up like a piece of crystal, he says, "There's a lot of things happening here, and there are a lot of little branches here. And a beautiful tight little bud up here, and I want to say the road isn't exactly straight right now, but be patient, take your time, and when you come to a crossroad just turn off your thoughts, because you have good people as spirit guides to help you and you'll know which road to go, and it's going to be all right, because I see here good growth all the way up and the tight bud will become a beautiful flower. Do you have a son living?"

"Yes, I do," she says in a concerned voice.

"I see here that there might be something that he wants to go ahead with, as far as work or business is concerned, because I want to say to you that the time isn't quite right here." His fingers travel up the main stem. "If I go up here a little farther I see a very light shade of green up here, and it gets better, and I feel if he can just weather the storm he'll go ahead toward strength and he'll be much more successful."

"All right," she says. "I'll tell him."

"But you know, before I leave you, I keep seeing a gentleman walking in front of me, walking back and forth, and he wants to be recognized and he won't stop. I don't know who he is, but he had something to do with the military before he went into spirit because the flags are at half mast, and he wants to bring you greetings in that particular way. I don't know if he was killed in the service, but there was some sort of military funeral because the flag was there." He searches her face for confirmation.

"I understand," she says.

"Hey, stop that," he says, laughing, to some invisible being at his side. Then, to the woman, he says: "There's a little boy who wants to keep coming here, and he keeps pulling on my trousers here, I feel his presence here and I feel he just wants to raise the devil. I think you feel his presence around you on the earthplane."

She nods.

"He says to tell you that he pulled the puppy's tail," the minister says, with an I-don't-know-what-this-means inflection. "Do you understand that?"

She nods and laughs, says, "God bless you. Thank you." The helper gives her her flower.

Next he picks up a large stem, studies it for a moment, remarking on how complex it is, gestures to the woman in the black cloche hat at the side of the room, who says, "Yes, God bless you."

"I have a gentleman here whom I'm very conscious of and I have to ask you a question: Did your father leave this world sort of quickly?"

"Yes," she says quietly, with a catch in her voice, "he did." A shiver runs across my neck. I know that voice. Moving a little to the left, I can see her more clearly: a pleasant face with brown eyes, straight bangs, strong nose, small mole to the left of her upper lip, and a look of tense belief.

"Okay, because this is the gentleman I have here. He was here one minute and he left all of a sudden into the spirit world and he wanted to talk here to you. But, you know, as I look at this flower I see a lot of things—over here is new growth, here is a beautiful new stem here, and down here I want to say there are a lot of things progressing down here in your vibration in a material sense, and I feel good about that, even though I feel right now you're closed to it—do you understand that?"

I drop my eyes and listen for her answer. "Yes, I do," she says. It is Louise, I'm sure of it. I'd know that soprano, slightly sandy voice anywhere. But this is the first time I've heard her speaking in a relaxed register. How did she rally enough to drive out here, walk in, be so composed?

"... but over here there's a lot growth possible, and I want to say: Go for it! Because everything will be there when you need it. You know, as I touch this stem here, this little bend in it, I feel as if you're going through a period of time right now when you're down, when you get a little bit depressed..."

A *little* bit?

"...because of the conditions around and about you—do you understand?"

"Yes," she says.

"...but I'm going up this stem, and there's all new growth here..." He holds it up to her, as if she could see the green force that he sees. Does she? "...which assures me that the depression is going to be behind you. So just look at the positive. And I want to say that this bud here is tight, and even though you're feeling tight right now, I want to take a load off of your shoulders—do you understand that?—because I can't see the spirit entity talking right now but the spirit is saying

'Don't blame yourself.' I don't know what the spirit's talking about, but whatever it is, don't blame yourself. And I feel good because these are all new beginnings. So when you're looking at the bad, just look at things in a good positive way and that will build a positive future here for you."

See the bright side? Don't blame yourself? Heaven knows, people have tried that with Louise and it didn't work. Does she listen differently to this minister than she does to SP's counselors or to her friends? If so, where does the difference lie?

"...And I want to say that there's a lot of spirituality within you; you have a lot of good thoughts you want to send out to other individuals on this plane, which makes you a very spiritual being. God bless you."

"Thank you," she says, and receives her carnation, touching it lightly to her nose. I do the same with mine. No scent.

For the next hour, the minister continues giving messages until he has criss-crossed the room and spoken to everyone. "I think I want to be with the lady back there," he says at one point, "but let me ask you a question first: Is there a grandma in spirit? And she didn't walk well? I wasn't sure if it was you because I wasn't sure if the light was falling on you or on the woman behind you." I look at the two women. Neither is sitting in visible light.

At last he finishes, exhausted, which doesn't surprise me, since everyone in the congregation is exhausted just from listening hard for so long. It was interesting how he used flowers to prompt each person's reading—like peering at tea leaves, I suppose—and felt that the spirit led his hand to the flower meant for each person. All the messages were healing, uplifting, encouraging, though he was a little tougher with the two men, admonishing one not to be so stubborn, and the other to keep a better eye on his health.

As the service closes with a benediction, he reminds all not to expect full sentences, or even coherent words from beyond the grave, because the dead "will communicate with us, if we seek them, through any of our senses, through touch, smell, vision, hearing, any of the senses, not just through words." The organist plays. As people leave the chapel, Louise passes close by me. She's a little shorter than I imagined, her hair darker and straight, her eyes brown not hazel, and her skin looks burnished. Perhaps from gardening. She often talks about how much pleasure she finds in gardening. I didn't expect her to look quite so intact, though she does seem distracted, trapped somewhere inside herself, as she walks out into the failing light. All right, I've seen her. Now what? I rise and follow. It would be easy enough to introduce myself as a neighbor, say we met at the summer festival or at some other local gathering. Then what? Befriend her? Offer her more intensive support? That wouldn't be fair to her. She has the right to make her own destiny, to call for a counselor's help when she needs to and on her own terms. I know she already has friends in whom she confides. She only seeks help from us when her mood becomes extreme, too extreme to impose on friends, or to handle alone. What if I discovered I couldn't help her any more than I already do? Worse yet, what if my friendship added to her problems? What if she became dependent on me and I felt responsible for her life? Here she is, upright, coping, attending church from which, presumably, she absorbs something valuable. At the moment, she seems to be all right. When she doesn't feel that way, she'll phone. I hope. Or is it cowardice on my part, not to become entangled in her troubles? Quite a few of SP's counselors become therapists, and I've often wondered if that estimable trade doesn't tend to attract people who crave deep intimacy without the usual risks. I remember a counselor friend (who went on to get an MSW) confiding how much she liked the limited intimacy of SP work. In most situations, becoming intimate must lead somewhere—to dinner, or an evolving friendship. On the phones, the intimacy is profound but also temporary, it doesn't become complicated or expanded. Being an anonymous caregiver has clear advantages. There are one-way mirrors to peer through, thick walls of silence to hide behind, changing roles to play, a hundred masks to wear. But something else, more disturbing, occurs to me. Maybe I need to think about whose pain I'm really trying to ease. What right do I have to intrude in her life, just because her suffering is hard for *me* to bear? At the moment, she's handling her pain remarkably well. I'm the one who isn't. Nonetheless, I hate leaving her. My instinct is to try everything when someone dear to me is suffering. Has she become that dear to me over the past years? I guess so, though I've never met her, seen her but once, and only ever heard her in the death grip of depression. Even within those limits, you can get to know someone, respect them, cheer their triumphs, lament their hardships, hope for their success. Walking in an awkward stroll, as if her pockets were unevenly balanced with fieldstones, Louise meanders along the gravel path. I am walking unevenly, too, since the ball of my foot still hurts with each step, which means thinking about walking too much to be able to do it well. The stones remind me of how Virginia Woolf committed suicide: by filling her pockets with stones and strolling into a river. In the parking lot, I pass a white Dodge "Spirit" with a license plate that reads: I 4 C. Below it a bumper sticker says: PROTECTED BY ANGELS. Thank heavens, someone has a sense of humor. A carnival of tree frogs, leopard frogs, pickerel frogs, toads, and crickets have been filling the air with plucks, snores, rattles, pops, rasps, and moans. Night is falling so fast it's hard to tell where ground ends and sky begins. As I drive away, I watch Louise grow smaller in the rearview mirror, then vanish suddenly as she steps between shadows.

CHAPTER 11

The World Unwound

A flutter of wings and a struggle catches my eye. At the end of the yard, where mown grass meets woods, a hawk swoops down, grabs a chipmunk from atop the metal fence, throttles it in midair, and dashes it on the ground. "Unbelievable," I say to myself, to the squirrels, the hawk, the chipmunk, the wilderness. I can see the hawk clearly—a beautiful, regal, voracious, brown-and-white speckled head with a rounded chest of sable feathers. The stuff that shields and coats of arms are adorned with. For a moment it sits still, choking the life from its prey, then it lifts off in a great upsweeping, a slow-motion flutter silent as snowfall. A hawk in the backyard. All one needs is a small piece of wilderness—two acres of woodland will do—and it becomes an ark for deer, skunks, hummingbirds, raccoons, and so many other forms of biomischief.

Both the hawk and the chipmunk are caught in the talons of a crisis—one flailing against hunger, the other fighting a disemboweling death. Humans rarely intervene in such dramas. We find the life-and-death catastrophes of other animals natural, acceptable, not to be intruded upon, even a form of beauty. Allowing animals to abide by the laws of nature, however cruel, we even claim it would be unethical to interfere, since nature is holy, in a sacred balance, and must be left to its own themes and unravelings. People used to swear that animals don't suffer, but now we recognize that lie for what it is, one of the many lies we tell ourselves out of emotional laziness. It's exhausting enough to feel for other humans, the unspoken logic goes; where will it end if we have to feel for animals, too? But in our hearts, we know we are all in the same breathless fix, all part of a bona fide struggle to stay alive and raise families. All balancing on a knife blade. From whales to gray squirrels, animals face crises similar to our own, propelled by the same basic motives and hungers. I ache for them. I would not have them suffer. When I look outside, I see a kingdom of neighbors, and yet we live in a moral twilight about animals. We find all of their behaviors—including violence—poignant and beautiful. Narcissistic and curious, we stare into the well of their familiar ways. Teach us about ourselves, we pray. And they do, allowing us a deeper look into life's cluttered attic, where we hope to discover antiques, objects of wonder, and, ultimately, a fuller portrait of life on Earth.

Although a thin line trembles between fascination and disgust, I know it is the nature of a hawk to kill a chipmunk. If hawks met to decide on codes of ethics, they would regard killing chipmunks as morally good. Thinking again in horror of the woman who shed her life by feeding herself to lions at the National Zoo, I still do not blame the lions, driven by instinct to maul and feed. But I could no more have witnessed that butchery than watched two human beings fighting to the death. Neither drama would fill me with a sense of privilege at beholding a natural spectacle—even though I respect the ways of the lion, and I know it is partly the nature of humans to kill.

When humans enter the life-and-death equation, we revise our moral code. Human suffering seems alien and unbearable, as does death, fear, anxiety, illness, sorrow, or prolonged pain. We fight those torments with a formidable arsenal of wits and compassion. Human crises are frightening, and we try to avert or resolve them. Appalled by their disruptive vigor, we label them bizarre, catastrophic, or insane. But when animals' lives unfold from crisis to crisis, we accept it as healthy. Our own sagas, catastrophes, and triumphs stand out against a backdrop of the acceptable crises of nature. Why do we apply different standards to ourselves? Perhaps because we are a renegade species that has evolved beyond its genes. No other animal I can think of refuses to be bullied by its biology, insists on suppressing some instincts and amplifying others, and worships choice. We are dancing a dangerous and thrilling tango with evolution, in which we sometimes lead, sometimes follow. Our desires have evolved faster than our bodies, our ideas outrace our genes. So it is also our nature to act fairly, mourn for those we kill, empathize with other life forms, "forget" where our meats come from lest we feel like murderers, suffer guilt over real and imaginary crimes, make sacrifices for strangers, admire the strong and handsome, but also cherish kind hearts, altruists, and saviors. Life may be short, unjust, and end badly; but we fight back by becoming the opposite: nurturing, generous, fair, forgiving, kind. One of the most popular bumper stickers of all time proclaims *Practice random acts of kindness and senseless beauty.* Those efforts may grease the wheels of society, as anthropologists argue, but they also enoble us, and that gives us power. Through compassionate altruism, we defy the harsh laws of nature and become benign gods to one another, or at least benign stepparents. It is the most we can manage, being responsible to and for other humans, and for nature in general, especially if we refer to its eternally pregnant and rotund source as a simple and loving entity—a human mother, whose good breasts dispense "the milk of human kindness." Occasionally, we also feel responsible for specific animals. Saving every whale, bat, and dingo is beyond the means of most people, although I do know some valiant naturalists who try.

Nature neither gives nor expects mercy, and yet we strive to be moral, compassionate, seemly. One of the major ways in which we differ from other animals, indeed part of our signature, is that we suffer the pains of others as if they were our own. We are compassionate beasts. Of course, as the many wars now in progress declare, we are also brutal, territorial, fiercely competitive, selfish, sadistic, easily frustrated, and given to violence. These extreme contradictions fascinate me. How can we possibly balance the two sides of our nature?

Animals are always busy living. It's only humans who wander the world like outcasts, feeling lonely much of the time, wondering what they're here for. Part of our sense of isolation and emotional hunger comes from having exiled ourselves from nature. We evolved to live in extended families, cued to seasonal time, part of a living fabric. We evolved to play meaningful roles in a social group. Much of that impetus we have lost, and the absence disturbs us. Something unnameable is missing from our lives. There is a hollowness at the center of society. We search for meaning, purpose, a sense of belonging. We battle boredom and loneliness. We evolved to fit intricately into nature and family. Alas, we also evolved to be violent and territorial. This combination produces a terrible sense of alienation, people at war with themselves, at war with the world. Looking at human behavior from a wider perspective is not just part of an emerging Zeitgeist—I believe it is one of the things our age will be known for. Searching for a spiritual, holistic view of life to embrace as a secular religion, people hunger for the revelations, tenets, and wisdom of an earth ecstasy older than culture or civilization, whose values sleep in our memory.

—

No squirrels have shown up at the feeding station this morning. Their living larder is full of black walnuts, mock hickories, corn, seeds, and other delicacies—why bother with handouts? They don't seem to have noticed the death-dealing hawk, or they don't care. While drinking my morning tea, I watch them cavort in the yard, paying special attention to their best-known feature. Few things in nature are as marvelous as a squirrel's tail. Or as transformable. Almost half the squirrel's body length, it's an all-purpose appendage: a balance pole, a scarf on cold days, a semaphore flag. Squirrels can sit in their own shade. Indeed, the name "squirrel" comes from the Latin for "shadow tail." When marking its neighborhood, a squirrel flicks its tail in an arpeggio of twitches, then moves a few feet up the tree trunk or along the branch and marks again. Sometimes, in strong winds, squirrels' tails blow forward over their foreheads and they look like balding men who have combed their hair all to one side only to find it blown straight up in a breeze. It's amazing the way a squirrel can clasp itself on the back with its tail, embrace and comfort itself. Humans do that, too—hug themselves when they need nurturing and no one is around—and sometimes people rock back and forth in that pose, as if their arms belonged to another who was happy to cradle and soothe them. When it rains, squirrels fold their tails up over their heads as umbrellas. As they sit and eat, they settle deep onto their haunches and throw their tails over their backs like scarves to keep themselves warm. Tails are cozy as sweaters—the squirrels can wrap up in them when cold or lay them aside when warm, or wrap them around small offspring.

It's a cool morning for biking, so I toss a pair of gloves and a face mask into my kit, and pull on a windbreaker over my sweater. For a change, I take my favorite bike route in reverse, starting with a long gradual climb beside a cornfield where someone has installed a dozen bluebird houses. As I approach Freese Road, I hear a clear *meep, meep,*

meep, meep, meep. Not a complex or wiry sound. Hawk, my mind says. Another hawk! Again the call. Tracing the sound to the woods across the road, I see a large fawn-breasted hawk sitting on a branch. Stretching its wings overhead, it tilts them like a parasol, then flaps away, helloing as it planes low over the cornfield, circling once before it flies off. Two hawks return its call. Three hawks in so small an area is a treat, and one in the backyard astonishing as a benediction. But it is migration season, and the sky is full of red-tails.

Going downhill, I use all my high gears, the wind snarls around my helmet, and my speedometer reads 25 mph. I like that combination of speed and control. In high gear, you move fast but can still pedal and feel the bike securely in hand. The corn tassels, glistening tawny gold, shine against a blue sky and the encampment of clouds on the horizon. Some trees have begun to color, but most surge with the shadowy green one finds in Goya's paintings. Yellow butterflies barnstorm the meadows, now thick with goldenrod, ragweed, chickory, Queen Anne's lace, and other wildflowers. Must remember to gather dry milkweed pods for my mother. When I was a teenager in Pennsylvania, she filled our autumn house with milkweed pods spilling their silken parachutes. Now that my parents live in Florida, Mother misses the change of seasons. I'll send her milkweed in a box filled with wax-covered fall leaves. Even riding fast, I can smell wood smoke, apples, and mown grass. It's warm in the sun, but chilly whenever I enter a tunnel of tree shade—in short, a typical fall morning.

Today I pass a dead deer beside the road at the cornfield, a dead squirrel at the Varna bridge, a dead bird beside the goldfinch woods. That visual litany of car-crushed animals produces a shiver. A thug-like fright slams through my mind at intervals: what a sudden impact—as of a car hitting me—would feel like. Not a fantasy exactly, more an hallucinated supposition, it feels real and frightening nonetheless. I can sense the impact. Quickly, I chase the image out of my mind and rebuke myself for such perverse and masochistic thoughts.

Funny how the mind teases and taunts, and how ashamed we are to let others know. Last night, though, embarrassing thoughts spilled freely at my support group meeting. A mainstay of SP are its four support groups, each led by a local therapist. No one is obliged to attend, but it's strongly encouraged, and most counselors enjoy the chance to share problems and explore agency matters. Thirteen people showed up for last night's meeting, held at the office, where we sat around a conference table laden with fresh grapes, apple cider, and cookies. Someone had painted the dingy walls a fresh green, flecked with sedgelike filaments of paler green—another dream field to match the one upstairs.

"Did anyone have any interesting calls this month?" Bea Goldman asked to get the ball rolling. An attractive divorceé who divides her time between working with sexual abuse victims at a facility in a nearby town and a clinical practice locally, Bea was an SP counselor for years, and then crisis-line coordinator, before she decided to return to graduate school for an MSW. As support group leader, she brings an energy and candor that's much appreciated. Each group has its own personality. Attendance is casual. In mine, eight to fifteen people usually show up, and they range in age from twenty-four to eighty-three, with varied backgrounds and sensibilities. Some are quiet, some outspoken, some practical, some feisty, some wealthy, some low income, some just out of training, some who have been counseling for years. Some have only finished high school, and others have many letters after their names, but no one waves credentials. The mix worked exceptionally well last night. Joyce began by revealing how frustrating she finds talking with one frequent caller, a highly intelligent man who is impulsive and manipulative and prey to large mood swings. Maggie chimed in that she gave that caller time limits, and politely but firmly ended calls after fifteen minutes. Joyce confessed, in an exasperated tone, that the last time she spoke with the caller they ended up quarreling. As usual, the caller demanded that Joyce praise him by using certain quirky and colorful phrases, echo his ideas and feelings, and swear to be his friend. When Joyce said she wasn't comfortable saying such things, the caller became adversarial, blaming Joyce one moment, criticizing her the next. Inevitably, such a call ends badly, with the caller peeved and the counselor feeling foolish. "He really knew how to push my buttons," Joyce sighed. Across the room, a long-time counselor got angry: "Look," Vicky said, "I never let him dictate to me or browbeat me. That's how he manipulates everyone he knows. They feel as horrible about it as I do, and they ultimately dump him. Then he starts drinking and gets depressed. That's his life story. I think it just makes him worse when we encourage that kind of behavior. He's always depressed or angry about losing friends. I think we should help him see that his demands aren't reasonable, and try to explore with him how his actions drive people away."

"Yes, but that's a therapist's job," Marty said.

"You bet it is," Vicky said with conviction, "and I don't mind doing it a bit." People frowned.

It's hard to know how best to handle a manipulative and angry caller. Sharing techniques that have worked, or potential blind alleys, are always useful. But more important is the mutual wringing of hands. A sense of inadequacy can grow fast in the hidden caverns of self-doubt, and it helps to know others are equally stymied. From that caller we went on to several others, which led to mulling over the role and limits of being a counselor. I could feel the tension, even anger, when some callers were discussed. Three counselors—all of them senior—confessed to a sinful secret. At one time or another, in the midst of a marathon, rambling, circling call from a frequent caller who was monologuing, they were tempted to use a free line to dial SP, so that the caller would hear the second crisis line ringing. Then, of course, it would be easier to insist "I *have* to go now. Please call back another time." I was glad they revealed how tough it was, even after years of experience, always to be in control of a call. This was a good meeting because some of the counselors were able to voice dark feelings—

anger, frustration, hostility—that sometimes arose during especially tough calls. If they weren't able to do that, they would burn out fast. A couple of the counselors confessed that they've done a write-up before the call ended, while the caller was rehashing an all-too-familiar story. Robert suggested in a friendly tone that a better alternative might be to engage the caller in a way that reflected that he or she was obsessing, point out that they had covered the same territory repeatedly without getting anywhere or it seeming to help, and then end the call. Robert's tone was friendly, but his content was critical, and it stung. Of course, he was right; counselors shouldn't be lazy or space out. But a frequent caller who phones to rant about life or harangue the counselor, who obsesses over a few details, wants to stay on the line for an hour doing so, and calls four times a day, can test your patience and good will. You can end up dreading calls from certain people. You can wind up being critical of the very people you pledge to help. These are shameful secrets, almost never mentioned. In training, counselors learn to be long-suffering, sympathetic, good at bracketing their troubles, wholly nonjudgmental, able to picture themselves in the caller's shoes, paragons of compassion. Putting those ideals into practice isn't always easy, and counselors can feel horribly guilty if they nod. Each of us has days when we're convinced that every other counselor is more capable, talented, virtuous, and sincere. So it really was good to ventilate dark feelings. They rarely get voiced. On the other hand, we talk openly about burnout.

Calls can sometimes last two or three hours and become very emotional. Then you've done what you can do, maybe sent rescue after a hair-raising near miss, maybe resolved a traumatic problem for the time being. It's late at night, you haven't been to bed, and when you hang up you're totally wrung out, brutally exhausted, drooping in the chair. The phone rings. You pick it up and you hear sobs, and you think: *Oh, no! Here we go again! I'm not ready for this!* New counselors start fired up, full of the warmth of human kindness, powerfully focused, a steady flame of altruism. But, regardless of their good will, they can exhaust themselves. The match of their kindness, which flares hot and colorfully at first, can burn out, leaving only stale smoke and the scent of phosphorus behind. It has taken me years to understand that such feelings are normal in such a high-stress job, not signs of weakness or bad character, but only too human.

Some disquiets are predictable, though still a surprise when they happen. For example, one of our most frequent, and at times irritating, callers abruptly disappeared. We haven't heard from her for six months, though we know she was calling other services closer to where she lived, and that she planned a move from New Jersey to Texas. Yet I find myself worrying about her from time to time. Toward the end, I didn't relish her calls, which could be abrasive, racist, blaming, circular. A "yes, but"-er, she frustrated many counselors, and had the bad habit, whenever a counselor finally tried to end the call, of suddenly saying she was suicidal—though she wasn't—just to keep the counselor on the line. Hers was a sad case for many reasons, and I felt great sorrow and compassion for her, although I didn't like her as a person. Now I'm amazed to find myself worrying about her. Not knowing what eventually happens to callers nags at us, especially if someone calls only once with a grievous problem. That sense of incomplete connection, of having to accept that your concern will be truncated and unresolved, hurts like crazy—so we discussed it last night.

We also considered, yet again, if the agency's name should be changed, perhaps to something simple like "Lifeline," or "Crisis Service," which is how many of the counselors answer the phone. My support group feels strongly about this issue, and counselors often bring in new accounts of people in trouble they urged to phone SP, who countered with, "My god, I couldn't call a place with *suicide* in its name! I'm not suicidal." "It's a crisis service," we tell people, "you don't have to feel suicidal to use it." But many people feel ashamed of calling with less-than-suicidal problems, or feel guilty burdening suicide counselors with more general calls. Or they aren't ready to face how seriously depressed they are. Or they feel being identified with suicide, even a suicide hotline, means admitting to total powerlessness and lack of self-control. Or they think of suicidal people as crazy, whereas they feel sane but temporarily troubled. Or they are superstitious about putting themselves in the category of possible suicides. They don't know that only a small percentage of our calls are actually related to suicide.

A good support group session, that. We all let off steam, picked up some tips, socialized, and shared secret fears and misgivings. With any luck, these monthly meetings will help us avoid burnout. But it's hard to know. Although the turnover rate is high, with about two years being the average length of service, people leave for many reasons. New jobs take them away; school ends; they need to work full time; their families require more from them; illness saps their strength; personal problems begin to mortgage their spare time; their own struggles with mental illness intrude; they get bored; yes, they burn out.

At last I reach The Plantations and bike across the raised wooden boardwalk out to the pergola in the middle of a lily pad-thick lake. A hundred mallards rest and sleep on shore. One male tucks his head into the feather pillow of his back, where purple chevrons flash in the sunlight. What looks like a white eggcup rolls up over his eye: pulling down the shades, he goes to sleep. A roller-blader skates by using cross-country ski poles, and the clattery noise wakes the male duck. When two more males join him, the three stand beside the pond like gents at a urinal, looking straight ahead as they casually quack-chatter. One by one, they dip their bills into the water, ladle up a bit of its rich broth, tilt their heads up, and swallow. Occasionally they preen, sometimes removing breast feathers. Then they settle down and snooze.

I love watching animals fall asleep. A duck begins to breathe more deeply, its back feet sprawl behind it like still paddleboat wheels, it nuzzles its bill into its breast feathers, its eyes close, its tail twitches and settles, and it becomes a feathered bellows as its whole body slips into a thick heavy breathing. If a preening neighbor accidentally wakes it, it stretches out one back leg in a body yawn, swallows a few times with its eyes closed, and sinks back asleep.

The lake looks oil-painting luminous today, reflecting the trees and sky, filled with lily pads and ducks and perfect white wakes trailing behind them in the many-greened water. What stillness—the living mirror of the pond, the quiet broken only by a few duck calls and the occasional sparrow. One duck stands on an orange leg, holding the other in a tai chi pose, then switches feet. Now and then a duck will call out in a loud frantic kazoo of three to seven notes. Quiet falls again. I say quiet, though the air burbles with noise, and below the surface of the water minuscule life-and-death dramas are playing themselves out.

My odometer reads 320 miles. Not bad for one month. Most of those miles I've added on weekend bike trips with Cathy. Where should we bike to this weekend? Last Saturday, we drove over to Watkins Glen, half an hour away. There we began at the State Park and biked uphill along Lake Seneca until we entered the wineries country. Miles of grapevines were strung out on wires like martyrs. Still heavily hung with grapes—beautiful, late-fruiting Concords— they saturated the air with perfume. It was like biking through pure grape juice. Plucking a grape from a vine, I closed my eyes and in- haled its deep rich scent. Then I popped it into my mouth and crunched through tight skin to the clotted pulp and seeds, which felt separate from the skin. So sweet. Using a bike tour map, we continued on to the hamlet of Logan, then Burdett, and finally down a long steep hill back into Watkins Glenn. As we traveled through the wineries, I was reminded how often beauty emerges from twisted, tortured- looking plants. True for grapevines and apple trees. Also for frankin- cense bushes, which grow rattled, wind-ravaged, sand-scarred, and yet sweet incense pours from their veins. For some reason, I thought of Van Gogh at that moment, his gnarled mind and his life contorted by woe. That's what we talked about for a while as we pedaled past a dozen small waterfalls and endless scenic vistas—the beauty that can spring from troubled limbs.

We also talked about Cathy's work, and mine, and her childhood, and mine, and her relationships, and mine. For this trip she packed cheddar cheese, slices of sourdough bread, marzipan-filled croissants, leftover Halloween candy, carrot sticks, and two apples. I packed V8s, grapes, Cheshire cheese, biscotti, and hummus. So, between us, as ever, we had a feast.

Thinking of food makes me hungry, and I head back home for a snack and shower before I go on shift.

—

Stepping carefully—more out of superstition than caution—I climb slowly toward the counselor room, up stairs whose varnish reminds me of the resin I used to drag over the catgut strings of my violin when I was in junior high school. I loved its sweet smell, amber luminosity, and thick sticky feel. The creaking wood announces me, which is probably why I find Bob already packing up. Lifting a hand in greeting, he says, "Hey, babe, howsit hanging'?"

I can't quite picture this anatomically. "It doesn't hang on girls. Didn't your dad teach you that?" I set my satchel down on the desk.

"Now there you go again, puttin' the shuck on me," he says in a Ronald Reagan parody, as he tightly rolls an issue of *Psychology Today* and fits it into his knapsack. Giant hands. I always forget how big they are until I actually see them handling objects. I bet he could touch fingers around a cantaloupe.

"*Shuck?* Are we talking about about safe sex or cornstalks... or both?" I ask, sitting Indian style on the daybed. The coverlet is wrinkled from where a body lay, and it reminds me of a poem by W.H. Auden, part of which runs:

> Who goes with who
> The bedclothes say

As I and you
Go kissed away,
The data given,
The senses even...

"Ha!" Bob says formally as he tosses his head. "Hey, I bought a new dog yesterday." He pulls three Polaroids from his kit and hands them to me with all the zest of a new parent. Not only are the photos poorly composed and slightly out of focus, but the dog is hideous, hideous in a way I didn't think was possible for dogs. Its head is square and blunt, its short legs too thin for the shape of its body, and it looks slightly porcine.

"Oh, what kind is it?" I ask cheerfully.

"It's a mongrel—part French poodle, part pit bull."

"That's an unusual combination." Fortunately, he takes this as a compliment. I hand the photos back to him, and he puts them away.

"Yeah," he says, hoisting the knapsack onto his shoulder as he heads through the door. Then, poking his head back into the room, he adds: "Not much of a guard dog, but it's a *vicious* gossip."

With that he jogs heavily down the creaking steps, and a few seconds later strides through the front door, the glass rattling as it slams. On the Hot Sheet today, a counselor offers advice about a recent caller, who just needs a sympatic ear, not efforts at problem-solving. Her life is in such disarray that counselors sometimes are tempted to tell her what to do, what *they'd* do in her place. The Hot Sheet advises: "Make supportive little mewling sounds...in fact, anytime you are tempted to make a suggestion, make a supportive sound instead." Good advice, but hard to follow when you desperately want to wave a magic wand and fix things for someone, even if you can't know what will work in the caller's life, and the caller isn't ready to take action anyway.

5:32 P.M. A thirteen-year-old boy calls to talk about how his father, drunk and out of work, has been beating him and his little sister. A thick blanket of guilt spreads over everything he says. He keeps returning to how he must deserve the beatings, must be doing something terribly wrong. Victims of abuse so often feel guilty, as if somehow they provoked their harsh treatment. They grow up thinking there is something organically wrong with them—a character flaw, a savage evil, an unpardonable sin both absolute and undefined—not that something is wrong with their abuser. As the boy talks, his hurt resonates in my memory, but I don't wallow in the feeling. I touch my own experience in passing, the way a baseball player touches a base as he is running, and focus hard on the boy's predicament until I am sure he is safe, feels heard-out, and has a plan of action. After we hang up, I spend a few minutes taking stock of the call, and making peace with my helplessness.

"God, I hope he's all right," I say to the walls, as I file my write-up.

6:00 P.M. An elderly man calls because he is feeling flustered about a social situation. A college student has sort of adopted him, has dinner with him every few weeks, and generally seems to be keeping an eye on him. Last year, the student took him to the Syracuse Fair, which he enjoyed, and this year the student called to invite him there again. But he has a bruised hip and doesn't feel up to it. He's worried that the student may already have bought the ticket and will be out of pocket. He can't figure out what to say. I ask him to get out a pencil and paper and I help him write down a little speech in his own words: "I'm calling because I was thinking about you. I wish I could go to the fair with you, but I'm afraid I'm not feeling well enough. But I'm concerned that you might have already bought the tickets, and I don't want you to be out of pocket. If you have, let me know how much mine was and I'll give you the money for it. Give me a call back to let me know, would you? And we can choose a day next week when you might come over for dinner."

It seems just right to him—concerned and grandfatherly—and he sounds clearly relieved. I can hear his breathing become more regular and his panic retreating. He says he is going to call right away and leave the message on the student's answering machine. Knowing how flustered some elderly people can get, I feel good helping him in so straightforward a way.

6:23 P.M. A powerfully angry woman calls to tell of her frustration, disappointment, and sense of betrayal. Like bold, heavily saturated pigments, her emotions are easy to identify. She knows what they are, why she's feeling them. One year ago she married a widower with a sixteen-year-old daughter. It was a second marriage for her as well, and she desperately wanted it to work. But soon after she moved in, to her horror she discovered that she was entering a household that, in effect, already included two longtime spouses. Father and daughter had rigid, well-established roles, and there was no room for her in that equation. The daughter ruled the house and battled her new step-mother. When the daughter informed her that she intended to skip school for a few days to go to a rock festival in a nearby state, the caller told her that was out of the question. Volatile and disrespectful, the girl had a temper tantrum and hit her hard, then went crying to her father, who agreed to give her a note for school saying she was sick. When the caller complained to her husband about the girl's violence, he said the caller must have provoked it. Constantly in trouble at school, the girl was known for her truancy, fist fights, and disrespect to teachers. Guidance counselors begged the parents to exercise discipline, and also to enter family counseling with their daughter. But the girl swore she was innocent of all accusations, and her father took her side. Now she tyrannizes her stepmother whenever her father is at work. Abusive, violent, she grows more dangerous each day. When the caller reports such events to her husband, he says she's making them up out of jealousy. Then he yells at her and threatens to divorce her if she doesn't stop "causing trouble." She wants the marriage to work, but she's also in a precarious position financially. They live in her house, paying off a large mortgage. Her husband doesn't make much, and he quickly depleted her savings. Uneducated and untrained, where is a woman in her fifties going to find a job? she asks fiercely.

In many ways, this is a simple call: a woman in the last desperate at-tempts to save a marriage before an inevitable divorce. Bursting with anger, she talks fast, articulately, and only needs a sympathetic lis-tener for most of the call. We even do some problem-solving, and come up with a few possible strategies she might use for bridling the daughter. When she off-handedly mentions suicide, I suggest we con-sider some other, less extreme options. We discuss divorce, agencies such as Displaced Homemakers, who could help and advise her, and various plans that, while they aren't wholly desirable, would at least give her some element of control.

The call, which lasts for over an hour, is a good one. The woman sounds a little calmer and less frantic when we hang up. But some-thing curious happened. My empathy for her was so great that her rampaging anger, upset, and frustration transferred to me. I took on her suffering, which reverberates throughout my body. Like an emotional lightning conductor, I'm trembling with anger. I feel an irrational urge to grip metal or stick my finger in a light socket to discharge the violent energy surging through me. Although I man-aged to exorcise some of her demons, I absorbed them. My sharing her distress lightened her burden a little and made mine heavier. In sympathy, one receives the caller with compassion and concern. In empathy, one enters the caller's emotional dwelling. If that world is a vortex of pain, and you go in too far, you can lose your footing and ache all over. For hours I stay tense and agitated from borrowed grief.

At last it occurs to me to try jogging in place. Maybe I can exhaust the anger, sweat it out. That does help a little, but not enough. Sitting on the couch, I try meditating. Broiling summer sun. Sandy beach. Gray Arabian mare. I'm riding bareback in the surf, cantering slowly. Smell the ocean air. The brisk winds carry thick aromas of salt, sea-weed, decaying fish. Hear hooves splashing in the surf, while gulls whine overhead. Feel the sun on my shoulders, and the mare's heart beating along my naked legs.

When the phone rings, my pulse jumps and my mind clears all at once. 9:02 P.M.

"Crisis Service," I say. "May I help you?"

"I'm just really confused," a man says.

"What are you confused about?"

In a whisper, as if to himself, he says, "This isn't any good. This is just not a good situation. I don't know what to do." The voice is young—maybe a high school or college student?

"You sound confused," I reflect. "What are you confused about?"

"I just don't know what to do. This is the last place I'm going to try. This is it for me. I don't know what else I can do now." His combination of frustration and despair worries me.

"You sound upset and frightened. What's happening?"

"What do you mean?" he asks, suddenly older and more formal. Maybe I've jumped to a wrong conclusion.

"Why have you called tonight?" I try again: "You sound very anxious."

This time the key fits the lock. He sighs. "There's no one else to turn to. Nobody listens to me. Everybody says, 'Oh, you can deal with it. Just deal with it!' I can't *deal with it* anymore, though. I was looking through the phone book; this seemed like a place to call."

"What is it that you're hoping to deal with?"

A longer sigh. "I don't know where to start. I'm just lost."

Casting around for a way to help him get started, I say, "Have you been feeling this way for long?" On a piece of scrap paper, I start doodling with a felt-tipped pen—a sod-roofed Scandinavian farmhouse soon floats in a sea of white.

"I don't know, something feels like it just snapped." I don't like how weak his voice sounds, especially when he adds, "I'm just losing control here. I don't know what to do."

My pen hovers above the drawing, still incomplete, awaiting the otherworldly flowers. I could reflect once more that he sounds confused, but I'm starting to worry about his safety. "Where are you now?" I ask in a quiet, even voice. Sometimes when I ask this of dis-traught callers they get panicky.

But he responds easily. "I'm in my room."

"Are you there alone? Is anyone nearby?"

"He just left. That's why I can call you right now. I couldn't call if he were here."

Who the hell is *he*—a roommate, a lover, a father? I doodle a man's face with huge, hooded eyes. Is this another domestic violence call?

"Do you feel safe?"

"Yeah, right now I am. I don't know when he'll be back though. I don't know how much time I've got, because he could come back any-time." His words trail away, and I think he may be looking down a hallway or out a door. Or perhaps he's on something. There's a funny sluggish quality to his sentences. He says he's frightened, yet he's talk-ing slowly. It doesn't make sense. Through the window, I watch a man park his car beside a culvert filled with orange daylilies, take some-thing like a rug out of the trunk, and set off across the field.

"You're sounding pretty overwrought. May I ask you if you've been drinking something or taking something?"

"*Me?* Me *drinking?*" His voice strengthens with surprise. "No, no it's not me. I wish I had been."

Back to square one. Laying down the pen, I cover my closed eyes with an open hand, and peer deep into the blackness. Talking softly, intimately not seductively, I try to convey my concern. "What's mak-ing you so upset tonight?"

Strained breathing. This must be difficult for him. Suddenly the gates open and he lets out a flood of words: "My roommate, *he's* been drink-ing—which he usually does—but tonight I think he *snapped*. He started to take it out on me and then he left in a huff, babbling things, scream-ing things, slamming the door. And it was just a wicked, wicked sight."

In my mind's eye, I can see him standing at a wall phone in a nar-row room (that has been painted with bold stripes, Mondrian style), the roommate (a big burly guy with a football player's physique), and the caller (a slender man of Asian descent). "You say your roommate has been drinking, and he began taking it out on you—in what way?"

"I was sitting on my desk and he just lunged at me like a wild man, and he grabbed me by my sweatshirt and threw me across the room and right into the bookcase. Man, it freaked me out."

That does sound bad. Now I see him wearing a red sweatshirt, his hair brushed up into a crewcut, his roommate slamming him against the furniture. "Are you hurt?"

"I'll probably be black and blue in the morning," he admits with a touch of embarrassment. "Nothing's broken."

"I see. Does this happen very often?"

In an urgent voice, he says, "It's never been this bad before. He usually just goes nuts and runs out for a while and comes back and goes to bed. But this time he...I don't know when he's coming back. He could do anything."

When I open my eyes, I can still see him, like a mirage floating in front of the filing cabinet. Is he safe? "That sounds very frightening," I say. "Are you afraid that he might really hurt you when he returns?"

"If this continues the way it has been, I'm sure he's going to do something. To take it out on somebody."

"Have you spoken with him about this and tried to get him to stop?" What a stupid question.

The caller answers it nonetheless. "He's messed up, totally messed up. There's nothing you can say to him. It just bounces off him."

"When was the last time you tried talking with him?"

"A few minutes ago. I said, 'What's your deal, man? Just chill out, will you.' He didn't want to talk about it. He just grabbed me and threw me across the room and kicked the garbage can so hard it hit the ceiling, and called me a 'lame sonofabitch,' and slammed the door, and took off."

Did I ever find out what the caller's relationship to his roommate is? "This is your roommate, you say; are you living in an apartment or in college?"

"I'm in a dorm."

"In a dorm. What year are you?"

"Freshman."

Wow. First year away from home and he gets a drunken and abusive roommate. That must be scary. He probably doesn't know the social protocols yet, what's usual, what he's supposed to endure, let alone where to turn. "Is there someone, a counselor or Resident Advisor, you could talk to about this? Maybe your roommate needs to be living alone." Picking up the felt-tipped pen, I add fecund flowers to the doodle.

"Well, I have talked to my RA, but he just sorta said, 'Well, if he doesn't do anything dangerous, it's okay, you'll just have to learn to live with him.' Only... This is the first time he's grabbed me. He usually just kicks a chair or pulls a drawer out or something. It's been scary but he never hurt *me*, so I said, fine, that's just the way he deals with things, everybody deals with things in their own way. I've never had a roommate before. I figure live and let live, you know?"

"So it really seems to have gotten out of hand tonight?"

"Yeah, I'd say so. He's just working too hard. He's a Fine Arts major and he's working too hard. School is pushing him over the edge. It's been going on for four days now. He's started in on the No-Doz thing, and he took one every four hours, and then he started one every hour, then every half hour. And now he's drinking on top of that."

Running my fingers through my ponytail, I unconsciously begin pulling out small tangles. "What do you think would happen if you went to the RA and explained that things had escalated a bit with your roommate, that he'd been drinking hard and taking a lot of pills, and coming after you, that you were concerned that he could get even more violent. How do you think the RA would respond? Do you think he'd be receptive?"

The caller isn't sure, and he also feels guilty about ratting on his roommate, guilty about not being able to help him cope.

I say, "We've been talking about a number of things over the past few minutes. One is your concern for your roommate. You've said you feel a sense of responsibility, and you want to help him. You sound frustrated about that. Another is the possibility that he could hurt you worse, since he's been so violent already."

"Yeah," he says with a shiver in his voice. "I guess five days of not sleeping, and all that stress...I'm his roommate and his friend, it's my job to help him. I should be able to deal with it, but I can't."

"You're very worried about him. You want to be a good friend and a good roommate, and you wonder how to help him."

"Yeah. Don't you want to help your friends?

I refuse to picture my friends in my mind's eye. "You sound frustrated because it's so hard to help him all by yourself."

"I should be able to deal with him," he says again, defeated.

"Well, I'm concerned about how difficult this is for you. It's hard enough to be in school, and here you are worried about your friend, and you don't know what he's going to do. It really sounds like you're under a lot of pressure. And I'm concerned that you might be in danger when he returns."

Suddenly agitated, he says, "What am I going to do? This has got to stop!"

"What about going back to your RA and telling him how serious things have become since you last spoke with him?" I suggest again. "When you spoke with him before, things weren't as bad as they are tonight, so he might not have understood how serious a problem your roommate has—or what a threat it might be to you. It could be helpful for you to have an ally."

"If *you* had a friend in trouble, wouldn't *you* want to help him, not report on him but help him? Wouldn't *you*?" the caller asks.

Of course I would, but we're encouraged not to personalize calls, and my version of helping a friend might be different from the caller's.

"You sound like a really good friend, a very concerned friend. It's tough to watch a friend in trouble. You've already made contact with your RA; he's not a stranger to you. Would you feel comfortable returning to him and talking with him?" I know I'm being directive, but I'm worried the roommate might return.

After a few moments, the caller says, "I guess I could talk to my RA. He's a nice guy."

Thank heavens. "Is he there now? Could you go see him now?" I pray I don't sound as worried as I feel.

"I don't know. It's late. What if he's asleep? I don't want to wake him up." Unbelievable. The caller is concerned about everyone but himself; I'm sure he *is* a great friend. I just wish to God I could get him out of his room and some place safe. He's got to do it for himself, though; otherwise he won't know what to do next time this happens. But new in town, new to college, he's understandably tentative.

"That's his job, to be on hand when people need him. That's why he lives in the dorm," I say.

"Yeah. That's right," the caller says. I can hear a little bit of conviction in his voice.

"Why don't you go do that now, and if he's not there or if you're not comfortable after your conversation with him, call back and we'll talk a little more and see what else might be possible."

"Will you still be there?" the caller asks, and my heart breaks. For the first time, he sounds little and afraid. It reminds me of a film I saw last night on television, a documentary about grizzly bears on Kodiak Island in Alaska. In one scene, a mother bear was crossing river rapids with her two cubs, one of whom was swept downstream by the current, tumbling and splashing until it washed up on shore beside a strange and dangerous adult bear. The mother rushed after it, fought off the danger, and led the cub back upstream. There, safe but frightened, the cub tried to nurse, even though it had been weaned a year before. As the mother bear shoved the cub away, a narrator explained that the mother was being protective but not indulgent. Nothing was said about how instinctively the cub regressed when it was frightened.

I wish I could assure my caller that I'll be here, but I don't know when he'll call, or who will be on shift. "It might not be me. But, if you like, someone here will know what the circumstances are. I'll make sure of that."

"Okay. You think I should go now?" He asks like someone just needing one more nudge.

"It might be a good idea to talk with your RA while your roommate is still out. What do you think?"

After a long pause, he says, "Yeah, I think that might be a good idea. Before he comes back."

"Okay. If the RA is not there, you could see him first thing tomorrow. And if you're not feeling all right at any point tonight, call us back. Okay?"

"Yes," he says firmly. "I'll go see if he's there."

"Okay. Good-bye for now," I say, implying that we'll talk again soon. Who is on overnight shift? I wonder, after we hang up. Checking the schedule, I discover that it's Connie, a lovely young woman who works with handicapped adults at a residence downtown. Perfect. I hope the rest of the caller's night is calmer, but I don't see how it can be. Sending him to his RA was good; he needs an ally. But what on earth will happen when the roommate returns, drugged, drunk, and angry? I hope the RA will stash the caller somewhere else tonight, and tomorrow, when the roommate is sober, take whatever action is necessary. My guess is the caller will be given a different room. Anyway, I pray that's what happens. I'm worried about the roommate, too, but he's not the one who called.

Counselors are nothing if not partisan. At one point during the call, the caller had wanted me to tell him how to help his roommate. He thought the problem was his roommate's, not his. This is what we call a "second-party call." He wanted help for someone else. We get such calls all the time—parents who seek advice for troubled children, spouses who want to help their partners with a problem, friends or teachers of people who are suicidal. The problem is, we don't know anything about those other people—who may not be real—we don't know their habits or personalities or strengths or resources or mental states. The caller is our client. Even when a teacher calls about a potentially suicidal student, our job is to bring the conversation around to how the caller is feeling, how the caller is coping, what the caller can do to feel that he or she is acting responsibly. The student may indeed be in danger, but it's the teacher's distress about it that prompted the call. We can't work with the student unless the student calls us (one of the things we suggest). The caller is our client.

In training, we practiced the protocol for handling second-party calls, which felt cumbersome at first. Actually, all of training felt strange, since it meant learning a new dialect of listening skills. I can still remember how nervous I was during the first half of training. I didn't know then the many octaves of hope and despair I would listen to. Even on my first shift I began learning an important lesson: the range of what's normal. It was like stepping into a locker room for the first time, and discovering a kaleidoscope of bodies, all of them fascinating and beautiful in different ways. The anatomy of each call is different, and every caller has a unique story to tell. It reminds me of Ray Bradbury's futuristic novel *Fahrenheit 451,* which concludes in a renegade village where each person is memorizing an outlawed book. Pairs stroll through the village, urgently reciting, while the air bustles with colorful stories. The collective sound is the literature of a people.

But those are artistically invented stories. More surprising is how much of a person's life is consumed by storytelling of one sort or another. Today, for instance I told dozens of narratives: to people, about people, to myself about myself, and to myself about others and events. For instance, I told Paul about the indefatigable dog that ran after Cathy and me when we were biking along the east side of Owasco Lake, how I clocked the dog running at 25 mph, how it stayed with us for miles and wouldn't go home, how it threw itself in front of my bike and how I skidded to a falling stop as a result. We discussed possibilities for dealing with dangerous dogs in the future—each one a small imaginary drama. That was only the briefest moment of the day.

In our own private mind theaters, we are constantly talking to ourselves, yelling at a boss, beseeching a lover, scolding a workman, exchanging witticisms with celebrities, rehearsing different versions of encounters, talking through problems, confiding in ourselves. Children as young as three years old conduct conversations with themselves and invent curious stories. The moment a child is born it is told stories by adults, and it learns what role it plays in the saga of the family. Sometimes the stories are simple: "Your daddy is mowing the grass," or "Here's a little bear that's coming to see you." Sometimes they're angry epics of trouble. Children are steeped in narratives. Then they tell their own and add them to the storytelling sounds of the entire human race.

Our stories help us understand a terrifyingly confusing and dangerous world, most of which is riddle. For the world to feel safe, we need to make sense of it, especially when we encounter setbacks and misfortunes that shatter our confidence. Telling anecdotes to friends, we reveal our true natures, we're not just offering the what and when of our lives. How was your trip? someone asks. The answer gives more than the whereabouts and the weather. It includes encounters, small triumphs, accidents, embarrassments, revised attitudes. Anecdotes alert our friends and loved ones to our basic values, biases, qualities, and concerns—and also how those vital pieces of identity are changing over time. The more we learn about ourselves, the more we revise the facts to fit our evolving sense of self. As the vocabulary of life changes, we need our memory to say something fitting, something that makes sense in a newly ordered world. How we tell the story influences how we feel about ourselves. Change your story and you change your identity.

That's why, Jungian psychologist James Hillman observes, psychotherapy really amounts to "a collaboration between fictions." People go into therapy to find a "plot to live by," psychotherapist Susan Bauer agrees. "They come as if to a professional biographer" to remodel their past and discover a plausible history. Bauer describes the process in *Confiding*:

> Both client and therapist use their skills as novelists as well as historians or detectives as they labor to get a story to work right and feel right. After a long tug of war, a new story, invariably called "How Things Really Were," is pulled from a mixture of old facts and new dreams. Hopefully this new account is more intelligent, more inclusive, and more cohesive than the story originally brought into therapy. If it is more imaginative, it may lead its narrator in directions he or she had not yet dared explore.... The therapist as historian, humbled by the new understanding that any account of a client's life ... is but one of a hundred possible versions, collaborates with the eyewitness.

According to studies done by James Pennebaker at Southern Methodist University, confiding strengthens one's immune system. So by simply listening to the confidences of a caller, we perform a lifesaving act. Callers sometimes refer to us as their friends, who offer them genuine support and make them feel less alone. But there is also the benefit of venting one's troubles instead of stewing in them. When people clarify their troubles, turning them into a narrative, and giving them just enough order to communicate to someone else, the fog lifts briefly and the world becomes a place that can be better understood, even if it isn't fully enjoyed. Writing books is a form of confiding, too, a way of continuing the conversation with oneself in public. In Pennebaker's studies, people who didn't confide were more prone to disease and stress and early death. Much of their physical energy went into containing and hiding emotions, and that led to high blood pressure and a weaker immune system.

Why should describing an event change our feelings about it? By telling stories we assimilate frightening or unexplained events, and fit them into a world where action is possible. One becomes less helpless.

Suddenly there are many options for escape or relief, many explanations for how an event that may have turned the world upside down can fit comfortably into one's life. The student who called this evening did not expect his roommate to be an alcoholic, pill-popping Goliath who could murder him in a rage. By making sense of the situation, telling the story repeatedly until it fit right, he could integrate that unexpected terror into his life, and we were able to discuss possible actions he could take. At that point, his panic fled. But he will need to tell the story over and over, to authorities so that they can take action, to himself so that he can rehearse ways of coping, to others so that he can organize and revise the events in his mind. When he tells friends, he will also be communicating what sort of person he is—the sort who doesn't feel comfortable ratting on a roommate, who feels guilty about not being able to help his roommate, who allows himself to be victimized by a bully, but only up to a point, and so on. The alternative is to worry, and he'll do that anyway, but it won't be as productive as confiding in others. To normalize the event, figure out what action to take, and feel good about how he handled it, or examine why he handled it poorly and what he could do differently next time, he'll need a listener. I think that's why many of our callers tell the same story over and over. Listening to their own stories, they understand parts of them better. The stories change over time, as callers revise them, or believe in them. As different counselors give them feedback, different parts of their stories take on importance or become clearer. The basic facts tend to stay the same, but the emotional relevance changes, depending on the caller's mood, or new circumstances, or gift for banishing a demon by repeatedly uttering its name.

CHAPTER 12

Desperate Measures

In the icicled dreamtime of December in upstate New York, the fields deepen in opalescent snow, horses wear platform shoes created by snow strata sticking to their hooves, and ice storms turn barbed-wire fences into a string of stars. Because the snow is bulky and immense, people place flags or colored balls atop car aerials to alert plows to the cars lying hidden under drifts. The streets look like bobsled runs. I love that sort of hard, gnawing winter. But, to tell the truth, I just love weather. Something about the ripening processes of a blizzard, the firefly-green sky of a tornado, or the humid bell jar of a hot August noon, reminds me of the weather in the cell and connects me to the atmosphere at the level of blood, bowels, and bone. So, unlike many Easterners, who feel imprisoned by winter and flee to hot spots with the mania of inmates out on parole, I never feel driven to leave home. Winter is an equation my body knows by heart. I love its snowy walls too thick to climb, its ice too sharp to handle, its cold painful as fire. Best to live like other animals, feasting on every windfall.

When love wanes, we lament how the object of our desire has "grown cold," developing an "icy stare" and a "stone-cold heart." Winter is a season filled with similes of scorn. Yet, in the high valleys, it's a lovely and tempting time. Bears eat tree-bark jerky instead of grubs and freshwater bass. Berries freeze to hard-centered nuts and snow roses point leafy digits sunward in scaly arcs. Foothills bristle like a boar's back. Summer pods are still visible under a dune of snow. Though there's little to fear from the wind's steel blades, the silver birches spin their addled leaves in the sun. The snow conceals, but also highlights and reveals. It's fun to watch a shrew tunneling beneath the snow, leaving its long, narrow designs all over the yard. Or find a hieroglyph of bird tracks. There's nothing like riding horseback through deep winter woods, among towering pines, or along creeks crusted over like caramel brickle. In the summer, light saturates open fields and is brightest from above, but winter light quivers off snow-banks and water, shooting up from the ground and striking at odd angles.

In upstate New York, the winter lakes and rivers become miles of white, sun-stricken crystal. View a length of the furious Susquehanna, with ice-knots snarled from shore to shore, and the blinding glitter will make you grow faint and forget everything but sparkle, as javelins of light lie broken on the river among bolts of candy floss, icy geodes, and massive pearl tusks. Then thought rises off like a clutch of fleas, and all that remains is *ice*. Cannons of ice. Tumbledown ice. Flirty, lucid, and shattery ice. Ice walls with ice filling every chink. Muscle-bound ice. Ribs of ice. Stunt ice looping the loop over ice. Boiling new ice climbing elder ice. Upsprung, bony, and ricepaper ice. Ice overcoats with ice in their pockets. Shortbread ice. Armored ice. Ice tongs dropping ice into ice. After that ice bath, my hot mind blanks and fills with ice caves of australopithecine ice, where our kind warmed their frigid buttocks at a fire while busily stitching and inventing, driven to resourcefulness by ice.

———

Early one bright and windless December morning, I throw my cross-country skis into the car and head for the undulations of a nearby golf course. It has taken me a while to figure out how many layers of clothing to wear, what sort of protection to keep close to the skin, what shell can be looser and more voluminous. We are so vulnerable in the elements, and yet being outside is what we crave. When I first began cross-country skiing, I piled on layers—two sets of long underwear, a turtleneck, pants, a fleece tunic, an anorak, a pair of Thinsulate mittens, two pairs of socks, a fleece hat with earflaps, and a fleece face mask. I was essentially a bed on the move, except that little of me could move inside all that Lycra, fleece, and down. I soon discovered how excessive all this was, a throwback fright to our fear of being alone and unprotected in the elements. After only a few minutes I would begin to sweat lightly, and then a hard sweat would soak my bangs and pour down my spine.

Standing still in the cold, before the first stiff stridings across the snow, it's hard to foresee how the body's furnace will blaze after only ten minutes of skiing. That requires faith in a future state of energy. We are good governors of our inner climate. Unconsciously, we know in what a narrow range of temperature we can survive. It is only a cross-country ski trip, but to the body it is life and death. Another pair of socks? Another layer of pants? We consider the air temperature, the wind, the distance, the time we'll be out, the sun and clouds, and how all these things may have changed by the time we return. Standing idle, it is hard to picture a future which is all action, drama, process, in which the body is a furnace, producing energy and heat.

Being able to imagine ourselves in a future radically different from the present is one hallmark of our species. But the mechanism can go awry and the brain snag, obsessively picturing a dreadful future that may not happen. A surprising number of our frequent callers at the Center are obsessives, chewing on a past or possible event like a terrier with a shoe. Most people obsess in a transforming way, fantasizing different versions of a drama, each one leading to different responses from key people, as well as alternate plots and outcomes. In time, the story gradually changes until it becomes absorbed. But a small number of people obsess fruitlessly—year after year exactly the same details plague them, in exactly the same words. Nothing changes. There's no way in or out of their mind-cocoon. I wish I knew how to break through that snarl, wish I knew how to rechannel a "one-track mind." It does seem sometimes as if a switchman were routing signals down a single track; that image might even evoke what happens in the neurons. Worry helps us rehearse and prepare, but in large doses its ropes coil heavily around us until we can't move or see past them.

Today I wear little and worry little about it—only one pair of long johns, a thin loose pair of stirrup pants, a fleece tunic, an anorak, a light pair of gloves, a wide headhand. But when I reach the golf course, even those feel too hot, so tomorrow I'll try paring down further until I discover the minimum. If only it were that easy with one's ego: peel off the heavy defenses and strip down to the barest adequate protection. Gliding out over the snow at last, I slip naturally into a track left by another skier. In cross-country skiing, it's always easier traveling in someone else's rut. Sometimes a slick crust, sometimes soft powder, yards of pearly snow flow beneath me as I sprint toward the trees, speed down shallow gullies, and return more slowly, my poles stamping hoof shapes in the snow. A perfect wake-up. I can't take long, though; the squirrels will be hungry.

Sure enough, I return home to find them waiting outside the garden room windows, some perched on hickory branches, some prowling on the ground. Even though I've been studying them now for two

years, it's hard to choose what I like best about squirrels. No other animal looks so much like eagerness incarnate as a squirrel standing up
on its hind legs, stretching, sniffing, erecting its ears, hands at its chest,
eyes wide and wet. *Did that human just drop something edible?* its whole
body seems to say, as it watches me toss apple slivers and sunflower
seeds onto the snow. A relaxed squirrel looks like a relaxed spaniel:
sprawled out with all four legs splayed, tail on the ground, head
lolling between its paws. But there seems little relaxation in the world
of the squirrel. Rainstorms soak the fur, crows and raccoons steal the
young, food must be found for both now and later. If chased, a squirrel often runs straight *at* a tree, then does a Fred Astaire move—leaps
against the trunk and springs away. When squirrels get frightened,
their palms sweat the way humans' palms do. After a long, aggressive
standoff, as a squirrel moves aside, you can sometimes see small palm-
prints on the stones.

Another wonderful thing about the squirrels in my yard is that they
keep the same hours as hot-air balloonists—they're most active at
dawn and sunset. In late fall, despite the cold, all the squirrels seemed
to be swept up in mating chases, spinning round and round the tree
trunks, waltzing round and round the yard. In a hormonal frenzy, they
would chase around, across, and over most anything, preferring tree
trunks of course; but two friends of mine were astounded one day to
find a pair of squirrels leaping onto *them,* spiraling fast around their
bodies, and leaping away. Confusing humans with tree trunks? You
have to be plenty distracted. When the females go into estrus, they
exude a fragrant hormone that scents the air. From a squirrel's perspective, the woodlands are drenched in the smell of sex. Healthy
squirrels tend to mate once or twice a year, and the pattern is usually
the same. Smell leads the male on. He sniffs around the nether parts
of a female. She coyly moves a step or two away. He follows and sniffs,
she steps away. He sniffs even the grass or branch where she sat. He
sniffs her shadow. She bolts. He follows. She slows down. He gains on
her. She waits. He grabs her around the middle, as if doing the Heim-

lich maneuver, she moves her tail to the side, and they mate. But only when and because she allows him to. A female chooses her mate from a posse of ardent, fleet-footed suitors, who have learned that speed, agility, and persistence win sexual favors. But females sometimes choose males that have already ingratiated themselves and accompanied them while feeding. Or, to put it in human terms, they prefer friends. Of course, a gigolo male may cozy up to several females, so that when the mating chases begin he'll be close at hand and familiar, and thus unlikely to be rebuffed. After mating, the male leaves the female to fend for herself while he chases other females elsewhere.

Today Collops sits and judges two nuts by weighing one in each paw, testing for the most value, but also for freshness. Squirrels are excellent greengrocers. Young squirrels learn to recognize different kinds of nuts, full ones from empty ones, fresh ones from weevil-infested ones, by both odor and weight. Blind for five weeks, nestlings rely heavily on smell, hearing, and touch. When they finally emerge from their leafy womb, they develop keen visual skills, but they can still smell their way along the arboreal highways, find Mom, and find food. All the mixing fragrances of the nest included Mother's unique fingerprint of odors, and the educational smell of her meals. Returning to the nest with food, Mother partially chews it, and the youngster puts its face right up to hers and sniffs what she's eating or actually takes food from her mouth. Mom likes it, the instinctive motto says, maybe I'll like it. We do the same, of course, giving our infants cut-up (instead of partially chewed) morsels as we dine. This morning I notice a smooth-barked tree wearing a tattoo of slip marks—three parallel lines—showing where a squirrel's claws couldn't quite catch. The length of the lines—about four inches—tells how far the squirrel slipped before its claws held. The lines crisscross, which may mean it took a few wild efforts to grab hold. Even squirrels leave their marks on the world, signs of triumph and struggle.

Some days, I could sit and watch the squirrels until nightfall. It's hard not to worry about them, especially in winter. Which ones will survive? Soon my *National Geographic* project will be finished, and I'll need to ween the squirrels and let them go about their ways. But not yet. Not in spring, either. Maybe in late summer, when nut-filled trees tempt them, flowers and berries are plentiful, and their world is an open treasury.

—

The afternoon shift begins quietly, with a request for a referral and two hang-ups. Then Saxman calls, very depressed, talking about suicide. Researching his medicines, he has discovered that overdosing on his insulin would do the trick neatly, with the least shock to his parents, who might assume it an accident. Although he's always vulnerable to depression, last night held a cauldron of woes. A fight with a potential girlfriend who got angry when he asked her to have an AIDS test was followed by a canceled performance at a club, which was followed by bumping into a cousin he hated at a bar—a man who had involved him, without his consent, in some tax scam. He also has a deadline looming. All week he procrastinated rehearsing for a concert at the marina tomorrow evening, and he feels completely unprepared. We talk about his diabetes: the flare-ups that produce temporary blindness, numbness in his hands, painful cracks in his foreskin and heels, and a grave fear of total blindness and loss of limbs. His illness is a culture. A disease can become the central point in one's life, around which fate, friends, and family radiate. It starts simply, with a clear disease whose restrictions, symptoms, and drugs make annoying demands. Then a parade of larger or smaller trials follows, each with new discomforts, doctors, drugs, side effects—until one lives in an endlessly exhausting labyrinth of doctors, medicines, and regimes. Diabetic since he was a teen, Saxman is understandably fed up with being sick all the time. The injections make him feel like a junkie, and he prays an insulin inhaler will soon be available, or better yet a genetic missile. We talk about his suicide plans; that helplessness has filled his house like a fog; the impending deadline; how worthless, witless, giftless he feels. I ask how he would feel if, by some miracle, he had already prepared tomorrow's concert, and when he allows that he would feel less stressed, we discuss triage. If he begins by rehearsing the easier tunes that could be transposed quickly, he could leave the tougher ones. At the very least, then, he'd have part of the concert prepared and not feel totally incompetent. And, who knows, if he did the easier ones first, he might actually get to some of the harder ones later. In his thinking-out-loud yet experienced voice, I can hear a mind fumbling and gauging a complex creative problem, testing it against the reality of what is possible in the remaining hours. As he talks himself into the future, and realizes that he can in fact master this one problem, his mood lifts a little. Toward the end of the call, he seems stronger, but I might be wrong, so I ask him how he is feeling, and he replies that he thinks he'll be able to manage the day. We make a contract: he promises to phone if he feels driven to end his life. But he sounds precarious. One good sign is that he started pychotherapy a few days ago; at least he's reaching out, creating a second lifeline. Apparently he interviewed four therapists and settled on a man who seemed insightful and sincere. Also a good sign. It takes energy and control to interview prospective therapists, as well as a belief that recovery is possible. When we say good-bye, I feel fine about the call, but also sad that he's been depressed for so long and haunted by suicide. Yet a thought dawns on me. I wasn't rattled by his talking directly about suicide. I took it in stride. True, I became more alert to possible warning signs, but I stayed reasonably calm as I explored his degree of lethality, trying to discover if he was in imminent danger or just wrestling with a bad depression that might slacken. I didn't begin by assuming the call was an emergency. More important, perhaps, I allowed him to be suicidal. I accepted that he might one day kill himself, that he might do it tomorrow, but that my job was to befriend him on this day, in this hour, give him comfort and concern, guide him to ways of coping if possible, but even if I couldn't do that, accept that he was headed for death sometime, somewhere. We all are. It's hard to live in the tense present with suicidal callers, and not try to peer around the corner or bolster them against some future threat, but accept the narrow corridor of the call. Befriend them in the moment. Save them in the moment. Try everything. Then let the moment go.

Thinking about this new threshold, I write up the call, file it, and brew a cup of decaf espresso. When the phone rings again, I hear the familiar voice of Endless Love, with "a huge heartache, a soul murder" that's tormenting him. A quick glance at the logbook: he phoned three times in the night, four times the day before, twice the day before that. When I ask gently what's causing the pain, he explodes with anger. "I need you not to ask any questions," he says firmly, adding that he also needs me to praise his virtues according to a few set phrases, express my unconditional love for him, "testify to the injured innocence" he has experienced, swear I will "hearten and restore" him "with words of strong faith," and assure him that God has a loving purpose for him. Ignoring his rigid rules, I listen for a few moments and unconsciously ask a small sympathetic question. This time he seethes with fury—didn't he tell me not to ask any questions! Don't I understand that my job is to do whatever he *needs me to!* Astonishing, I think, we help him out of the goodnes of our hearts and he yells at us and tries to make us performing animals. Anger whisks up inside my chest. I hate the feeling. Mentally, I identify it, move it out of my body and across the room. Don't react, *observe,* I counsel myself. You're feeling anger; it's what he does to people. Maybe Vicky was right. Can this really be any good for him? I explain calmly that I am not comfortable reciting his scripts. If he wishes to talk about his problems, I'm happy to listen, take his problems seriously, and give him whatever feedback he thinks useful, but, like most people, I am extremely uncomfortable being told what to say, or what grammar I may or may not use. It's too much of a straitjacket. I suggest we start over on a more relaxed footing, but he reads me the riot act. Splattering me with insults, he tells me that my job is to hear whatever he needs and to do whatever he needs. I politely explain that no, that isn't my job. If he needs to control me or yell abuse at me, the call really isn't going to work for either one of us.

Gently, I ask him again if he'd like to start over and talk about his "soul murder." Because I phrased it as a question, he explodes. Didn't he tell me I wasn't allowed to ask questions! It was hardly a probing one. It doesn't matter, he says, he's decided what I'm supposed to say, and my job is do what he "needs." Read *orders* for needs. I shake my head in frustration. How do I help this man? We've been shadow-dancing with Endless Love for years and, if anything, he's getting worse. It's not our job to make callers better, only to ease their suffering, but I'm not convinced he's profiting from his contact with us. He intimidates new counselors with his criticism and demands, and, because they truly wish to be of help, they usually comply. I think he may be phoning us because it's one of the few places—maybe the only place—where he can manipulate people and consistently get away with it. Are we making his predicament worse by encouraging that behavior? Although he comes from a large family (eight brothers and sisters, a posse of nieces and nephews, and one grown child of his own), and works at a diner among many potential friends, he says they all avoid him. For years, the central theme of his calls has been how people disappoint and abandon him, when he desperately needs only the simplest and most obvious thing in the world from them—"soul-mates who will fill their hearts with joyous devotion and unconditional love," for he is "a purely loving heart whom everyone betrays." If he makes the same demands on his family and friends that he makes on us, bullying them with absolutes, it's small wonder he drives them away. I'd like somehow to move the call around to discussing if I'm reacting to his demands the way his retreating friends do. But he hangs up in disgust before I have the chance.

Yes, I think, tapping my pen idly on the logbook, we mean well, but we may be making his problem worse by reinforcing his self-sabotaging way of dealing with people. And how about the well-being of the counselors? They're not required to endure abuse from a caller.

I didn't understand that when I first began counseling. Because I'm at pains to help callers, and sincerely wish to bring comfort, I sometimes assume that I have to put up with humiliation, insult, or manipulation, and that I'm being a lousy counselor if I don't let Edward Scissorhands curse at me, or give in to Endless Love's tirades and demands. Trying to dwell temporarily in the caller's world, I can become so empathic that if a caller criticizes me, part of me believes it. I know it may be a caller's modus operandi to insult counselors, just as other callers often thank us extravagantly. But nonetheless, I feel that I've "lost the call," failed someone in distress because of weak character or faint know-how. It's hard to accept that some people live in a world remote beyond my imaginings, touch, or help. I hear their turmoil, confusion, despair, insurmountable pain—however angry or hateful it might be—and a hot spur inside me keeps touching my flanks. *Keep trying,* a voice whispers as hope gallops on, *keep trying, keep trying, just keep trying.*

5:25 P.M. Louise calls. At least I think it's Louise: a charged silence that seems to be rising from a well, and a small female voice—not a child's, a woman's in extreme pain—a voice choking back tears while trying to breathe, cry, and talk at the same time, making little sounds like snagged nylon between audible sobs, and a whimper I know is her full effort at speech. Someone using her voice as an ax to break through the thick glass walls of a depression is what I hear. For a moment, it reminds me of the lady cardinal who used to hurl herself against my bedroom window on summer mornings. I brush the image from my mind, but a new one rushes into the void. The brain cannot help but try to make sense of sounds. Something about the catch in the throat I'm hearing sounds too much like the necklace catch on a single string of pearls, a string breaking in slow motion while the pearls spill to the ground, bounce hard, and roll in a hundred directions. I look at the clock. The minute hand hasn't moved. Words are all I have to ease her anguish, and they seem paltry. I love the invisible ink of language, staining people and things with a revealing light, love the mouselike cunning of words that swerve into mysterious half-lit corners, love the rich emollient of conversation, love the form of intimate confiding that authors do, love how each word teaches us about daily life in bygone eras, love how words caress fleeting moments and lavish care on unconsidered trifles, love using words as currency to pay friends their due, love the way words connect the inner life with the outer, and the self with the other, love the notoriety of language whose cabaret tricks provide jokes, admiration, and laughter, love the poultice of language, a remarkable healer. But I hate like hell being limited to words in the war zone of the heart. Instead, I wish I could convey a pure mineral comfort to Louise, steady her trembling for a moment, reach into her bones and install a rock bottom, the-world-will-wait, sheltered, safe feeling.

Rock bottom. For Louise, those words mean emotional vertigo.

"It sounds like you're having an awful day," I say at last, quietly, emotionally, as if I knew the details of her upset. All I know is that the details don't matter.

"I really am," she half whines, and then cries in a small staccato of pain. Some crying voices are ambiguous; there may yet be hidden strengths and resources to plumb. Some, like this voice, leave little doubt. I can hear the fast-fraying edges of hope in the way she gasps between cries. Her weak voice breaks up. Life slips like sand through her syllables. Her mood is deadly. I think this is Louise, and realize with surprise that I recognize her breathing pattern even more than her voice. Her face flashes into my mind, but not the composed face I saw at the Spiritualist church. Tonight she is beyond their otherworldly healing. I wonder if she sometimes pictures herself "on the other plane," as they say, a spirit guide who sends messages to the living. Do her suicide fantasies extend past death? In my mind, I see her standing at a kitchen telephone, leaning against the wall, shielding her eyes with one hand, crying into the darkness of her palm, then holding her forehead as if it would otherwise shatter. Quickly I withdraw from her kitchen, as if back up a telescope barrel, and return to the counseling room, return to the bare outlines of her voice. For some reason, my free hand has been floating an inch above the desk, so I set it down.

"I can hear how much pain you're in," I say, in an intense, intimate voice. "What's made it so rough tonight?"

A long silence, stretching into an even longer silence. Stay calm, I think. Don't lose her. Don't ask if she's all right. Don't speak just because the silence is uncomfortable. In a rackety world of traffic, music, appliances, and people, silence is most often an interruption of the constant noise that surrounds us, and so we find it disquieting. We tend to speak automatically, scattering and emptying ourselves of words, talking ourselves into the future, at pains to stay alive despite the desolation we feel. At first, when callers fell silent, I would nervously fill the gap with open-ended questions. But I've learned now to allow silence, which can be a positive part of a conversation. As philosopher Max Picard wisely observes, silence begins when speaking stops, but not because it stops. We live between two silences, the silence from which we came and the silence to which we go. Speaking, we are forever echoing those worlds. Speech came out of the fullness of silence. Death is woven into the fabric of language itself. Silence is eloquent and rich. Sometimes poets connect us to those silences. The silence around a thought can free it from distraction, give it perspective and dignity. Silence can be creative.

"Are you still there?" I say at last.

She laughs a dangerous laugh. I know exactly what it means. "For the moment," she says.

"Let's talk about the moment," I say, letting my voice fall into a conspiratorial whisper I hope will engage her and draw her nearer.

"Over all the hills is quiet/ Over all the dells you can hardly hear a sound/ All the birds are quiet in the woods/ Soon you will rest too," she recites in a disembodied voice.

I can't place the quote.

"All the heat is gone," she says. "It's so cold, so alone. Last night I saw a documentary on TV about penguins. They stand all alone at the edge of the world, outside human society. They just stand there like lonely beautiful spirits and stare out to sea."

I cannot tell her that I have seen penguins in the wild, and understand the cold, isolation, and wind-searing sound she identifies with those sentinel creatures. Unlike her, they aren't lonely, though, and when I visited their world, I didn't pity them. They were perfectly adapted to their environment. But in her mind they symbolize a powerful emotional climate, an icy wasteland where they endure the ravaging winds of daily life just as she weathers repeated brainstorms. In the Antarctica of her suffering, at the end of the known world, the vista looks bleak. Sometimes anchoring feelings with a metaphor can steady them. Sometimes you can rephrase feelings with words; if I change her words could I change her mood? Maybe I can detain her in an image, focus her mind on something.

"What do they watch for?" I ask.

"I don't know. An answer."

"Life doesn't seem to have many of those at the moment, does it?"

"No." Her voice crumbles again. "Only one..."

"It sounds like you're feeling as cold, isolated, and raw as those penguins."

"Raw," she echoes. "Like meat."

"With no protection from the elements..."

"No. In a completely colorless world."

I smile. She imagines penguins living among ice palaces in windswept rookeries of monotone white. But their world dances with minute prisms. More colorful than a rain forest, that never-ending white contains all colors, could we but see them. In extreme cold, when the surgical winds blow sharp and clouds can't form in the frigid air, snow falls in a confetti of diamond dust. Louise's daily world has color, too, from what I understand of her work, hobbies, and friends.

But it doesn't feel that way at the moment, just colorless, flat and barren, lonely, isolated, and cold.

"I've been thinking about ... the gorge ... then it would be over," she whispers. "The pain would finally be over. This long sorry mistake of my life would be over."

The bridge again. The long fall. What is it about humans that makes us want to hurl ourselves from heights? Imagining the pain of those brain-bludgeoning, flesh-ripping, bone-shattering rocks below gives me a jolt. Even deep water feels hard as a steel door when you fall onto it from a great height. San Francisco's chapter of Suicide Prevention celebrated a ghoulish anniversary this year: that of the thousandth person to commit suicide by leaping from the Golden Gate Bridge down 250 feet into the tumultuous waters of the bay. The first person was a forty-seven-year-old bargeman who walked the bridge's 1.6-mile length, then, tossing his vest and coat to an acquaintance, said, "This is where I get off," and jumped. The bridge had been open only three months. That was in August 1937. In 1973, fourteen people competed to be the five-hundredth suicide, including one man who dressed for the honor, wearing a T-shirt marked "500." The oldest person ever to leap from Golden Gate Bridge was eighty-seven, the youngest five. Some have left unusual notes. One said: "Absolutely no reason, except I have a toothache." Another wrote: "Do not notify my mother. She has a heart condition." A trained counselor on an antisuicide mission now patrols the bridge for at least eight hours a day. From time to time, San Francisco tries to reckon with the bridge's hypnotic lure by erecting barriers or proposing laws, but nothing stops the flow of despairing pilgrims. Its skeletal heights are a magnet. No one knows why. Something about how it spans the churning unconsciousness of water, straddling two shores? Its dual status as a progressive American icon and a shrine to self-destructiveness? Its presence as a petrified pathway? Or perhaps merely its availability, an easy stroll to deadly heights? Most people who commit suicide are emotionally abducted, trapped in a powerful but transitory depression. Therefore San Francisco's Suicide

Prevention Center has eight telephones on the bridge, for people who have second thoughts. When I visited that branch of SP last year, I was surprised to discover that their callers could easily have been our callers. They had the same issues, the same upsets. I had assumed that I'd hear a different emotional dialect in different parts of the country, or in a big city compared to a country town. But I was wrong. It doesn't seem to matter much where humans live. Needs and hungers stay the same, stress hits where we're most vulnerable, depression works its usual mischief, and hearts break in the same ways. Our essential nature doesn't vary.

Although I'm curious about what Louise meant by the "mistake" of her life, it isn't my role to ask. That's for the hard gardening of therapy. Her voice sounds angry, weak and sad. Her cries are the gut-wrenching sounds made by a wounded animal, and I want to reach down the line and hold her tight, pull her away from the gorge.

"You've been thinking of killing yourself in the gorge?"

She sighs. Often when a person is suicidal and you ask about it, you hear a sigh because no one else has believed them. They're relieved to discover that someone can listen to such awful thoughts. Friends and family get scared and don't know what to say or do, so they ignore it, or say, "Oh, you'll feel better." We take depression seriously and talk about it head-on.

"Yes," she says.

"How do you see it happening?"

"Flying. I would lean into nothingness, let go, and fly."

"Cold at the bottom," I remind her. Suicidal people get wedded to means. If you can disrupt the means you can sometimes disrupt the plan. A very specific and available plan, like Louise's, signals high risk.

"Yes." She cries. Silence. I know she is picturing it.

"What are you thinking?" I ask.

"About the frozen white glass of the falls, the cold rocks at the bottom, cold, cold, all that cold." Her voice shivers.

"What's made tonight so rough?"

Nervously, I begin fidgeting with a triangular-shaped pencil, pushing it slowly back and forth on the desk, but its flat pyramidal sides won't roll. Then I plant it point down in the pen-and-pencil cup, and begin tapping my fingers on the edge of the desk, lightly, as if in Morse code. For some reason, I can't banish from my mind the city bus I saw on Triphammer Road earlier today. It was traveling recklessly fast, and in the destination box over the front window were the words NO PLACE SPECIAL.

CHAPTER 13

A Last of Last Times

I'm afraid of losing Louise. *Losing her.* A shorthand for an avalanche of hurt, the phrase sounds too casual, the equivalent of misplacing a set of keys or an umbrella. I suppose it's my fundamental belief in the uniqueness of people that makes me cherish how irreplaceable they are. Louise has many talents, a lively mind, a quirky and unusual point of view, and a generous heart. I don't want life to lose her. I don't want society to lose her. I don't want to lose her from the pageant of humankind. We use only a voice and a set of ears, somehow tied to the heart and brain, but it feels like mountaineering with someone who has fallen, a dangling person whose hands you are gripping in your own. Saxman was very depressed, but within reach. With Louise, I'm not so sure. But if she truly wishes to die? We don't hear from her when she's not depressed. In stabler times, I don't think she would choose death. But I respect her right to choose, and I tell her so.

"Look, you can always kill yourself. That's one option tonight. Why don't we put that up on the shelf for a moment and talk about what some other options might be."

Because she feels bereft of them, I want her to have choices. Choice is a signature of our species. We worship choice, choosing often with purpose, but at other times simply for athletic reasons—to keep choice alive. We choose to live, sometimes we choose our own death, but most of the time we make choices just to prove choice is possible. We've created a culture to supply potential choices, to market them as necessities, though usually what is being sold are merely new opportunities to choose. Choice is what separates us from the ants. Not that I have anything against ants. At SP, we hope our callers will choose life, but they have the option and the right to choose death. It is their decision. That's why many counselors also believe heartily in Dr. Jack Kevorkian's efforts to help terminally ill people commit suicide. Above all else, we value the right to choose one's destiny. The very young and some lucky few may find their days opening one onto another like a set of ornate doors, but most people make an unconscious vow each morning to get through the day's stresses and labors intact, without becoming overwhelmed or wishing to escape into death. Everybody has thought about suicide, or knows somebody who committed suicide, and then felt: "pushed another inch, and it could have been me." As Emile Zola once said, some mornings you first have to swallow your toad of disgust before you can get on with the day. We choose to live. But suicidal people have tunnel vision—no other choice seems possible. A counselor's job is to put windows and doors in that tunnel.

"Options?" She says the word as if it were too large for her mouth. It probably seems tragically impersonal for what she is feeling. "You mean like eating dinner?" she asks acidly.

"Have you had anything to eat today?"

A dry little laugh. "I bought some lamb chops but couldn't face cooking them. I don't want to eat something more nervous than I am."

I laugh. Her delivery was perfect. She laughs again. It is barely more than a chuckle.

"Cold..." She launches the word like a dark cloud, not attached to anything special, a nimbus of pure pain.

"How come so cold and lonely tonight?"

"I'm always lonely, lonelier than life," she says faintly, then rallying a little, she explains, "When I worked at Montessori, I used to meet people there, or when my kids were little, through their activities. Now I don't meet anyone. Not at work in that pathetic office. My job is horrible. Not hard, you know, just the same rain barrel full of soak everyday, boring and lonely, but it's the only one I could find. There's nothing out there for a middle-aged woman, and the minute they learn I've been hospitalized, they're afraid to hire me, like I'm going to napalm their filing cabinets or Crazy Glue their customers' thumbs to the counter or something."

A thought she has obviously entertained in some detail.

"I understand. You hate your job, you don't make friends there, and it's hard to find a new one. Every workday must feel like a wasteland."

"Oppressive," she corrects. Not too little of a good thing, too much of a bad.

"Oppressive. Maybe we can figure out some other work..."

"It's hopeless. I've tried everywhere. There's nothing."

Before I can reply, she swerves to: "...And I haven't had a date in years, haven't been laid since I don't know when. And then there are my kids. I mean, they're teens, and suddenly Mom's a drag. We fight all the time. About ridiculous things, small things. I don't even know what we're fighting about half the time. They don't want me to hug and kiss them anymore. I can understand that, but it hurts."

Breathless, she sounds like a child trying to tell a story faster than her tumbling words. I was rushing her. She wasn't finished with her lamentation. She still needs to be heard, so I sit quietly and listen, a borrowed heart.

"... There's no point to my life. I'm not doing anything of value with it. No one would miss me. No one would care if I were gone. Well, that's not true, it might change how a couple of people feel—give my ex a few sleepless nights, send a message to my Neanderthal boss, make my kids feel sorry about how cruel they can be..."

Magical thinking—the belief that suicide will change a relationship with someone. One of the warning signs. "I'm lonelier than life," she says again. She likes the phrase. "How do I get out of this?" she bleats. A primal cry, not a question. Then she says almost too low to hear, "I just want the pain to end. I only want to lose consciousness." A rustling noise: she is settling on a chair or a hallway step.

A mental inventory of her state alarms me. She's feeling unendurable pain. Her needs for love, friendship, achievement, and belonging aren't being met. She's feeling helpless and hopeless. Although she's desperately searching for a way out, she's so depressed that her thinking has shrunk to absolutes—life or death—and life has lost its tang. No wonder she wants consciousness to end. In her narrowed world, she's blind to variety, so only one solution remains, one direction in the tunnel. She openly talks about killing herself. Eighty percent of suicidal people give clear messages. She is ambivalent. With all her heart, she wants to live. Just as ruthlessly she wishes to die. Though opposite and irreconcilable, both feelings are equally true. Should I send the police? We have met at this crossroads before. The terrain is the same, the emotional whirlwind is the same, but is *she*? Is anything different?

"What a heavy burden that must be. I can hear how low you're feeling, how meaningless life seems, how bleak things look. I'm so sorry you're suffering like this."

"Promise you won't send the police," she says, reading my mood.

"How about if I promise that I won't, and you promise not to give me reason to?"

She doesn't answer.

"Too much?" I ask.

"Yeah," she says. Kindly, not critically. Her tone says: We are in this together. "I just don't want to be alone right now...in these last minutes." I think she said minutes. Her voice dropped when she sniffled. Every call has its own pace, and this one moves slowly, with long pastures of thoughtful silence followed by tears or words.

A hastily committed suicide, before all alternatives are exhausted, is the ultimate tragedy. I don't want Louise to miss the chance to recover and live happily, but I also hate the idea of her abandoning life while she feels so terrible about herself. That's a tragic ending to a life. Her bare mortality reminds me of a bittersweet day last summer. Walking in the cool of the morning, I was rewarded by culverts filled with daylilies, a city of snails clinging to blades of grass, and a huge luna moth camouflaged so well that at first I confused it for a leaf or wad of paper. By the roadside sat a marvel as big as my hand, its lime-green wings spread open like a cape, trimmed at the top in a thin stole of yellow fur. Its neck was golden, with two gold waving feathers atop its head. It had long raspberry legs shaped like a dancer's, and on each shoulder a small perfect human eye. When I reached out to touch the legs, it didn't move. A bead of dew sat on one damp wing. Perhaps the air was still too cold for it to fly. For an hour I sat quietly beside the moth while it dried its wings in the sun. Otherwise it would have been easy prey for the birds filling the sky with a menagerie of liquid warbles and chirps. Prisms of dew wobbled on a nearby leaf. Goddess of the moon and protectress of animals, perhaps Diana watches over all moon dramas and beings, including lunatics (the moonstruck). I suppose it makes sense that I've gradually evolved from studying animals to studying the human animal, from nature to human nature, and back to nature again.

With sheets of amazement pouring off me like sweat, I sat in the dirt and crawl of the roadside, amid shards of broken glass and ant bites, my focus narrow as a shaft of grass. Luna moth. I could not fill my eyes enough with it; even after an hour of admiring it, each look was a surprise. That luna moth was in her summer dress (the spring form has a raspberry stole). By midmorning, I realized that it was the end of the moth's season; its life was dwindling away before me. Reason enough to be its hospice and guard. I would not touch her or pin her or keep her. I just kept her company and praised her for the rest of her brief life, thinking that every moon moth deserves its day.

Tonight, I hear Louise huddling by the roadside. "I'm worried about you," I say. "How about if I send someone over to be with you?" The tinkling of ice cubes against glass, and a small sip between sniffles. I didn't realize she was drinking. She doesn't sound drunk, but the alcohol won't help her mood and it might give her the wrong kind of courage.

"I'm not at home," she says. "Anyway, it's too late for that. I put my coat on, but I don't need to, do I, to be warm when I fly." She sounds wrung-out, exhausted, giving up. "At least it won't hurt much.."

"Won't hurt much?"

"I took a bunch of Tylenol…"

My heart starts to pound, and with a huge effort at control I ask: "How much Tylenol did you take?"

"I don't know," she whines, "a bunch, enough."

Prodding her once more about the pills, she again answers vaguely, saying she's not sure how much Tylenol she has swallowed. It may not be much. She doesn't sound ill. She doesn't mention the pills with dread or in ominous tones. The gorge is her weapon, not the pills. But she may not know how dangerous an elixir Tylenol is—even a small overdose can do permanent damage to the liver, and a large one be fatal. Taking them is one more preparatory act. That's it. I can't stand the risk any longer. Every call with Louise has seemed this dire, a last call for help, and she has survived. But suppose tonight is the exception, suppose this is the last of last times? What is different tonight? I'm not sure. Then it dawns on me. Something small. I'm frightened by how often she has been using the word "only," a word tight as a noose. Without letting her hear, I notify the police to trace the call and accompany her to the hospital, where a doctor will give her yet another type of medication. She has tried eight different antidepressants over the past years, all mind-scrambling in their start-up phase, plagued with side effects, and, unfortunately, not effective in the landscape of her unique chemistry. But she has been willing to try them, God help her, and she has called tonight, with however faint a heart. The life-hungry part of her has phoned for help. If we send rescue, and she survives tonight, will she be afraid to call the next time? That may be a moot question. A trace can take hours, and doesn't always work. She said she isn't home; a remote lake house would be impossible to find. On principle, to preserve a caller's anonymity, we don't have caller ID. Thus traces are laborious, hit-or-miss events, which may include several telephone systems. We rarely initiate them. I busy-out the second telephone line so that no one can interrupt us, because I'm not sure Louise would stay on the line if I answered an incoming call.

"I'll stay with you." Which problem to focus on? Which section of the tunnel to drill windows in? Her job? Her family problems? Maybe her sense of isolation. The outer one, I mean, the one that can be eased by friends and acquaintances. The inner one is another matter. So often loneliness comes from being out of touch with parts of oneself. We go searching for those parts in other people, but there's a difference between feeling separate from others and separate from oneself.

"You said no one would care if you died. But *I* would care."

"I bet you say that to all the callers," she says, mustering a touch of coyness.

"Not so. You and I have had some good talks over the past few months."

Leaning on the desk, I focus my eyes on the wood grain's many streaks and knots. If it had color, it would look like a Navajo blanket. Hard as I try to concentrate solely on hearing, sights keep trickling in.

So does the fragrance of coffee brewing in the kitchen. The long vowels of the wind. The chatter of the venetian blinds against a drafty window frame.

"Yes," she says, "you've been swell. You've been my only friends, well not friends exactly, not to you, I mean I'm just one of…"

"You'd be surprised how well you can get to know someone over the telephone. I bet you've gotten to know me a little, too, and the other counselors."

"Yes," she says, "I have actually. *You* always sound so calm and even. I envy how together you must be. My life is shooting out of my hands, and I wish I could have your…spirit level."

"I'm not always level. Believe me, my life has problems, too. It's easier to be calm when someone else is in trouble."

"Oh," she says, with a mixture of surprise and relief. "Anyway, you're a good person: patient, and kind, and strong…"

"So are you. All those things."

"Strong? That's a good one. If you could see how weak I am…" Her voice trails away.

"Amazingly strong." Be careful, I think, not to use the past tense. She might interpret that as an obituary. "Look how you've been fighting the torrents of depression—for years. That takes such courage. You've been working during that time, raising two kids, surviving the nightmare of an ugly divorce. Okay, you've lost jobs, but you've picked yourself up and found new jobs. You've even volunteered during the flood—filling sandbags and making sandwiches, I think you said once—and you've found the time and energy and heart to do volunteer work with the Hangar Theater and the Summer Festival, and the a capella group, and helped other people in trouble. You've been heroic. You're being strong tonight, calling us. Given how bad you're feeling, that takes real strength. I admire your courage."

"Admire?" she says, letting the word hover a long moment while she considers it. "You wouldn't want to live my life. It's only bad choices…except…" Sniffling.

"Death is always a possibility, but not the best."

"Do you know something about it I don't know?" she says with a morbid touch of sarcasm.

"Maybe so," I say gently. "It's hereditary, it's irreversible, and you don't need to keep a day free for it."

Silence. I can feel her thinking it over.

"*Lonelier than life,* you said. Why don't we think of a few ways to help you solve that problem," I suggest. Broaden the perspective. The hardest job when someone is depressed.

"There aren't any."

"Sure there are." Off the top of my head, I list some ways for her to ease her loneliness—through classes, volunteer work, athletics, music, nature centers, city projects, and such. Not one appeals to her. I didn't think any would. Nonetheless I ask her to consider the list and arrange it in order of preference, "even though we'll agree that you're too tired and fed up to do any of them and they all sound bad anyway." Despite her strong resistance to each item, she goes through the motions of ranking them, and that distracts her a little. Arranging them in descending order, she objects to each one, pointing out its drawbacks and her inability or lack of interest. I remember suicidologist Edwin Shneidman observed that "Life is often a choice among many unpleasant possibilities, and the goal is to choose the least unpleasant one." That's all I'm doing with Louise, rummaging around in undesirable choices for the least undesirable, but it opens a few tiny windows in her tunnel. And suicide is nowhere on the list.

"Will you hold on?" she asks abruptly. "There's someone at the door."

Damn, the police. That was fast—she must be at home after all. Maybe I didn't need to send them. And she'll be angry, she'll feel lied to and betrayed. She does. I hear her screaming at me, at the telephone, at the world. She calls me a liar, and she's right. I lied to her. Not about what mattered, only about the trace, and only because her life is in danger, and only because I deduced that some part of her craves life or she wouldn't have called. "False in part, false in whole"—isn't that how jurors are advised to consider the testimony of a perjurer? How can she trust any of my sincere concern if I lie to her? Her crying hits me like a ton of heavy drapery. I feel ashamed, I hate having lied to her. The next voice I hear on the line is a policeman's, and I ask him about the Tylenol. He finds an empty bottle by the phone next to a glass redolent of alcohol. Everything follows quickly from there. She's furious at me, but she does go with them to the hospital. Mad as hell, she is, and very lethal, but also just ambivalent enough to let them transport her to safety. Thank God for that. Suppose the hospital releases her right away and she heads straight for the gorge? Knowing and not knowing about callers, that's what gets to me. Maybe I could have calmed her and talked her round? Maybe someone else would have prevailed, someone who can do this slow tango of life and death with more grace and cunning. My chest feels rigid as a boat hull, my ribs tense. Taking a large breath and letting it out slowly, I press my open palms against my face, rub the eyebrows, then the cheekbones and jaw, and laugh. Not a ha-ha laugh, a small sardonic one, the kind we save for the ridiculous, as I catch myself slipping into a familiar trap. I did fine. I did the best I could. Maybe the best anyone could tonight. Did I guess wrong about the extent of her lethality? Who's to say. Surely it's better to err on the side of caution. My next duty is to phone the hospital and alert a doctor to her imminent arrival, telling him of her emotional state, previous suicide attempts, and general psychiatric history. Not the details of our conversation or her life; she'll tell him those if she wishes, or she'll leave them in the well of this exhausting night.

My shoulders feel skewered, and a long grinding pain twitches down my right side. Rolling my head in slow circles, twisting my shoulders, stretching my arms, arching my spine, I realize that during the past two hours my back never touched the chair. The perfect recipe for backache. She'll hate me, hate me, I think, as I get up stiffly and go to the kitchen for tea. Yes, but she'll be *alive* to hate me. Until the next time, anyway, the next rock-bottom night when she longs to fly. Helping Louise survive is always an ordeal. Tonight she sounded even more determined and deathbound than usual. It was the right choice. I think. Maybe. On the write-up sheet, under "Caller," I write "Louise," put the letter H for "high" in the box marked "suicide risk," attach a yellow Lethality Assessment sheet, and add a few details of the call. I don't mention the penguins, her private metaphor for depression's bone-chilling expanse. Leaning back in the chair with my feet stretched out and resting on the desk, once more I think of the luna moth, that beautiful being struggling in slow motion through the last moments of life. I cherished it, protected it, and when it became clear I could do no more, I left it where it fell. For some time, though, I felt a conflicting sense of wonder and loss. Imagine, we mourn even the death of a moth. Pressing my fingertips to my face, I push again on the brow bones, as if I could rearrange them, but they ache from a place I can't reach with my hands.

CHAPTER 14

Before the Dawn

With three feet of snow on the ground, the streets look like a tobog-
gan run. The whole city is really and truly ice-in-your-socks bliz-
zard-bound. Seven snowstorms hit in a row this month, accompanied
by sub-zero weather. Snow piles high on every roof, and huge water-
fall-like icebergs cascade from the eaves. All over town, the houses
look tusked, part of a mammoth herd. Everyone's roof is leaking, and
mine is no exception. In my bathroom, ice water has begun to drip fast
from an overhead heater; slowly along the skylights; plunkingly from
a doorjamb; silently as it seeps from under a baseboard; and in wavering rivulets down the inside of the window frame.

I've constructed an aqueduct out of aluminum foil, a stepladder, cardboard boxes, and a variety of plastic wastebaskets. This directs the water into the bathtub, but now and then new drips start and the aqueduct has to be repositioned. Paul tends the contraption after I go to sleep, but one hour of potential catastrophe remains between five and six. The window-frame trickle is the hardest to capture, and so I've pressed a small parachute of aluminum foil tightly against the wood, allowing water to ebb over it into a loaf pan. After a few seconds, surface tension holds the foil secure against the wood until (sometimes days later) the leaking stops.

Why an epidemic of roof leaks for the first time in fifteen years? Because so much snow blankets the roofs, with no warm melting weather between storms. If a house is poorly insulated, the roof warms from the furnace and the lives beneath it. The lowest layers of snow melt, and ice dams forming along the house eaves hold the water in place. So, in effect, many houses have ponds on their roofs—sometimes as much as six to twelve inches of standing water—and no shingles can withstand being the bottom of a lake. Right in the middle of the bathroom ceiling, a large pendulous belly of water formed, which Paul bayoneted to save the ceiling from even worse damage.

Insulation, I think, as I pedal along freshly plowed roads. That's what it's all about, finding a way both to protect yourself from and be in harmony with the elements. Today, wearing a knitted cap and mask under my helmet, I'm a Ninjalike apparition amusing the neighbor children. Even though my broken foot hasn't fully healed yet, which means no hiking for a while, I can bike for hours on end (a non-weightbearing exercise), and it feels wonderful to be outside. The sun casts a golden spell over everything, but especially on things pale and dry like seedpods, grasses, and dead leaves still attached to trees. Sunlight hits them like an emollient and makes them glow. As I pass a red barn, the sun glazes the weathered wooden slats with a strong light, clarifying the bare wood, and giving painted wood a deep patina. Few things are as bewitching as the way sunlight spackles rough wood, filling the cracks with gold, glittering off higher splinters, burnishing still reddish parts to a radiant burgundy. All the washings and hesitations of light illumunate the barn like a great text, and reveal in the flaking wood an inner depth and unfurling message. The barn walls rest on a foundation of uncemented, unmortared, perfectly poised fieldstones. Because the beauty of the sight fills me with a tincture of joy, I stop for a while and stare at the tones and shapes. Goethe was right, "One searches in vain beyond phenomenon; it in itself is revelation." *Bare attention,* Buddhism calls it, a pinnacle of meditation, a path to freedom from pain and suffering—not by fleeing the world, but by being fully available to it. *Disponibilité,* André Gide named a related attitude. Phenomenologists label their version of "bare attention" *phenomenological reduction.* But it's interesting how many of the world's religions and philosophies urge us to live in each silvery moment, while resisting the temptation to skim over, take for granted, or ignore the impromptu sensations that give life its vigor. Forget meaning, this attitude says; practice *being.* Feats of disciplined awareness wouldn't be necessary if we weren't in such a hurry to die and shed the burden of our senses, those permanent houseguests that keep us tipsy or tormented throughout our lives. Slow down, our sages advise, slow all the way down to the pace of stone and shadow. How long can you watch sunlight flash across threads of spider silk stretching between two limbs of an evergreen? How long after the tree appears to be full of tinsel? Can you observe it longer than that, with continuous pleasure and surprise, but without remembering a Christmas? Without planning gifts or visits? This is the tinsel test. Poets tend toward bare attention naturally, and are usually able to address one facet of the world with such devotion that, as Blake described it from the depths of his own supple vision, it is possible to "see the world in a grain of sand, / And a heaven in a wild flower, / Hold infinity in the palm of your hand, / And eternity in an hour."

On sweet vagrant days, I find myself in a state of alert calm as I bike, undisturbed by thought, all my senses open, regarding the sun dapples on macadam, or pastures of horsetail-shaped clouds above, without trying to construe them, without dwelling on personal matters. I know how fortunate I am to possess this receptive gift, and I never take it for granted. It's one of the reasons I love biking, a sport that allows me to dally at speed. However, I do wish I could regard life's problems with bare attention, too. Perhaps I should give the Buddhist monastery a call this afternoon, and see what controlled meditation is like. Can you *invite* rapture? It has always befallen me at unexpected moments, and not always when I am sitting still. But I do go to places where rapture may happen. I make room for it. Then I remove the distractions of self, listen affectionately to the voices of the world, and want nothing, search nothing, judge nothing. I guess that qualifies as an invitation, and also as a Zen discipline, "the discipline of acceptance."

At the Crisis Center, we also practice a discipline of acceptance, pledging not to judge callers, regardless of their views or values. That's the ideal; in practice, it's not always easy. When men phone from a nearby prison, as they occasionally do, I don't inquire about the crime that has condemned them to years of confinement. Better not to know if they stole or killed or raped or embezzled or prostituted or injected or brutalized. If I don't know too many details, I can try to understand how cramped they must feel, how bored and lonely, how full of anger. Picturing them standing or sitting at the telephone, I imagine their lot and listen to their suffering. When people call who are bigoted, sadistic, or wrongheaded, we try not to judge them, but of course that's difficult. We all have buttons that can be pushed, tripwires that explode the hidden landmines of self-esteem or morality. For me, racism is unconscionable, and I'm not good with racist callers; I lose my neutrality. A saintlier person would embrace all, even the worst hate-mongers, but racism disgusts me, disgusts me at the deepest level, where I believe in the sanctity of life and the perfectibility of people, threatens the dignity I behold in all living things. It doesn't scare me, it puts my worldview in peril. Fear is danger to your body, but disgust is danger to your soul. Ideally, I should be able to ignore my disgusted soul while I'm counseling. If I could resist all biases, past experiences, and personal values when I speak with a caller, I think I might feel a sense of communion rare among mortals. I might leave my self and travel into the caller, insert myself into his psyche, walk with him a while, truly share his burden. I try to do that anyway, but sometimes my self intrudes and I stumble.

Soon Flat Rock comes into view, with its churning, sun-polished waters. It's amazing how many different versions of stream there are, how the water, broken up and transfigured by rock bed, is propeled at several speeds, assumes different poses, reflects light in a pageant of shimmer and glare. Here gooseflesh rises, ripples, sings forward. There a swell rushes backward with the slightest quiverings. In another spot a sinewy white froth forms where the current slides around a jagged rock. A few yards on, the water puckers and dashes ahead. Beside that, a flat calm area looks like skin on pudding. Next to that white caps flee toward a buttress of rocks. A small insinuation of current outlines a boulder, while large flat shards of ice float by. Though only twenty yards across, the stream changes complexion a dozen times. So many temperaments of water mingle, all of them involved in different dramas, yet all part of the larger movement of the stream. They combine in one onrushing whole, one gushing organism made up of varying strengths and weaknesses, whose past pools in the mountains, whose future pours through the imagination. How life carries us all along, despite our differences and eccentricities, in one ongoing froth of lives. Pulling over for a moment, I jot down these metaphorical thoughts and some others for a poem, then continue on up Freese Road, pedal hard past the Hawk Woods, and coast most of the way home.

———

When I toss out nuts, they parachute through deep snow and twenty-five squirrels rush in and out, digging for treasure in one spot, nosing

around in another, on a sort of mystery hunt. Because they are sometimes lucky enough to strike peanut gold, they keep up the search for
quite a spell. I'm certain they'll find every nut. Now that the snow has
begun falling thickly, with flakes big as bumblebees, I don't expect the
squirrels will be out and about for the rest of the day. I'm glad to see
them active and well-padded, but the Pleader has been missing for
nearly a month, and this time I think he may be gone for good. Poor
fellow, what hardships did he encounter? Collops has vanished, too,
and I'm just as worried about her. A plump, friendly squirrel, she's the
great matriarch of the yard, the most frequent breeder, with many offspring and, I would have thought, a fresh batch of pups at home. Is she
injured? She always arrives along the telephone-wire highway between the house and an outlying building. Could she have slipped on
an icy patch? What will become of her pups? I cringe inside when I
think of four pink squirrel pups naked and cold, their eyes not yet
open, blindly squealing for their mother. Maybe Collops is still alive
but unable to make her way to the house. Just in case, I'll start leaving
a small pile of seeds and nuts out in the deep woods, closer to her tree
nest.

An article in the newspaper mentioned how many squirrels were
showing up dead on the highways, and the writer asked in all seriousness if it wasn't perhaps a form of suicide. Suicide is not only a human
phenomenon; other animals commit suicide, too. There are termites
that explode on purpose, protecting their nests by pelting invaders
with the putrid contents of their guts. There are sick rodents that iso-
late themselves and then starve to death rather than infect their relatives. There are uniquely patterned butterflies with a knack for
camouflage, whose elders might attract the notice of predators, alerting them to the secret camouflage code of the young; after they finish
breeding, the elders leave hiding and beat their wings exhaustively
until they wear themselves out and die. There are sickly blind mole
rats, which exile themselves to the toilet area of the burrow and starve
rather than contaminate the tribe. Most touching of all, though, are

the many species of nonhuman primates, which become hideously depressed by life's losses and stresses, and react in familiar, melancholy ways: becoming listless, not defending themselves when attacked, taking life-threatening risks (swinging recklessly from dangerous trees, for example), or refusing food until they wither away. In a compelling study of free-ranging rhesus monkeys, scientists discovered that about 20 percent of them were vulnerable to profound depression during their lives. That's the same average one finds among humans. What precipitated depression most often among the monkeys was loss of parents, offspring, and mates, or loss of social status: some of the same things that cause us stress. Monkey depression looks so much like human depression that scientists give melancholy monkeys antidepressants like Prozac, which work well to lift their mood. In a heartwrenching story, Jane Goodall tells of a young male chimpanzee who mourned so profoundly after the death of his mother that he refused to leave her dead body. Paralyzed by grief, he couldn't rally enough to eat, and in time he starved to death from loneliness and despair, or, as Goodall put it, he died of a broken heart.

Contrary to popular legend, lemmings don't hurl themselves into the ocean in a single-minded mass suicide. Frantic when the urge to migrate calls, the plump, tawny rodents scramble wildly on, sometimes without noticing that they're heading right off a cliff until it's too late. Then, like an ill-fated Air Force aerobatics team, the mob follows blindly without sensing the danger. This strategy works if lemmings are leaping small boulders or fording streams, but not at cliff heads or on the edge of oceans. Lemmings aren't suicidal, they're simply unswerving followers and lousy navigators.

I've never observed self-sacrificing squirrels, but stressed ones, confused ones, embattled ones, exhausted ones, frantic ones, belligerent ones, competitive ones, affectionate ones, loyal ones, problem-solving ones, ones who weigh risk against advantage, ones who anticipate, playful ones, resilient ones, skillful ones, ones who cleverly manipulate humans, defeated and melancholy ones: yes. *Wild* is what we call them, the word tottering between fear and praise. Wild ideas are alluring, impulsive, unpredictable, ideas with wings and hooves. Being with wild animals—whether they're squirrels in the backyard, or heavily antlered elk in Yellowstone—reminds us of our own wildness, thrills the animal part of us that loves the feel of sunlight and the succulence of fresh water, is alert to danger and soothed by the familiar sounds of family and herd. Yet we pretend that we alone feel, we alone worry, we alone form affectionate attachments, we alone know disappointment, sorrow, and desperation. It's sad we don't respect the struggles and talents of other animals, but I'm equally concerned about the price we pay for that haughtiness. Monarchs may be powerful, but they rule alone. We've evolved to live tribally in a kingdom of neighbors, human neighbors and animal neighbors. Kith and kin, we all travel the same byways.

And what of the squirrels dying on the highway? In late fall the numbers were highest, and I think that's because squirrels were eating fermented apples and other fruit, then staggering around in a drunken haze, crossing roads but not watching for oncoming cars. I'm serious. Yard animals sometimes get tipsy in the fall. Chipmunks, squirrels, deer—I've seen all of them wobbly after a feed on fermented apples.

What a year it's been, I think as I sip a mug of tea. Each morning, I've been studying the ways of squirrels, deer, birds, and other animals, whose struggles sometimes echo problems I find among humans at the Crisis Center later in the day. In both arenas, I've tried to ease the suffering of the world a little, but I've also found a perspective on life that fascinates me. At this crossroads, it's possible to see the human world and the world of nature meet and become one. Observing the tumult, mysteries, grandeur of the seasons, the plight of animal families, and the Crisis Center emergencies, sometimes it feels as if I'm living in a novel, the setting of which is the sprawling, heavily haunted mansion of nature. Part of my mind lingers on the sometimes catastrophic phone calls I'm dealing with. Another part rejoices in the antics and struggles of the squirrels from day to day, from the way they master the obstacle courses I built for them to how they strip off tree bark and lap the sweet sap, from their aerial courtship and mating rituals to their warfare, from the schooling of their young to their frenetic and ingenious preparations for winter. Meanwhile humans are gathering and preparing for winter, too, also schooling their young, triumphing over obstacles, courting and mating at considerable risk. What a marvel that these two realms of behavior exist at the same time in the same universe for essentially the same reasons. What a marvel that they differ in unique and prismatic ways.

———

When we enter a public building we lose some of our own wilderness, and the relaxed eccentricity of an unobserved life. Nonetheless, I hurry down to the Crisis Center, skidding along roads slick as silk. Carrying my hastily packed lunch of Swiss cheese on a bagel with cilantro and mayo, a can of apricots, and a Coke and a straw (so that I don't make drinking sounds over the phone), I tap the secret combination into the door lock, go in, and climb the stairs. Fred, the overnight counselor, is already awake, quietly doing write-ups at the desk. He looks scrunched-up, sleepy-eyed, and boyish first thing in the morning. One usually sees a man that way only when he is family, or a lover, so there's a touch of tenderness about the scene, of our waking up together on the ledge of the morning, able to tumble right back into bed. Fred is gay and in a longstanding relationship, about which we occasionally talk. There's something about working with exposed, vulnerable callers that creates a bond of intimacy among counselors, who are quick to drop pretenses and façades. This morning, Fred and I chat amiably, and then he heads home to finish sleeping. The logbook reveals that it was a quiet night for him. Four hang-ups, one call from an anonymous female. The hang-ups came at regular two-hour intervals, just often enough to wake him every two or three hours through the night. Edward Scissorhands? Possibly, but at some point he would have vented his rage in familiar ways. As usual, I scan the bulletin board for notices, and a new postcard catches my eye. On one side is a reproduction of the Edward Hopper painting *Nighthawks*, in which three lonely souls sit drinking coffee in an overlit diner. A cliché of American alienation, it's still riveting to view in person, as I once did at the Whitney Museum. Although you can't see it clearly in reproductions, I remember being startled by the way Hopper painted eye sockets. Both colored and carved by brushstrokes, they expressed the hollowing, ratcheting pain of a loneliness that tunnels right into the skull. Turning the card over, I find a neat, even handwriting, in blue ink, addressed to the agency. *I'm writing to thank whoever the counselor was I spoke with*...Notes to SP frequently begin that way. But when the large open loops and rounded *d*s mention the day and hour, my thoughts quicken. That was *my* shift. My eyes slide to the signature. It's from Louise, who has signed her real name. Sitting down on the couch, I read the card carefully, and learn that she went from the emergency room to a psychiatric hospital in Pennsylvania, where she spent three weeks "in palatial bedlam." When she returned to town, she met an acquaintance who volunteers for Displaced Homemakers; Louise discovered a genial group of people there, and even took a paying job at the agency. A month later, she's "finally in a good place," by which I know she means several terrains, including her job and her mood. I cross the fingers of both hands and tap the interlocked fingertips together. May this small placard be true; may she find peace. She blesses the soul who "took my life in her hands that night," thanks us all for our good work, is just writing "to let you know what happened—I bet you don't hear very often." We don't.

Soon after 9:00 A.M. the phone rings. An older woman says, as if interrupted in midsentence: "Oh, I guess I'm just calling to hear a human voice." She sounds sad and tired. It's surprising how quickly a voice can reveal one's age. A low soprano, hers has thickened over the years and grown a little gravelly, but not wheezy or frail. She's in her early seventies I'd guess.

"How are you feeling this morning?"

Voice breaking, she says, "Not so good. I've just had to pay the hospital bill..." She struggles to hold her voice steady even though she's crying, but it's like trying to lock up a hurricane in a barn.

In a softer voice, I ask, "Hospital bill?"

Her voice catches a few times. "After my husband died," she says at last, "all these bills started arriving...the electric, the insurance, the car, the funeral home, the hospital, everything. He always paid them. I don't even know where the insurance coupons are, and then the bills arrive and..." Her voice dissolves into tears. "I remember so much."

"That must be painful. The bills are overwhelming in themselves, but worst of all they keep reminding you of his death."

"Yes," she says, exhaling the word. "It was such a shock." Her voice wavers, trying not to break. "He had a heart attack when we were out shopping at the mall. He just fell down dead. Collapsed. He fell so hard. The *sound*. I'll never forget that sound."

In the mall? I picture them walking hand in hand past the Hallmark card store, and her husband dropping like a big animal. "That must have been frightening for you."

"It was such a shock."

"When did he die?"

"Three months ago."

A fresh loss. All the trees planted over a lifetime in the garden of her marriage, an emotional landscape she relied on and took for granted, have been ripped up in one of life's severe earthquakes. "So there was the shock of his death, and now there are lots of aftershocks as the bills and paperwork come in?"

"Yes. I never learned how to do them." A familiar story.

"You're feeling overwhelmed by them?"

"It's so much. The car needs to be fixed. Dave always used to take care of that. I get his social security, but that's all, and it's been reduced now that he's gone."

"That's terrible. Your husband is gone and they reduce your income?"

"It *is* terrible. I don't think there's enough to pay the telephone and electric this month. I've called them, and they've agreed to give me more time, but where will the money come from? And I'm so confused about things. I make notes so that I won't forget to do things."

"That's good that you make notes." The shortest pencil is the longest memory, my Uncle Lou always used to say. "Does it help?"

"A little," she sighs.

"You get easily confused?"

"I do."

More than anything, what she needs now are friends and loved ones. We weren't meant to mourn alone. "Do you have family or close friends, perhaps, who can give you a hand getting through this tough time? Someone to lend a little emotional support?"

"No. No one. My husband always said when we'd fight, *You'll miss me when I'm gone!* And he was right. I do." She begins whimpering.

Her raw animal sorrow touches a nerve in my throat and I make an instinctive sound of sympathy, then add, "It's really hard to have him gone, isn't it?"

"*So* hard."

Where are her friends? "Is there a woman friend you can call to talk with a little?"

"Not really. My husband hated me to have people over. Dave wouldn't socialize at all—except now and then he'd bring home some guys from work. They were never friends of mine. I was stupid. Now I don't have anyone." She sounds angry, angry at him, but also angry at herself.

"You're wishing you had some friends now..."

"I really am. I was so stupid!"

Another familiar pattern—men who keep visitors from the house, discourage their wives from making friends, and leave behind widows with no community, no confidantes, nowhere to turn when they're feeling isolated and alone.

"Maybe this would be a good time to make some new friends," I suggest, wondering if it wouldn't help her to feel part of the human tide. Especially since she spent her marriage feeling forcibly unsociable. Having friends might be a novelty, offer her the tonic of intimate relationships, and generally help buttress her crumbling spirits.

"Maybe."

"How would you feel about trying a support group of women who have also lost their husbands?" Instantly I regret my choice of words. *Lost their husbands?* It sounds doomed, and suggests how at sea the survivor feels, how confused and hopeless, how imperiled. When a loved one dies, the world does seem all subtractions. One feels impoverished, a terrible draft blows through every room, simple objects assault one with memories, and time loses its momentum. But others see the survivor as a whole person: pained, sad, struggling, grieving, yet also continuing on the unpredictable journey of her life. *Lost their husbands* sounds too close to *lost their identity*, or *lost their sanity*, or *lost their way in the world* for my liking. I don't know what a better euphemism might be, but emphasizing how helpless, dead-end, and destroyed she feels doesn't seem the best solution. On the other hand, maybe my caller isn't as sensitive to labels as I am, maybe she isn't as vulnerable to suggestive words. I should just follow her lead, and use whatever term seems the most palatable to her.

"I called Displaced Homemakers," she says, "and they have a widows' group meeting this Saturday. I was thinking about going but haven't made up my mind."

Good, she used her initiative. I wonder if she spoke with Louise? It's vital that I persuade her to go.

"A widows' group—that sounds good. You'd meet other women there who understand what you're going through, and they might be able to give you some practical advice," I offer. "But it might also be a good place to meet some nice people, maybe make some new friends."

"Yeah, that sounds like a good idea. I'm going to go there."

Thank heavens for that. "There are a few days between now and then. What are you thinking of doing today?"

How obsessively we define, measure, and even sell time, yet its elasticity amazes me. Quilting the days together with work, chores, decisions, appointments, phone calls, meals, hobbies, and family, we rarely worry how to make day become night. If anything, the days gallop away when we wish we could rein them in. But, for a number of our callers, each day is a desert to be crossed inch by inch, and filling the gritty hours takes planning.

"I don't know," she says, crying, a small fright in her voice. "I have errands."

"Is there anything you can do to be good to yourself, anything comforting? Maybe stop for a cup of hot cocoa or tea somewhere?" The tea cure. Something about the ritual of tea, and its fluid warmth, brings comfort.

"I don't know if I can afford it. I know it's only pennies, but I just don't have anything right now. I've had to quit my watercolor class, which I really liked. It was only twenty-five dollars a month, but...all these bills. I don't know how to cope."

"It sounds like it really feels overwhelming sometimes."

"It is. Sometimes—ha! all the time—it's just an avalanche. And I'm always thinking about Dave, about his just falling suddenly. Everything reminds me. I can't seem to get on with my life. Or want to. I'm so confused, so worn out."

"I can hear what a tough time this is for you. It would be for anyone. What you're going through is normal. It takes time, and unfortunately it really hurts."

"Is it normal to be this overwhelmed?"

That's what most people want to know when they're struck by grief. Is it normal to feel such extreme pain and despair, or am I just screwed up and trapped in hell forever, with no way out and no control? Normalizing the pain reassures them a little.

"Yes, it is."

"That's good to hear. I thought I wasn't handling it very well. Sometimes I'm so confused."

"Everyone handles grief differently. There's no right way, no best way, no right amount of time. Eventually you'll find your own timetable, your own way of coping. There's no rush."

"Calling you guys has been helping me get through," she says tearfully.

Glancing up, I follow a small crack to the light fixture, beside which a large spider sits on a kite-shaped web. The same spider has sat there for over a month, and no one has killed it. Suddenly, the spider rappels down a silk cord into the middle of the room, reconnoiters briefly, then scrambles back up again. Unless I'm the only one it favors with such visits, I presume it often drops down for a look-see. Although I like spiders, it's eerie not knowing when one might land on my shoulder. And what of those counselors who find spiders frightening? Surely they fret about one dangling overhead, only a silent free fall away. Lifting a hand to my forehead, I salute the spider, which every counselor on every shift for the past month has spared. Then, turning around to face the desk, the telephone, the window, I return my thoughts to the caller.

"It's tough going through a crisis like this alone," I say.

"It really is. You're never prepared. I don't know how to *be* anymore."

"...to *be*?"

"Now that I'm on my own, without my husband."

I wonder if I can put what she's dreading into a more positive light. "Now that your life is changing and you have new responsibilities..."

"Yes."

"It sounds like you've been handling quite a few of them."

I try to imagine how scary it must feel, being swamped with unexpected and arcane *obligations*. There's so much for her to master, since her husband protected her from the sordid details of bills, due dates, legalities, and small print. Although she dutifully tended him and ran the household, she must also have felt a precious sense of being protected and looked after. Now she must look after herself. I don't envy her the transition.

"Oh, yes. That's kept me busy at least."

"And taught you new skills."

Laughing, she says: "And how! Never thought I'd be running the house, getting the car fixed ... everything."

"How does it feel to know that you *can* do these things?"

"I'm surprised that I can. Hell, I'm amazed that I can. But it's just too much right now, all at once. And I still can't believe he's gone. Except for all the paperwork. Boy, that'll make it clear!"

"It's still hard to believe, isn't it, a big shock, a big change in your life?"

"That's what it is." She sounds fearful.

"Why don't we take a couple of deep breaths," I suggest.

She laughs. "Okay." I hear her taking two slow deep breaths.

What next? Back to crossing the desert of her day.

"Have you got any tea you might make? Maybe listen to the radio for a minute or two? Or watch a movie? Maybe plan your trip to the support group on Saturday?"

"Yes, I could make some chamomile tea. I will go on Saturday. It's on Green Street. I'll park in the church lot."

"Would you like us to call you later, just to check in on you?"

"No," she says gratefully, "but thank you for offering. I'll be okay for a little while now I think."

"Okay. Please do call back when you find you're having some trouble coping. This is hard to go through alone. We're here whenever you need to talk to someone."

After hanging up, I immediately call my mother and ask if she knows how to run the house, pay the bills, and so on. My father is eighty-six, and my mother has gradually allowed him to run the business of family life. He's very good at it and enjoys the responsibility, but she would be at sea if he were gone.

"Don't you think you should drive the car sometimes, just a little to keep in practice?" I suggest to her.

"Oh, your father drives everywhere. I don't need to, and the traffic down here scares me!"

The enclosed kingdom of their condo sits on a quiet street, at the end of which sprawls half a mile of shops. "How about just down to the mall at the end of the street, maybe to the grocery store and the drugstore? I mean, what if Dad were laid up sometime? You'd feel cut off, wouldn't you?"

Even though she understands my worry, and agrees that it makes sense for her to learn how to run the house now while my father is alive to teach her, the possibility spooks her and she changes the subject. But at least I planted it in her thoughts.

10:06 A.M. A male caller stumbles awkwardly as he tries to convey his grave depression. Though he urgently needs to make contact with someone, crossing the threshhold of intimacy and trust is frightening, especially with a stranger. Slowly, I try to draw him out. He has lost his job of fifteen years, and with that his income, his food, his self-esteem, and his reason for getting up each day. Little is left of his bedraggled sense of future. His work defined him, and now he feels no connection to society or life. For nearly an hour, I concentrate on the man, his story, his pain.

When we hang up, after logging the call, I find my thoughts drifting again to the Pleader, so lethargic and low in recent months, though he did rally briefly. I've no idea where his winter tree home is, or if he's even in the neighborhood. Or alive. But, before I have much time to dwell on things, a call comes in from the next counselor on shift, who has a crisis of her own—a chest pain she's convinced is nothing more than a hiatus hernia or a muscle spasm. But her daughter is going to drive her to the doctor for an EKG just to make sure. Last-minute cancellations are nearly impossible to fill, so I agree to stay a little later.

12:05 P.M. A call comes from a frequent caller with an erotic obsession. He tries to trick counselors into saying the word "prick" as often as possible. A conversation might begin with his saying, "I feel like such a prick today."

"Why do you feel that way today?" I'll ask.

"What way ... ?" He'll inquire, hoping I'll say back to him: *like a prick.* I never do, and that annoys him, so he continues trying to trap me, and when that fails he angrily accuses me of being inhibited and prim, the source of all of society's troubles. Then he tries another ploy. "Do women talk about garter belts?" he asks. "What do they say about their garter belts?"

Sometimes when Garter Man calls I try not to think of the word *prick,* try not to picture garter belts (especially those I've owned), but the effort always boomerangs and reminds me of them nonstop. It's hopeless trying to gag the mind. Don't think about a pink elephant with woolly legs. Once before when I talked with this caller he admitted that he calls so that he can masturbate afterward. We have a few callers who are desperate to hear us say sexual words or refer to fetish objects or articles of underclothing. It's a strange, fascinating obsession.

"Look, there's nothing wrong with masturbating, and there are a lot of numbers you can call for that service," I say, "but it's not one we provide. So I'm going to hang up now." I do.

1:00 P.M. An Owego woman calls who says she's been drinking heavily and is probably drunk, but she doesn't sound it. She does sound convincingly suicidal though, and I discover she has attempted suicide twice before, and knows that she's right at the edge, close to the no-turning-back point. Her husband died three years ago in a mining accident. Her two children (ages four and six) were taken away from her after her last suicide attempt and put in the custody of their grandparents in Horseheads, with the understanding that she could regularly visit them. But her new husband won't allow her to see them. She says he wants her full attention and is jealous of the children. Does he honestly believe he can win this contest? Maybe so. After all, thus far she has forsaken them on his orders. He also insists on always knowing her whereabouts, and he polices her in other ways. Before I ask, she says emphatically that he doesn't hit her, and the way she says it, defending him, sounds suspicious. But at the moment she is her own would-be assassin. When I ask if she has a plan, she reveals that she's holding a bottle of Valium and means to swallow them. They're what she ODed on before. Even though she sounds sober, the alcohol is a wild card. She may not remember this conversation to-morrow—if she lives until tomorrow. I need her address, and it would be best if she gave it to me, but she's frightened of her husband's tem-per. Among the many laws of conduct by which she must abide, she is not allowed to summon help. He has threatened "to O.J." her, by which he means slash her throat and not be convicted. She's terrified of his rage if he finds out she phoned. So terrified that dying seems preferable.

For a while we tussle with words in a gentle tug-of-war, as she in-sists she's in a quagmire, and I keep suggesting ways to climb out of it. Her young children need her, she moans, they need their mother. But how can she leave her lover? A sip at something. The alcohol speaks in melancholy extremes, as she vacillates between swallowing the pills or accepting help. At last she agrees to go to the hospital. When I offer to send the police to escort her, she hesitates so long I'm afraid she may be taking the pills after all, but then she says all right, and gives me her name—Marjorie—address, and phone number. Instantly she regrets it. Her husband will be furious. Using the other phone, I call her local police, explaining telegraphically: "I'm a counselor at Sui-cide Prevention. I have a woman on the phone who has been drinking heavily and who is extremely suicidal. She needs to go to the hospital right away. Could you possibly transport her there?" They're eager to help. Then I keep talking with Marjorie as we wait for the police to arrive. Maybe this drama will shake up her husband enough to respect her needs more. Maybe she'll find the courage to leave him and straighten out her life. When the police car arrives, I wish her luck, say good-bye and call the hospital to tell the emergency room and the mental health unit of her imminent arrival.

My adrenaline continues pumping. Alcohol screws up the whole equation. She could have popped the pills at any time. When the business line rings, an Officer Randal from Owego asks for me by the counselor number I gave his dispatcher. He was the officer who escorted Marjorie to the hospital. Because it's a small town, he knows a mutual friend who says her husband was beating her up—regardless of her denials—but he couldn't see any obvious signs of abuse. What do I think? I think it's likely, but she didn't confess abuse to me. The officer is still at the hospital, where the husband arrived mad and nasty. It's clear Randal wishes he could bust him. Did I know, he asks me, that the caller's father killed himself? I didn't. Did I know she was a thirty-five-year-old mother of four, not two, whose children have been wrenched away from her? I didn't. That must be agony. No wonder she's drinking. No wonder she clings to her home life, even if it's abusive. Finding my voice familiar, he asks if we might have met at an After Suicide group. No, I answer, and ask what took him to that meeting. His mother-in-law attended for a while, he explains, and he drove her there, but he doesn't say why, and I decide not to pry. Owego...Owego...I search my memory for a suicide in Owego. After we hang up, I do remember, and it was a horrible death. A young woman, vertiginously despondent when her boyfriend jilted her, shot herself in the head in her boyfriend's driveway, blowing half of her skull away. I read about it some months ago in the newspapers. Officer Randal was her brother-in-law.

Walking over to the window, I pull aside the blinds and look out at the night, the fields, the city, the quiet. After a death, quiet is the greatest horror, the fact that the world doesn't stop, the sky doesn't split open. Instead, the world goes on its green evitable way, crocus and baby bloom. But priorities arrange themselves automatically. The calendar begins filling in its own pages. What matters shines like a gold coin someone has dropped in the sunlight. I'm not surprised Officer Randal phoned us, unable to let the incident go, or chalk it up as a simple police event on a snowy evening. The first time around, when the comet of desperation passed through his own family, he missed sight of it. But now he's only too aware of the trajectory Marjorie's life seems to be taking, and wishes he could do something somewhere somehow some way to help her change course. It won't bring back his wife's young sister, but, long after a suicide, survivors continue to wage a war with their guilt, and sometimes with destiny.

4:00 P.M. The phone rings, and before I've finished saying "Suicide Prevention and Crisis Service," an hysterical young woman gushes about a suicidal male friend who has been visiting her for the weekend.

"I don't know what to do!" she cries. "He's just run out of the house, and I think he's going to kill himself, I think he's going to jump off a bridge—WHAT SHOULD I DO?" she says, almost screaming.

"What happened?" I ask firmly.

She gives me a fast summary: For days he's been hideously depressed, crying and agitated, in a death trance, insisting that she alone can save him—not through talk or concern, but by allowing him somehow to attach his life to hers. Curled up in a corner of her dorm room, he would cry for hours on end, eat nothing, and sleep little. She hasn't slept a wink either, and she fears he is obsessed with her, fixated on her. He kept insisting his life lay in her hands, his death would be her fault. But he wouldn't respond to entreaties, wouldn't let her take him to the hospital or to the Mental Health Clinic. He's a high school student from her hometown in Vermont, who drove in for the weekend, supposedly to check out the college, and supposedly to return home by 6:00 P.M. today. Although the boy sounds as if he's in horrible pain, I don't know him and can't reach him. The caller is my client. So I begin working with her as I would in any second-party call.

"I can hear what a nightmare this is for you. It's hard enough trying to cope with school without something like this happening."

Slipping down a time chasm, I remember my freshman year in Boston in the late sixties, when chewing too many morning-glory seeds sent one of my friends into a suicidal tailspin. Drugs, bone-bashing music, depresson over a recent break up, and hallucinations of blood pouring from the clouds, all mixed into a deadly brew. It took half the night to beg, talk, and drag him away from the window ledge. I'll never forget how inhumanly strong he seemed, and what a wreck I was, how frightened and ill-equipped for such a drama. At one point I was so mad at him, so exhausted, so frustrated, so fed up with his antics, that I actually hoped he *would* jump. I exhale heavily. Even after all these years, I still feel ashamed of that fleeting thought. What a chaotic time. In the caller's situation, at her age, I'd be a wreck.

Her voice fights me off. Not her words, which insist he's "emotion-ally blackmailing" her in what's become "a total nightmare." But her voice sounds knotted up like muscle. Confused as she is about what to do, her voice resists me. He left a note, and she's frightened he may be heading for a bridge, but she's not sure, because she also thinks he may just be playing a mind game with her. I'm not sure either, and after all, she is my caller. Too agitated to hear, she waves aside my concern. Her voice staggers with fear as she starts to repeat her story again, which isn't an unusual thing for a caller to do, but this time she in-cludes one more small fact.

"He left a note, took off his watch and put it next to the note, and then he just ran out of the building. I read the note, and ran after him but I couldn't find him. WHAT SHOULD I DO?"

"He took off his watch? He left his watch?" I ask.

"Yes," she says.

The watch hits me like a sledgehammer. He intends to stop time. I believe the boy is going to kill himself right now. Everything changes.

"Okay. I want you to phone the police immediately and give them his description and tell them to go to all the bridges. Call them right now! Then call me back and we'll talk about what to do next."

When she hangs up, silence falls in wide, heavy, suffocating blankets. Will she call back? Will the boy survive? What will happen to *her* if he doesn't? I feel utterly helpless. Should I have called the police for her? No. I didn't know what the boy looks like or where he might have gone; and if this ends well, knowing that she took charge will help her recover. But if it doesn't end well? Some euphemism, I think, as I collapse on the daybed. All I can do is wait. There isn't enough air in the room. Walking over to the window again, I open it wide and stare out at the street, where snow glimmers like silk in the moonlight, then over to campus, whose several towers impale the night. A picture postcard of snowbanks, stone buildings, and slate roofs. Who would guess the invisible suffering of the visible world? Somewhere in that landscape a teenage boy is dissolving his life, and a teenage girl is fighting to save him. He's so young, he's so damn young. I remember the gut-wrenching emotional havoc of being fifteen. How trapped you can feel. Last year over a million teens made suicide attempts. Reported ones, that is. Experts say the real figure may be three times that many. A million children in agony. Not all of them lucky enough to be found in time, or accidentally live through it. Some of our counselors, like me, are ones who survived, people who lived to see their lives turn around, and who relish life more because they came so close to losing it. *What was I thinking!* they may now say in horror. But they understand the belly of the beast, the choking logic, the terror of not dying, the holy proclamations of destruction a suicidal person feels. They know the sleepwalker's path down to that icy dungeon. Some counselors, like my caller, had suicidal friends or relatives, who tortured them with worry while alive and left them the emotional carnage of a violent death. But, chastened by what happened and determined to help others in distress, these counselors are not obsessed with suicide. One of the reasons for *not* becoming a counselor is a morbid fascination with suicide. Our work would worsen the obsession; and we also don't want callers in other stages of crisis to be misdirected or misunderstood. Whatever happens to the boy tonight, my caller may well volunteer for crisis line duty one day. Her harrowing experience is a classic one for inspiring volunteers.

Twenty minutes of explosive silence pass, then the phone rings with such a clang I jump. The girl, calling back as she promised. She contacted the police, who immediately dispatched a squad car and two officers who found the boy! Although she has no details, she says they took him to a hospital for evaluation. The county hospital across the lake? She doesn't know. The police only told her that they'd found him and need her to stop by their office to fill in various details.

Thank heavens. My palm feels icy as I run it over my forehead and capture my brain in the forceps of thumb and fingers. I press in against the sides of my eyebrows, but it doesn't relieve the tension. We continue talking, this time about how traumatic the weekend has been for her, how frightening it was to watch her friend literally climbing the walls, then curling up into a fetal position, continuously demanding from her, but not being able to talk with her. He refused her offers to take him to the Mental Health Clinic, and said that his parents hate him, don't listen to anything he says, ignore him for weeks on end, and wouldn't care if he lived or died. She is his only lifeline. Meanwhile, she has prelims tomorrow. She is only eighteen, a freshman. It is her first time away from home. School is demanding enough. She feels extremely guilty, feels that she has failed her friend, feels that if he dies it will be her fault. I wish I could impress upon her that she doesn't have that power, is not responsible for his death or his life. Ironically, it's a power I don't seem to have with her.

As gently as possible, I urge her to call the boy's parents later on (they'll be at work now) and explain why he won't be returning tonight as planned. She's reluctant. They'll be mad at her, she thinks. After all they don't care about him, right? I ask her if she thinks this could be true, or if it might just seem that way to him in his depressed state. Wouldn't she be worried about a suicidal son? Maybe enough to get him the counseling he needs? She agrees to call. I suggest she talk with her professor about taking tomorrow's prelims later in the week. Now the toughest part. I need her to go to the Mental Health Clinic to see a therapist for her own distress. She refuses, says she'll be fine, doesn't need psychiatric help. I know what I can't tell her in a way she'll understand—that she won't be fine if she doesn't get help. A sly tactic is needed, so I propose that she talk to someone at the clinic about a strategy for dealing with her friend in the future. I'm not a therapist, I explain, I can't advise her on the best way to handle him if he does this again, and it would be helpful to have a plan. She agrees. Before she goes I tell her how wonderfully she has handled this emergency, how she had the concern to work with her friend all weekend, trying to help, then when she realized that was impossible, she wisely called us, then when she realized events required it she reliably called the police. She handled everything beautifully, with great presence of mind, and she should be proud of herself. In a quiet voice, she admits she did handle everything well. It surprises her. Does she have a confidante in her dorm? She does. I don't imagine she'll be calling us back, but if she relies on her friend and goes to the clinic for counseling, she'll probably be fine.

Even though the emergency is over, my heart keeps racing, my adrenaline keeps pounding, and my body can't seem to accept that peace has been declared and all is calm again. Strained hours pass without a call. When I look up, I'm startled to see a man with a crew cut wearing a state police uniform, a gun, and a badge. I didn't hear anyone walk in, and I didn't know we had a state trooper as a counselor. What he reveals stuns me.

"I was the one who found the fifteen-year-old," he says. "He's okay. In the hospital. His mother is flying in. But when we found him, man was it tense! Two of us were in the squad car, and we could see a boy fitting his description climbing onto the bridge but we were stuck at a light a block away. We were afraid that if we put our siren on he'd jump, so we sat there for what seemed forever, and then we rushed across to him and jumped out of the car. But by that time he had one leg over the rail, and we had to drag him off of it. Man did he fight us! He kept trying to jump. Thirty seconds more and he would have been gone. Great work!" He shakes my hand. "Great work!" He points to my chest, at heart level, whispers: "You did it. *You* did it. Great work!"

One foot over the rail. Thirty seconds later and he would have been gone. A fifteen-year-old. And, only an hour before, the thirty-five-year-old woman in Owego. My eyes fill with tears of fright and ful-fillment. Talking with both callers, I had sensed my way along as usual, not confidently, not tidily, but tentatively, advancing little by little, wandering from one edge of the trail to the other, wondering what to do. In retrospect, I did everything right. Not perfectly, by a long shot, but right enough. What if I had known there was only a window of less than thirty seconds? A chill soaks through me. I would have been petrified. Yet two troubled, complicated, pained people now have a second chance. With any luck, both will turn their lives around. We rarely learn the outcome of our calls, but today grace has delivered to me two officers with shining news.

The state trooper, Ben, goes on to say that when he had the co-ed come in to advise them about her friend's parents, background, and so on, he took the opportunity to counsel her for an hour. She didn't know he was an SP counselor. Then he called in a therapist who is also one of our support group leaders. She will be taken care of; a support system has been put in place for her. When this officer took the boy to the hospital, talking during the drive over and while waiting in the emergency room, they bonded enough that the boy settled down some, said he wanted to live, and thanked the officer for saving his life.

"They're only children, children asked to save the lives of chil-dren," he says, his face tense and upset.

We both marvel that the system worked again, the training worked. We learn it piece by piece, and are still amazed when all the pieces fit together and lives are saved. When Ben leaves, I am surprised to discover that I'm drenched in sweat. For hours I have been sitting still, but my mind has been sprinting, my heart has been pounding and clenching. The long day has been filled with animals and humans facing the rigors of their environment, each in their own unique way, and at times in nearly identical ways. A powerfully disturbing day. It's Ben's handshake, though, that means so much. A job well done from the man who caught the boy in mid-jump.

"You did it," he says again as he stands up to leave; and shaking his hand firmly, joyously, I reply, "We both did."

With a wave of the hand, he leaves for his evening rounds. I thought I knew most of the crew, but not Ben with his gun and badge, a secret counselor, a sorrow ranger.

CHAPTER 15

Close Calls

"Want something to eat?" a voice behind me asks. I hadn't realized that Barbara was sitting on the couch, eating a bagel and sipping a cup of steaming coffee. A small blue Samsonite suitcase stands at her knee. So much for listening skills—I didn't hear her walk in. A glance at the clock. Ben left twenty minutes ago. I have no idea what I was thinking or doing since then. Time simply evaporated.

"How about moon on the half shell, and a side order of stars?" I say wearily, as I get up and crawl into an ankle-length down coat.

"I see," she says, laughing. "Another busy evening on planet Earth, huh?"

"Yes, indeed." When she reads my write-ups, she'll see.

Outside, I drink in long strong drafts of cold air as if it were the rarest thing in the world. Driving home through the tunnels of the night, I avoid the route that would take me past the bridge. There's no emotion left in me to spill. My eyes keep tearing, I still feel tense and ready to sprint. The moment I walk in the door at home, the phone rings—Marty heard what happened, asks if I need to talk. It's one of the strengths of the agency, how attuned people are to the trials of the job and counselors' needs. My support group meets next week; I'll pour out my emotions then. Or tonight over dinner with Paul, although I can't tell him the details. Or after dinner, when Cathy and I set out on our long-awaited sublunar trek.

———

At 8:00 P.M., Cathy and I rendezvous at the golf course with our cross-country skis. The moon is full and blazing, a toy in the Cracker Jacks box of the night. Mars is up, too, nearby the moon and also Venus. But the brightest spark in the sky is Sirius, a blue-white star loud as an outcry. Sirius, the Dog Star. It's easy to find if you remember that the dog nips at Orion's heel. And Orion strides clearly across the sky tonight, his belt stars (Arabs dubbed them "the golden nuts of Orion") visible, and his long sword curving low.

On the golf course the moonscape looks like a meringue hardened into craters. I've brought along a boom box and a tape of Beethoven's *Moonlight* Sonata and when we're all set to ski I set the boom box on the hood of my car, turn the volume up high, and we glide away across the pastures of ice as the melodies rinse the cold air with lushness. The moon showers an eerie fluorescence over everything and casts long shadows. For some reason, I've never noticed moon shadows before, but they're even more precise than sun shadows. Every turn I make, a shadow swivels and glides behind me. I cannot escape them, but I can influence their path.

The wild blackberry stems are beautiful in the winter woods, even at night. In winter, the branches are slender, arcing, magenta-colored, dusted with a powdery lavender bloom of the sort one sees on peaches. Those branches will bud in the spring and produce what locals call "black caps." On this wooded edge of the golf course, the woods are full of blackberry canes, and I make a mental note of where they are, in case I want to go hiking there next summer and eat them as soon as they start fruiting.

After an hour or so, we grow too cold to ski and return to the car to find the boom box slurring sound, its batteries stricken. No matter. Climbing into Cathy's car, we turn the heat on, pop the tape into the tape deck, and continue our full-moon concert while drinking thermoses of hot chocolate and eating chocolate cookies. One of her clients checked himself into the hospital's psychiatric unit last night, and she's happy he took control of his life. I share my temporary relief about Louise, and tell her of the afternoon's two rescues and how distubed by them I still feel. You wouldn't think there could be a musculature of emotion, but as I've learned, it's possible to sprain your emotions, leaving them too weak to work in their full range. Although our counselors have saved many people over the years, two rescues on one shift is rare. Something about those thirty seconds, so flimsy a tightrope, so narrow a filament of time, and yet life or death hangs by it. Barbara was right. It has been a busy day on planet Earth. A busy year. Almost everything dangerous or poignant that can happen to human beings has prompted a call to SP in the past year. Suicide, murder, addiction and overdose, sexual or physical abuse, depression, domestic squabbles, confusion about sexual identity, flashbacks from war, the ordeal of being in prison, student pressures, poverty, isolation, insanity, child custody battles, dire loneliness, various stages of grief, and all the trials, uncertainties, and conflicts of love. I've encountered a pageant of human hopes, terrors, and predicaments. It's been like sitting in a chair in the middle of a war zone. Over two hundred branches of SP receive calls from millions of people every year. Callers confide the most intimate details of their lives, the most desperate moments, the most shameful acts. And counselors listen to their stories, validate their pain, try to help them survive with grace— or just survive. Most of these events happen without the townspeople noticing, while babies are being born, gardens being planted, people cursing or blessing their bosses, and every family's Joan or John speaking a first word or packing for college. When we think of a town's personality, we focus on its gleaming, face-to-the-world demeanor, and don't include its struggles, frustrations, darker facets, and hidden networks. But, as I now understand, many of the people I pass on the street work secretly with the Center, have counseled there in the past, or use our crisis line and other services.

My arms ache, as if a year's worth of calls has accumulated in my bones. I feel shot through with every caliber of fatigue. But also satisfied. The planet is full of hurt people, angry people, lost people, confused people, people who have explored the vast cartography of trouble, and people stunned by a sudden grief. Someone has to help them; and so we become our brothers' allies, if not their keepers. We nourish them, and they inadvertently nourish us. The minute one imagines oneself in the victim's predicament, and moves to save him or her, it becomes an act of self-love. Outside, the night is a coliseum of stars. For a few moments, I sit and just behold those distant worlds—each one trembling, beautiful, and full of drama. Tonight they look closer than ever, and the darkness seems to burn with their small urgent lights.

Heartfelt thanks to the volunteers and staff of Suicide Prevention and Crisis Service—an extraordinary group of smart, concerned, bighearted people. I will always be grateful for their guidance and insights, and I cherish their friendship.

I'd also like to thank Suicide Prevention of San Francisco for their hospitality. They do superb work in the Bay area, and visiting them was fascinating.

My two-year-long squirrel study was funded in part by *National Geographic*; I published my results in the November 1995 issue of the magazine.

The musing about hummingbirds in Chapter 8 led to a brief essay entitled "Mute Dancers," which appeared in *The New York Times Magazine*, May 29, 1994, pp. 34–35.

I visited Walt Whitman's birthplace in Huntington, Long Island, in the fall of 1985, and wrote about the experience in an essay entitled "Where America's Poet Was Born," which appeared in *Parade* magazine, December 22, 1985.

Some thoughts about the history of bathing, and about women and strength, are loosely based on essays entitled "My Place" and "Getting Physical," which appeared in *New Woman*, March 1995 and October 1995.

The passage about my caravan of selves in Chapter 7 is included in the anthology *Who's Writing This? Notations on the Authorial I*, edited by Daniel Halpern, Ecco Press, 1995.

If no listing for a crisis hotline appears in your local telephone book, call Information and ask the operator to put you in touch with the one closest to you (some calls chronicled in this book came from people in distant cities). You can also contact your local Department of Social Services, Human Services, or Mental Health Association.

Although I'm no longer a counselor at my local branch of SP, I'm now a member of their board of directors, and I continue telephone counseling in a different city. People who phone SP won't find me at the other end of the line, but they'll find people just like me, perhaps people like themselves.

INDEX

Ackerman, Diane:
   childhood and adolescence of, 16, 50,
      78, 96, 101, 116–17, 154–55, 173, 213,
      220, 285
   counseling chosen by, 19–20, 22
   counseling rewarding to, 16–17
   counseling sessions held by, 8, 10, 11,
      13–14, 24–25, 34–36, 38–42, 47–50,
      58–59, 75–77, 99–109, 113–16,
      147–50, 170–72, 176, 177, 192,
      221–31, 242–63, 295
   depression of, 42–44, 151–52
   education of, 154, 155, 174
   family of, 49, 63, 96, 173, 181, 191, 199,
      213, 279–80
   home of, 27, 31, 52, 53–54, 55, 142,
      264–65
   journal entry of, 172–73
   as poet, 132–34, 151–52, 169, 174–75,
      181, 267, 268
   training of, 20–22, 232
adaptiveness, 12
After Suicide group, 283
Agent Orange, 14
Al-Anon, 9
albatross, 71
alcoholism, 9, 180, 181, 182
Alexandra (author's friend), 78–79
alienation, 89, 211, 273
Allen (caller), 10
Alliance for the Mentally Ill of New York
   State, 179
altruism, 210
amphetamines, 153
animals:
   captive, 124

crises and, 11, 27, 124, 209, 210
depressed, 123–25, 136–37, 270
listening behavior of, 10
naturalists and, 31
pets, 125
in spring, 27
suicidal, 269–70
in summer, 82–83
therapists for, 124–25
water and, 52–53
workers and, 59
in zoos, 56–60, 123–25
see also specific animals
Anna Karenina (Tolstoy), 100
Annie (author's friend), 77–78
anoles, 79
anorexia, 46
antidepressants, 39, 150–54, 270
   see also specific medications
anxiety, 86–89, 153
   in animals, 124
Aristotle, 180
armadillos, 80
artists, *see* creativity
asylums, varieties of, 130–31
Auden, W. H., 220–21
Aztec culture, 143

babytalk, 85
Barbara (counselor), 291
"bare attention," 266
Bath, 53
bathing, history of, 52–56, 111, 295
bats, 159, 160
battered women, 24–25, 156
Bauer, Susan, 234

DIANE ACKERMAN, a poet, essayist, and naturalist, was born in Waukegan, Illinois. She received an MA, MFA and PhD from Cornell University. Her poetry has been published in leading literary journals, and in the books *The Planets: A Cosmic Pastoral; Wife of Light; Lady Faustus; Reverse Thunder: A Dramatic Poem,* and *Jaguar of Sweet Laughter: New and Selected Poems.*

Her works of nonfiction include *The Rarest of the Rare,* in which she explores the plight and fascination of endangered animals; her panoramic *A Natural History of Love;* the critically acclaimed *The Moon by Whale Light, and Other Adventures among Bats, Crocodilians, Penguins, and Whales;* and *On Extended Wings,* her memoir of flying. Her bestseller, *A Natural History of the Senses,* was the basis for a PBS television series, *Mystery of the Senses,* in which she was featured as host and narrator. *Monk Seal Hideaway,* her first children's book, appeared recently, and she is writing other nature books for children.

Honored as a Literary Lion by the New York Public Library, she has received many prizes and awards. She has taught at a variety of universities, including Columbia and Cornell. Her essays about nature and human nature have appeared in *National Geographic, The New Yorker, The New York Times, Parade,* and other journals, where they have been the subject of much praise.

ABOUT THE TYPE

The text of this book was set in Janson, a mis-
named typeface designed in about 1600 by
Nicholas Kis, a Hungarian in Amsterdam. In 1919
the matrices became the property of the Stempel
Foundry in Frankfurt. It is an old-style book face
of excellent clarity and sharpness. Janson serifs
are concave and splayed; the contrast between
thick and thin strokes is marked.